# BUDDHISM

AND

# ITS CHRISTIAN CRITICS

# BUDDHISM
AND
# ITS CHRISTIAN CRITICS:

PAUL CARUS

GYAN

*Published by*

GYAN

Gyan Publishing House
5, Ansari Road
Daryaganj, New Delhi-110002
Phone: 011-47034999, 9811692060
E-mail: books@gyanbooks.com

*Distribution Network*
gyanbooks.com
India, USA, Canada, UK, Australia



ISBN: 978-93-7014-256-5 (HB)

First Published, 1897

2nd Impression 2025

*Printed at:* Gyan Press, Delhi.



**BUDDHISM AND ITS CHRISTIAN CRITICS**
Author: PAUL CARUS

# BUDDHISM

AND

# ITS CHRISTIAN CRITICS

BY

DR. PAUL CARUS

1897

# CONTENTS.

# PREFACE.

Comparison is the best method of acquiring comprehension; and comprehension involves both the discrimination of contrasts and the recognition of similarities. Differences are upon the whole at once apparent while similarities are hidden; but the import of differences can, at the same time, not be appreciated until the similarities are seen. Thus, the discovery that the course of the moon and the fall of a stone are both phenomena of gravitation, becomes significant only when the difference of both phenomena can be traced to a difference of conditions.

For this reason every religious man should study other religions in order to understand his own religion; and he must try to trace conscientiously and lovingly the similarities in the various faiths in order to acquire the key that will unlock to him the law of the religious evolution of mankind.

The present book purports to be a contribution to comparative religion, and it is one-sided because it is addressed mainly to Christians, viz., to those Christians who are anxious to acquire an insight into the significance of Buddhist thought as it is at its best.

Buddhism and Christianity are in many respects

so similar as to appear almost identical; in other respects they exhibit such contrasts as to represent two opposite poles; and it is on this account that a study of Buddhism is indispensable for a proper comprehension of Christianity.

But what is true of Buddhism in its relation to Christianity is not less true of Christianity in its relation to Buddhism. When I think that this book may be read by such Buddhists of Japan, Ceylon, or Siam as are only superficially acquainted with Christianity, I feel like adding to its contents another chapter that might easily be extended into a book, in which I would refute their various misconceptions of Christianity and urge them to send emissaries to Christian countries, especially to the Protestants of Germany, England, and North America, for the sake of investigating Christian modes of worship, Christian institutions, and Christian ideals. The importance of Christianity does not consist of its dogmas, but in the spirit in which these dogmas are interpreted and applied to the home life of Christian congregations; and it is on these lines that Buddhists can learn many valuable lessons which Christian missionaries can only imperfectly communicate to them.

The main advantage of Christianity over Buddhism consists in the activity which it inspires. Buddhism has to a great extent (with the exception, perhaps, of some Japanese sects) favored a passive attitude in life. In spite of Buddha's injunction to be untiring and energetic, salvation was still sought by many Buddhist saints in the suppression of all aspirations. In spite of Buddha's rejection of asceticism, and his declaration that hermit and layman are alike, if they but free themselves of the illusion of self, the ethics of world-flight after the fashion of the old Yoga philosophers continued to be regarded as the highest goal of religion. In spite of Buddha's lessons of compassion, charity, and practically applied love toward all suffering creatures, the bliss of Buddhahood was frequently sought more in the state of an eternal, undisturbed happiness as is afforded only after the riddance of all corporeality in the abstraction of a pure spirituality and not in helpfulness and struggles for further advance. On all these lines Christianity, especially Christianity as it is to-day in the United States, marks a decided advance in the practical applications of Buddha's own principles. In Christianity the principle is dropped that the Buddha, the Christ, the Master, the Blessed One must at the same time be the Happy One. Bliss is not always happiness. In addition to the paradoxes of Buddha's ethics, for instance, that by giving away we gain and that hatred is conquered by love, we learn through Christ that the Blessed One may be the Suffering One, and that the man of peace may be the boldest struggler.

Christianity is less philosophical than Buddhism; Christ proclaims no theory of soul; he says nothing about the nature of things, and never enters into metaphysical inquisitions of any kind. The Christian theories of creation, of God's personality and trinity, of the nature of the soul and the mode of resurrection were made later on by the church fathers and church councils. Christ expressly declared that he spoke in parables. But this humbler method of popular teaching was more effectual than Buddha's philosophy. Whatever may be said in favor of Buddhism, its profundity, its cosmic universality, and the loftiness of its morality, the great strength of Christianity lies in the lesson of Golgotha, which means, salvation lies not alone in the attainment of the truth, but in struggling for it, in living for it, in suffering for it, and in dying for it.

The heaven of Christian dogmatology is too mythological for a scientist and the Nirvâna of Buddhists too abstract for the mass of the people. The former is in its popular form not acceptable in our present age of scientific exactness, and the latter is after the Asiatic mode of thinking, too much conceived in its negative aspects, and if the attempt is made to show its positive features, Nirvâna appears as mere being instead of doing; as mere rest instead of efficacy, as a state of abstract indifference instead of a definite condition of existence.

A comparison with Christian views will help Buddhists better to define their own faith. But what, above all, is most needful for both parties is the adoption of exact and scientific methods of investigation in the fields of psychology and philosophy.

There is a rivalry between Christianity and Buddhism, more so than between other religions, and the question is which will be the first to clarify our conceptions of the religious goal of mankind in plain terms, so as to suit the practical demands of life, the Christians or the Buddhists. Christians can learn much of Buddhism; and Buddhists can learn much of Christianity. The final victory in their competition will be with those who learn most of the other.

Christianity conquered other religions by adopting of them that which was good. It adopted of the Greek the Logos philosophy and of the Teutons the ethics of struggle and energetic endeavor. It is only since Christianity refused to assimilate new truths, that its progress was checked; and the same is true of Buddhism. The religious future of a religion depends upon the spiritual vitality of its representatives, and vitality means capacity of growth.

Mankind does not want Buddhism, nor Islam, nor Christianity; mankind wants the truth, and the truth is best brought out by an impartial comparison. There is probably no human mind free from error, but he who "proves all and keeps the best" is most likely to attain to perfection.

Missionaries are religious ambassadors. Their duty consists not only in the propagation of their own religion, but also in the acquisition of a perfect comprehension of the religion of those people to whom they are sent, and Christians can justly pride themselves on the fact that all their great missionaries, such men as Duff, Judson, Hardy, Beal, Legge, and others, every one in his field, did an enormous amount of work which served to widen our own knowledge of the religious views that prevail in India, Ceylon, Burmah, and China. Indeed, had it not been for their labors, comparative religion would have made little advance. And I would not hesitate to say that the most successful part of their work consisted, not in making a few converts abroad, but in widening the horizon of the people who had sent them. Such is the advantage of an exchange of thought on the most important questions of life, that it would be a blessing all around if the non-Christian religions also decided, on a larger scale, to send missionaries to Europe and America in order to have among Christians their faith worthily represented, to facilitate comparison and invite investigation.

Mankind is destined to have one religion, as it will have one moral ideal and one universal language, and the decision as to which religion will at last be universally accepted, cannot come about by accident. Science will spread, maybe, slowly but unfailingly, and the universal acceptance of a scientific world-conception bodes the dawn of the Religion of Truth, —a religion based upon plain statements of fact unalloyed with myth or allegory. In the eventual conditions of religious life, there may be a difference of rituals and symbols, nay, even of names, according to taste, historical tradition, and individual preference, but in all essentials there will be one religion only, for there is only one truth, which remains one and the same among all nations, in all climes, and under all conditions.

The law of the survival of the fittest holds good also in the domain of spiritual institutions. And let us remember that the greatest power lies not in numbers, not in wealth, not in political influence, but in truth. Whatever may be the fate of the various faiths of the world, we may be sure that the truth will prevail in the end.

# THE ORIGIN OF BUDDHISM.

## BRAHMANISM THE CRADLE OF BUDDHISM.

About two and a half millenniums ago, India was already in a very prosperous condition. The land yielded rich harvests; industries and arts flourished; and science kept abreast with the material development of civilization. Logic, however, and abstract reasoning had attained an unusually high development, for in these arts the ancient Indians were masters above all other nations in the world.

In those days the religious question was, perhaps, for the first time, recognized in its full importance, and led to investigations, discussions and various modes of solution. The central problem which lies at the root of all religion is concerned with the origin of, and the deliverance from, evil. We are thirsting for life, not only for life in general, but for individual life, for the preservation of our personal existence, its continuance, welfare, and further evolution; yet life involves us in pain, misery, labors, struggles, sickness, old age and death. The very contents of life seem to be made up of evils, as a means of escape from which religion was sought, and the religion of India was in those days, as it is now again, Brahmanism.

Brahmanism is a system of ceremonies, prayers and sacrifices by which men attempt to win the favor of the gods. The doctrines of Brahmanism are contained in their sacred writings called the Vedas, which were supposed to have been revealed by divine inspiration. The purpose of sacrifice was threefold: (1) we read in the Vishnu-purâna, "By sacrifices the gods are nourished," and (2) in the Tândya-brâhmana the limb of the victim consigned to the fire of the altar is called "the expiation for sins committed, by the gods, by our ancestors, by other men now living, and by ourselves." But the dearest hope of the Hindu was (3) to acquire through sacrifices supernatural powers.

The Hindu world-conception as it appears in the Vêdic literature may be called a loose monism. It is a unitary world-conception containing a polytheistic mythology, the meaning of which, however, is frankly declared to be pantheistic. Brahma is the One and All, and he reveals himself in all the various divinities. We read in the Isa Upanishad: *

> "Whate'er exists within this universe
> Is all to be regarded as enveloped
> By the great Lord, as if wrapped in a vesture.
> There is one only Being who exists
> Unmoved, yet moving swifter than the mind;
> Who far outstrips the senses, though as gods

* Quoted from Sir Monier Williams's "Hinduism," p. 45.

They strive to reach him; who himself at rest
Transcends the fleetest flight of other beings;
Who, like the air, supports all vital action.
He moves, yet moves not; he is far, yet near;
He is within this universe. Whoe'er beholds
All living creatures as in him and him—
The universal Spirit—as in all,
Henceforth regards no creature with contempt."

The social system of ancient India divided the people rigorously into four castes: the Brahmans or priests, the Kshatriyas or warriors, the Vaishyas or traders and agriculturists, and the Shudras, or the lowly class of the conquered population. The first three are Aryans; the last mentioned, the original inhabitants of India.

### THE DARSANAS OF ANCIENT INDIA.

There were six philosophies (Darsanas) in ancient India: 1. The Mîmânsâ, founded by Jaimini; 2. The Vêdânta, whose main representative was Sankarâchârya; 3. The Vaisheshika, founded by Kanâda; 4. The Nyâna, founded by Gotama; 5. The Sâmkhya, founded by Kapila; and 6. The Yoga. The first two, Mîmânsâ and Vêdânta, may briefly be characterized as an exegesis of the Vêdas. The Vêdas are said to be eternal and their authority is recognized as absolute. The aim of the Mîmânsâ is to explain unintelligible passages of the Vêdic texts and to give reliable information concerning the proper performances of ceremonies and sacrifices. The Vêdânta, which literally means the end or aim of the Vêdas, reduces the religious doctrines of the Vêdas to scientifically exact terms. Its trend is a philosophy which is called Advaita or non-duality, a spiritualistic monism, or rather a pantism, teaching the doctrine that Brahma, the universal soul, is the all, and the only true reality, while all things and individual beings are mere appearance, a product of illusion (Mâyâ) and ignorance (Avidya).

The Vaisheshika and Nyâna belong together. The founder of the Vaisheshika is only known by his nickname Kanâda which means "Atom-eater." The peculiarity of his philosophy consists in his method of classification. There are six categories: Substance, quality, action, generality of properties, particularity and inherence. The disciples of Kanâda add as a seventh category, non-existence. The fifth category, particularity (*vaishesha*), gave the name to the system. Reality is conceived of as an infinite variety of particular units or atoms, the infinite nature of which remains constantly the same. The atoms are self-existent, uncaused and eternal. An invisible force (*adrishta*) is the forming principle. Man's soul (*purusha*) is supposed to be without beginning and without end, all-pervading and omnipresent in space. The action of the soul depends upon mind (*manas*), which, in contrast to the diffused nature of the soul, is conceived as an atom capable of being in one place only at a time. This artificial idea of an all-pervading soul and a monad-mind, or manas, was invented to account for the fact that man can think of one thing at a time only, while he is at the same time conscious of possessing deeper spiritual resources.

The Nyâna philosophy is a mere extension of the Vaisheshika. It adopts the atomic theory and psychology of the latter and adds expositions of the method of inquiry. It might best be characterized as a system of formal logic applied to practical reasoning. Later representatives of the Vaisheshika and the Nyâna admitted a certain theism, but their god is not like the Christian God, the creator of the world, but only one extraordinarily powerful individual soul which has become omnipresent and omniscient through the accumulation of merit in former existences, and is now exempt from migration, enjoying the unfathomable bliss of needing no deliverance.

The Sâmkhya philosophy is dualistic, propounding the theory of a radical difference of self or soul or subjective being, and the objectivity of material bodies; it assumes the eternal existence and reality of both matter and soul, or rather souls, for Kapila assumed the existence of an indefinite number of souls. He argued: Impure matter cannot originate from pure spirit or *vice versa;* and he denied at the same time in unequivocal terms the existence of a creator, for there is no creation out of nothing, and all becoming is transformation according to law. Sâmkhya means "enumeration," which name has probably been chosen on account of the enumeration of the principles of Sâmkhya philosophy, which sketch the evolution of the present form of existence from the undifferentiated primordial matter called prakriti—the unproduced producer and the rootless root of all things.

The Yoga philosophy adopts the theories of the Sâmkhya, adding to them the practice of meditation and self-induced trances. The means of self-hypnotization consisted in abstraction from the outer world and the concentration of the mind on itself with the aim of isolating the soul from matter and thus gaining deliverance.

We might mention as a seventh school the materialistic philosophy of the Chârvâkas or Lokâyatas, founded by Vrihaspati. They recognize only sense-perception as a source of knowledge and reject the reliability of logical inference. They regard only the four elements—earth, air, fire, and water—as real, and consider intelligence as a transient product of these elements. Soul is to them identical with the body, and all phenomena are declared to be purely mechanical processes. They ridicule sacrifices as much as devotion and penance, and do not believe in the retribution of moral justice. The Chârvâkas have never succeeded in becoming a recognized school or producing any literary documents of importance. We know them only through the arguments of their adversaries who mention their theories merely for the purpose of refuting them.

There are certain ideas which cannot be credited to any one of the various schools, because they have come to be the common property of Indian thought; they are briefly stated as follows:

1. The irrefragability of the law of causation, which is said to be as rigid in the sphere of morals as in the physical world. It is called "the law of Karma, which means that our existence is the exact product of our deeds done in our present and in former existences, and that our sufferings are just punishments for sins previously committed, while the advantages we enjoy are the rewards for former merits.

2. The transmigration of souls according to their Karma.

3. The pain of Samsâra (the circuit of life), which means that the eternal repetition of soul-migration implicates us in evils of all kinds, especially birth, disease, old age, and death; or briefly, that life is suffering.

4. The salvation of Nirvâna, that is to say, the aim of all moral aspirations is to reach the calm and peaceful bliss of Nirvâna, which is a deliverance from the evils of Samsâra.

### THE SAMKHYA PHILOSOPHY.

The Sâmkhya philosophy is of special interest in so far as it forms the starting-point of Buddhistic thought. We cannot understand Buddhism without considering the great influence of the dualism and pessimism exercised on Indian thinkers by the Sâmkhya philosophy.

As in Sanskrit, soul and man are expressed by the same word (Purusha), matter was naturally compared to a woman, a favorite simile employed not only by many dualistic philosophers, but also by Giordano Bruno, the great martyr and champion of monism who stands at the threshold of modern thought. But while Giordano represents the female principle, matter, as passive and the male principle, spirit, as active, Kapila represents matter as active and soul as passive, reminding us of the quite modern view of some French psychologists who describe consciousness as a mere accompaniment of the physiological brain motions, which latter alone are said to be active and efficient to serve as causes in the bodily system. Soul, according to the Sâmkhya view, is the principle of apperception, while matter is that which produces effects in the world of reality. Their union as we find it in living organisms is compared to a lame man mounted on a blind man. Matter, the kind man, is said to be the faithful servant of the soul, the lame man. The exertions of the former are solely for the benefit of the latter. As soon as the soul becomes disgusted with the restlessness of the material world, matter ceases to be active; it is recognized as inane and becomes inert, while the soul after its separation from matter enjoys deliverance (Apavarga), which is the highest bliss attainable. At the close of the introduction of a Sâmkhya text-book (the Sâmkhya Pravacana-Bhashya) the following four propositions are added, which bear a close resemblance to the four noble truths of Buddha. We read:

1. That from which we deliver ourselves is pain.

2. Deliverance is the cessation of pain.

3. The cause of pain is the lack of distinction between soul and matter, which produces their continued union.

4. The means of deliverance is the discerning cognition.

Kapila rejected the methods of salvation proposed by the Brahmans, which were sacrifices, prayers and ceremonies. They may be granted to alleviate pain, but they do not free us from the cause of pain and therefore cannot make its return forever impossible. Kapila argues: Since pain lasts only so long as the soul is in connection with the body and the bodily organs, salvation can be obtained only by the absolute separation of soul and body, which must be affected through a cognition of the difference between soul and body.

The practical application of the Sâmkhya philosophy led to asceticism. Self-mortification, in the literal sense of the word, was supposed to be the means of salvation. The body must be killed. It must become dead so that the soul may live in a state of pure spirituality and the struggle for a painless existence became identical with the attempt of reaching a state of bodiless soul-life. Matter was denounced as the source of all evil, the three qualities of matter (the three *gunas*) which as they affect us in three ways were called good (*sattva*), bad (*raja*), and indifferent (*tamas*), were compared to a triple rope by which the soul is bound; but pure spirit was supposed to be free from pain, old age and death.

There were many serious men in those days who tried to realize the ideal of this ascetic dualism. Fasts and self-mortifications were carried to their extremes, and if, as a natural consequence, trances with ecstatic visions appeared, those morbid states were considered as the first hopeful symptoms of a partial deliverance of the soul. But a radical separation of body and soul and an actual deliverance from evil were not attained in this way.

The more the Sâmkhya ideas gained ground, the higher grew the repute of the yoga-practice of attaining deliverance by entering into trances.

### THE APPEARANCE OF BUDDHA.

The religious ideal of delivering mankind from evil had become so general that many teachers appeared, hermits, ascetics, and philosophical thinkers of all kinds, who pretended to have found the way of salvation, which would lead to Nirvâna, to the extinction of all misery, to peace and happiness; and a man who had attained perfect enlightenment so as to be able to show to mankind the way of salvation was called Buddha.

Among the Buddhas who appeared in those days there were two whose doctrines led to the foundation of religions which still exist. One of them is Vardhamâna, the son of Jnâta, frequently called Jnâtaputra, who lived at the end of the sixth and at the beginning of the fifth century B. C. He is the founder of the Jain sect, which at the present day numbers almost half a million adherents in India, most of whom are said to belong to the richest and most aristocratic classes of the Hindus. The other Buddha is Gautama Siddhârtha, the son of a wealthy land-owner at Kapilavastu. He is a younger contemporary of Vardhamâna; he lived in the fifth century B. C. and is the founder of Buddhism.

Buddha's religion has been and may be considered as a further development of the Sâmkhya philosophy, because it shows in many details traces of Sâmkhya terms and modes of thought. But Buddha changed the foundation of the system, overcame its dualism, and applied the new doctrine thus gained to practical life. He became the most powerful, the boldest, and most radical reformer that ever appeared in the history of mankind. From the Sâmkhya philosophers Buddha adopted the doctrine of the existence of misery and the attempt to deliver man from evil, seeking salvation through enlightenment. Like them he expressed his doctrine in a fourfold formula. Like them he acknowledged the rigidity of the law of causation, and pushed its application so far as to deny frankly the efficacy of prayer, rituals, and sacrifices. Indeed Buddha lost no opportunity of denouncing bloody sacrifices as unnecessary, cruel, and inhuman. He disregarded caste distinction and denied the divine inspiration of the Vedas, in consequence of which he was considered as irreligious by orthodox Brahmans. And yet his irreligious attitude was only a protest against religious superstitions and abuses. But Buddha differed from the

Sâmkhya philosophy not less thoroughly than from the Brahmans in ethics. His idea of enlightenment was not merely the recognition of a theory, but the basis for an energetic activity. Enlightenment, according to Buddha, teaches morality, and he rejected asceticism as injurious, showing his disciples, as he called it, the "middle way," which abstains from both extremes, self-mortification and self-indulgence. Having subjected himself to a rigorous asceticism, he came to the conclusion that by thus subduing the body the mind was crippled. The mind became dimmed after severe fasts, and deliverance could not be obtained. He recognized that our evil desire, and not material existence, was the root of evil, and proposed as a remedy neither self-mortification nor the beatific visions of the yoga, nor the prayer and sacrifices of the Brahmans, but the radical extinction of desire. Buddha saw for the first time clearly that the religious problem was a moral problem; that pain is only a transient evil which need not concern us; that the real evil is sin; that the root of sin is to be found in the lust of the mind; and that he who harbors no lust or ill-will in his heart will naturally walk in the path of righteousness. Take away desire and you destroy evil at its root.

Kapila's dualism proclaimed that a distinction existed between soul and body, yet Kapila regarded man's sensations and thoughts and desires as material. The soul was to him a transcendent being, which by a kind of sublimated body (similar to the so-called astral body of our modern theosophists, and supposed to reside in the material body) was implicated in the world of matter. This metaphysical soul-being of the Sâmkhya philosophy was supposed to be the apprehending principle in all psychic activities. It was said, that the eye does not see, the ear does not hear, and thoughts do not think, but it is that mysterious something called âtman, *i. e.*, self or soul, which is the smeller in the nose, the taster in the tongue, the seer in the eye, the thinker of our thoughts, and the doer of our acts.

Kapila assumed an innumerable number of souls, which made his system intricate and invited the criticism exercised by his great successor, Gautama, who went so far as to deny the existence of the âtman, a theory which is generally called a denial of the existence of the soul.

We have to add here that the translation of âtman by soul is very misleading. Buddha did not deny the existence of our feelings, sentiments, ideas and ideal aspirations. He only denied the existence of a hypothetical soul-subject which is supposed to be the principle or agent of our psychical activity. He denied the metaphysical soul-entity, not the soul itself. He rejected Kapila's dualism, but he did not fall into the opposite extreme of materialism; and strange to say, he anticipated the modern conception of the soul as it is now taught by the most advanced scientists of Europe.

Buddha's world-conception at the same time coincides with the theory of evolution. Every organism, according to Buddha, consists of samskâras, generally translated "confections," that is, soul-structures, formations or dispositions which through function have originated in a gradual development. All creatures are the product of an immeasurably long chain of deeds. They are the result of their Karma.

Man also is a bundle of samskâras; his eye is the product of seeing, resulting from sensation under the influence of light; his ear is the product of hearing, resulting from sensation under the influence of sounds; and in the same way all the organs of our bodily and of our spiritual organizations are the product of deeds transmitted to us either directly by inheritance or indirectly by education. These samskâras constitute our being. The eye sees, the ear hears; our thoughts think. There is no metaphysical entity behind them as their agent, but these samskâras, or soul-forms, constituting our existence are transmitted by action, word and example, to others. There is, accordingly, no soul migration, but there is rebirth; viz., there is a reappearance of the same type of soul. Our samskâras impress themselves on and they continue in others. Death is only the discontinuance of their presence in the special body of an individual; but death is not the annihilation of a man's karma, for his karma continues according to the law of causation. Death does not annihilate the samskâras who continue in following generations according to the deeds done during life. Thus death disappears in Buddha's soul-conception, and the realities of our psychical existence are recognized in their pre-existence as well as in their continuation after death.

The Buddhistic view of immortality which is based on the denial of the âtman is forcibly expressed in the Buddhist canon. Buddha, having attained enlightenment, met on his way Upaka, a young Brahman and a former acquaintance of his. Upaka said to Gautama: "Your countenance, friend, is serene, and your eyes are bright, indicating purity and blessedness." And Buddha, having told Upaka that he had attained deliverance, adds (according to the translation of Prof. Samuel Beal from a Chinese text): "I am now going to the city of Benares to establish the kingdom of righteousness, to give light to those enshrouded in darkness and open the gate of Immortality to men." *

Buddha's idea of salvation is ultimately based on enlightenment, and enlightenment is to him the recognition of the nature of things. We are confronted with evil and find the root of all evil in the waywardness of our own heart. There is the notion that our inmost existence is an ego-entity, but this is an error; it is the illusion of self, for the preser-

* The romantic legend of Sâkya Buddha translated from the Chinese Sanskrit by S. Beal, p. 245. The translation of the corresponding passage from the Pali reads, according to Rhys Davids, as follows: I am now going to establish the kingdom of righteousness. For this purpose I am going to the city of Benares, to give light to those enshrouded in darkness and to open the gate of Immortality to men.

vation of which we are so anxious. Selfhood is the source of vanity, egotism and sin. There is no moral wrong but it has its ultimate root in selfhood. Knowing, now, that selfhood is an illusion, that this limited individuality of ours is only a temporary abode of the soul, whose stream flows on uninterruptedly, we learn the transitoriness of the ills that the flesh is heir to, and identify the true self of our real being with those immortal elements of our soul which are not touched by death. Buddha's ideal, accordingly, is the utter annihilation of all thought of self and the preservation of all that is in conformity with enlightenment. The utter extermination of desire alone can afford a final deliverance from the evil of existence, leading to that absolute peace of mind which is called Nirvâna.

Buddha rejected the religious superstition that there was any merit in ceremonies and sacrifices; but he rejected also the monkish ethics of asceticism, proclaiming openly and without equivocation that holiness cannot be attained by self-mortification and austerities, but only by a radical surrender of all selfish desire.

Gautama Siddhartha, the founder of Buddhism, was what to-day would be called a freethinker, for his religion is different from Brahmanism, in so far as he promises no help from Brahma or any other Deity, but enjoins its devotees to rely upon themselves, and have no other guide but the truth. "Hold fast to the truth as to a lamp," were the significant words of Buddha in his farewell address to his disciples before he died. He bowed to no authority, and set up no creed, no dogma. He denied the divine inspiration of the Vedas, the sacred scriptures of Brahmanism, refused to recognize castes, rejected rituals as irrelevant, denounced sacrifices as inhuman, ridiculed prayer as useless, disdained worship, refused to believe in the creation of the world by an Ishvara (i. e., a good Lord and personal God), and denied the existence of a soul-entity or âtman. In a word, he opposed all the favorite notions of Brahmanism, the religion of his time. And yet he was not an irreligious man. On the contrary, he was deeply religious, and certainly more religious than any of the priests of his age who denounced him as irreligious. Such was the influence of his powerful personality that his disciples spread his doctrine over all Asia, and his religion has even in its aberrations preserved the moral earnestness of its founder.

Of special interest is the method in which the Brahmanical belief of Brahma as the creator, governor and Lord over all things is treated in Buddhistic literature. As an instance we quote from the Dîgha-Nikâya, XI. 67, where a certain priest is introduced who goes in quest of a philosophical problem. After having addressed all the sages, kings, and gods, he comes at last to Brahma himself. And Brahma says: "I, O priest, am Brahma, Great "Brahma, the Supreme Being, the Unsurpassed, "the Perceiver of All Things, the Controller, the "Lord of All, the Maker, the Fashioner, the Chief, "the Victor, the Ruler, the Father of All Beings "Who Have Been and Are to Be." The priest, having patiently listened to this self-definition, calls Brahma's attention to his question, saying: "My "friend, I am not asking you, Are you Brahma, "Great Brahma, the Supreme Being, etc.? but I ask "you a question which I should like to have an- "swered." But Brahma, instead of replying to the question, repeats his speech a second and a third time, and when the priest is not to be quieted in this way Brahma takes the questioner by the arm, leads him aside and says to him in a whisper: "O priest, these gods of "my suite believe as follows: Brahma sees all "things, knows all things, has penetrated all things. "Therefore was it that I did not answer you in "their presence. I do not know the answer to your "question. Therefore it was a sin and a crime that "you left the Blessed One and went elsewhere in "quest of an answer. Turn back, O priest, and "having drawn near to the Blessed One, ask him "this question, and as the Blessed One shall explain "unto you, so believe."

Concerning Buddha's atheism the following passage quoted from Max Müller's essay on "Buddhist Nihilism" is instructive. Max Müller says:

"As to Atheism, it cannot be denied that, if we call the old gods of the Veda—Indra and Agni, and Yama—gods, Buddha was an Atheist. He does not believe in the divinity of those deities. What is noteworthy is that he does not by any means deny their bare existence, just as little as St. Augustine and other Fathers of the Church endeavored to sublimize, or entirely explain away, the existence of the Olympian deities. The founder of Buddhism treats the old gods as superhuman beings, and promises the believers that they shall after death be reborn into the world of the gods, and shall enjoy divine bliss with the gods. Similarly he threatens the wicked that after death they shall meet with their punishment in the subterranean abodes and hells, where the Asuras, Sarpas, Nâgas, and other evil spirits dwell, beings whose existence was more firmly rooted in the popular belief and language, than that even the founder of a new religion could have dared to reason them away. But, although Buddha assigned to these mediatized gods and devils, palaces, gardens, and a court,—not second to their former ones,—he yet deprived them of all their sovereign rights. Although, according to Buddha, the worlds of the gods last for millions of years, they must perish, at the end of every Kalpa, with the gods and with the spirits who, in the circle of births, have raised themselves to the world of the gods. Indeed, the reorganization of the spirit world goes further still. Already, before Buddha, the Brahmans had surmounted the low standpoint of mythological polytheism, and supplanting it by the idea of the Brahman, as the absolute divine or super-divine power. What, then, does Buddha decree? To this Brahman also he assigns a place in his universe. Over and above the world of the gods with its six paradises, he heaps up sixteen Brahma-worlds, not to be attained through virtue and piety only, but through inner contemplation, through knowledge and enlightenment. The dwellers in these worlds are already purely spiritualized beings, without body, without weight, without desire, far above men and gods. Indeed, the Buddhist architect rises to a still more towering height, heaping upon the Brahma world four still higher worlds, which he calls the world of the formless. All these worlds are open to man, and the beings ascend and descend in the circle of time, according to the works they have performed, according to the truths they have recognized. But in all these worlds the law of change obtains; in none is there exemption from birth, age and death. The world of the gods will perish like that of men, even the world of the formless will not last forever; but the Buddha, the Enlightened and truly Free, stands higher and will not be affected or disturbed by the collapse of the Universe: '*Si fractus illabatur orbis, impavidum ferient ruinæ.*'

"Now, however, we meet with a vein of irony, which one would have hardly expected in Buddha. Gods and devils he had located; to all mythological and philosophical acquisitions of the past he had done justice as far as possible. Even fabulous beings, such as Nâgas, Gandharvas, and Garudas, had escaped the process of dissolution which was to reach them later only at the hands of comparative mythology. There is only *one* idea, the idea of a personal creator, in regard to which Buddha is relentless.

"It is not only denied, but even its origin, like that of an ancient myth, is carefully explained by him in its minutest details."

So far Max Müller.

Buddha thought it not necessary to play the part of a religious Don Quixote. He made no attempt to fight the windmills of mythological deities whose existence he knew to be doomed. But as soon as confronted with a serious problem, he made no attempt at evading it, but met it squarely, and gave to his disciples his solution without equivocation.

In spite of the contrast that obtains between Buddhism and Christianity in the formulation of their doctrines about soul and God, we are struck by the similarity of their ethical maxims. Both Buddhism and Christianity have remained to a great extent monkish religions, although neither Buddha nor Christ favored a monkish conception of life. Buddha said: "The layman and the hermit are the same when only both have banished the thought of self." *

Among the Buddhist sects of Japan there is one by the name of Shinshiu, which justly has been called the Buddhistic Protestantism. It is the most progressive and at the same time the most numerous sect of Japan. Their priests eat fish and meat, and are allowed to marry, because they claim that Buddha had refused to make any difference

* Sacred Books of the East. vol. xix. p. 182, ver. 1292 (Fo-Sho-Hing-Tsan-King) and "The Gospel of Buddha," chap. xviii. ver. 10.

between priest and layman, that austerities are of no avail, and that faith in Amita alone, in the infinite light of Buddha, can set us in that state of mind which ensures eternal salvation. Their opposition to a monkish morality is unquestionably in conformity with Buddha's simple teachings, the gist of which is contained in what Buddhists call the four noble truths and the eightfold path of righteousness.

The four noble truths and the eightfold path of righteousness are reiterated again and again in the sacred literature of Buddhism. In order to show the spirit of Buddhism in its original purity, without any admixture of our own interpretation, we here present a few unabbreviated paragraphs as they stand in Prof. Rhys Davids's translation of the Buddhist Suttas.*

### THE FOUNDATION OF THE KINGDOM OF RIGHTEOUSNESS.†

REVERENCE to the Blessed One, the Holy One, the Fully Enlightened One.

Thus have I heard. The blessed One was staying at Benares, at the hermitage called Migadâya. And there the Blessed One addressed the company of the five Bhikkhus,‡ and said:

* Sacred Books of the East, Vol. XI. pp. 146–150 and 150–154.

† The expressions "the kingdom of righteousness," "the glorious doctrine," or "gospel," etc., sound like imitations of Christian ideals, and yet those names are genuine Buddhistic terms and unquestionably older than Christianity.

‡ Bhikkhus, monks. The monks here addressed are the five mendicants who had waited on Gautama while he underwent austerities, and before he had attained enlightenment.

"There are two extremes, O Bhikkhus, which the man who has given up the world ought not to follow—the habitual practice, on the one hand, of those things whose attraction depends upon the passions, and especially of sensuality—a low and pagan way (of seeking satisfaction), unworthy, unprofitable, and fit only for the worldly-minded—and the habitual practice, on the other hand, of asceticism (or self-mortification), which is painful, unworthy and unprofitable.

"There is a middle path, O Bhikkhus, avoiding these two extremes, discovered by the Tathâgata *—a path which opens the eyes, and bestows understanding, which leads to peace of mind, to the higher wisdom, to full enlightenment, to Nirvâna!

"What is that middle path, O Bhikkhus, avoiding these two extremes, discovered by the Tathâgata—that path which opens the eyes, and bestows understanding, which leads to peace of mind, to the higher wisdom, to full enlightenment, to Nirvâna? Verily! it is this noble eightfold path; that is to say:

"Right views; right aspirations; right speech

* Tathâgata; the usual epithet for Buddha, and is explained as the Perfect One, or he who fulfils. Prof. Rhys Davids says in a footnote: "It is interpreted by Buddhaghosa, in the Samangala Vilâsinî to mean that he came to earth for the same purpose, after having passed through the same training in former births, as all the supposed former Buddhas; and that, when he had so come, all his actions corresponded to theirs."

right conduct; right livelihood; right effort; right mindfulness; and right contemplation.

"This, O Bhikkhus, is that middle path, avoiding these two extremes, discovered by the Tathâgata—that path which opens the eyes, and bestows understanding, which leads to peace of mind, to the higher wisdom, to full enlightenment, to Nirvâna?

"Now, this, O Bhikkhus, is the noble truth concerning suffering.

"Birth is attended with pain, decay is painful, disease is painful, death is painful. Union with the unpleasant is painful, painful is separation from the pleasant; and any craving that is unsatisfied, that too is painful. In brief, the five aggregates which spring from attachment (the conditions of individuality and their cause) * are painful.

"This, then, O Bhikkhus, is the noble truth concerning suffering.

"Now this, O Bhikkhus, is the noble truth concerning the origin of suffering.

"Verily, it is that thirst (or craving), causing the renewal of existence, accompanied by sensual delight, seeking satisfaction now here, now there—that is to say, the craving for the gratification of the passions,

* One might express the central thought of this First Noble Truth in the language of the nineteenth century by saying that pain results from existence as an individual. It is the struggle to maintain one's individuality which produces pain —a most pregnant and far-reaching suggestion. See for a fuller exposition the Fortnightly Review for December. 1879.—*Translator.*

or the craving for (a future) life, or the craving for success (in this present life).*

"This, then, O Bhikkhus, is the noble truth concerning the origin of suffering.

"Now this, O Bhikkhus, is the noble truth concerning the destruction of suffering.

"Verily, it is the destruction, in which no passion remains, of this very thirst, the laying aside of, the being free from, the harboring no longer of this thirst.

"This, then, O Bhikkhus, is the noble truth concerning the destruction of suffering.

"Now this, O Bhikkhus, is the noble truth concerning the way which leads to the destruction of sorrow. Verily! it is this noble eightfold path; that is to say:

"Right views; right aspirations; right speech; right conduct; right livelihood; right effort; right mindfulness; and right contemplation.

"This, then, O Bhikkhus, is the noble truth concerning the destruction of sorrow."

And when the royal chariot wheel of the truth had thus been set rolling onwards by the Blessed One, the gods of the earth gave forth a shout, saying:

"In Benâres, at the hermitage of the Migadâya, the supreme wheel of the empire of Truth has been

* "The lust of the flesh, the lust of the eye, and the pride of life" correspond very exactly to the first and third of these, and would be not inadequate renderings of all three.—*Translator.*

set rolling by the Blessed One—that wheel which not by any Samana or Brahman, not by any god, not by any Brahma or Mâra, not by any one in the universe, can ever be turned back!"

***

This is the essence of Buddha's doctrine. This is the Dharma in which Buddhists take refuge.

This doctrine of the four noble truths and the eightfold noble path of righteousness was taught by Buddha with the powerful authority of his impressive personality. He exemplified it in his personal conduct, and explained it in parables; and the mustard-seed of his noble religion has become a great tree, under the branches of which the nations of Asia have found a dwelling-place.

# THE PHILOSOPHY OF BUDDHISM.

## ORIGINAL DUALISM.

Buddhism originated, as all religions do, from the desire to escape the transiency of life with its incidental vicissitudes and to attain the permanent and enduring bliss of an undisturbed existence where there is no pain, no disease, no death, no incertitudes of any kind. As soon as the prevalence of suffering was recognized as an inalienable condition of bodily existence the first attempt at obtaining deliverance from evil was naturally made by a mortification of the body for the sake of benefiting the soul. The body was looked upon as the source of all misery, and a purely spiritual existence was the ideal in which religious men set their hope of salvation. The body is doomed to die, and was therefore considered as an animated corpse. Our material existence is a body of death of which man must rid himself before he can obtain the deathless state. Thus we read in the story of Sumedha, which serves as an introduction to the *Jatakas:*

> "Even as a man might rid him of
> A horrid corpse bound to his neck,
> And then upon his way proceed,
> Joyous, and free, and unconstrained;

"So must I likewise rid me of
This body foul, this charnel-house,
And go my way without a care,
Or least regret for things behind.

"As men and women rid them of
Their dung upon the refuse heap,
And go their ways without a care,
Or least regret for what they leave;

"So will I likewise rid me of
This body foul, this charnel-house,
And go my way as if I had
Cast out my filth into the draught." *

Sumedha says:

"What misery to be born again!
And have the flesh dissolve at death!

"Subject to birth, old age, disease,
Extinction will I seek to find,
Where no decay is ever known,
Nor death, but all security." †

The ideal of Buddhahood, accordingly, was in its original shape the attainment of a purely spiritual condition which it was hoped would afford a perfect emancipation from suffering. It was the same yearning as that of the early Christians, expressed in St. Paul's words:

"O wretched man that I am! who shall deliver me from the body of this death?"

* H. C. Warren, in his *Buddhism in Translations*, pp. 7-8. See also the passage quoted from Chapter VI. of the *Visuddhi-Magga*, p. 300.

† *Ibid.*, p. 6.

Even Luther, with whom the monistic era of Christianity begins, speaks of his body with the utmost contempt. The term *Madensack*, i. e., a bag full of food for grubs, is a favorite expression of his.

The religious problem, as it presented itself to the ascetic Gautama before he had attained to Buddhahood, was formulated on dualistic principles, but his final solution rested upon a monistic basis. We know little of his philosophical evolution and the phases through which he passed; but the outcome is unequivocal in all important questions that form decisive test-issues as to the character of his system. He was tolerant and showed extreme patience with all kinds of mythologies, even utilizing the superstitions of his age to the enhancement of his religion, but he was merciless in his rejection of metaphysicism and dualism.

### ANTI-METAPHYSICAL.

After Buddha had surrendered the old dualism, the traditional formulation of philosophical problems lost their meaning; they became what we now call illegitimate questions; and whenever Buddha was confronted with such illegitimate questions, he either refused to answer them or declared openly: "The question is not rightly put." * His refusal to answer such questions, which on his plane of thought had become unmeaning and irrelevant, nay, even mis-

* See, for instance, Warren, *Buddhism in Translations*, pp. 167 and 312.

leading, can be interpreted as agnosticism, or as a dodge and attempt at straddling, only by those who utterly misconceive the spirit of Buddha's doctrines. When bored with questions by a wandering ascetic, one of those frivolous wranglers who dispute merely for the sake of discussion, Buddha refuses to answer, but when afterwards Ananda accosts his master he explains why the wandering ascetic received no reply. The reason is here again the error involved in the wrong formulation of the question. Thus if he had replied in the negative, saying that the âtman does not survive death, the wandering ascetic would have said "the Buddha teaches that there is no after-life"; and if he had replied in the affirmative, saying that the âtman survives death, the implication would have been that Buddha believed with the Vedanta philosophers in the existence of an âtman.

Buddha's monism is not materialism; he does not identify soul and body, he only denies the separate existence of soul-entities. There is soul and there is body. There are consciousness-forms and bodily-forms, and both are changing and developing, both are subject to growth and decay. The body is dissolved, and consciousness passes away, yet their forms reappear in new incarnations. There is death and rebirth, and there is continuity of life with its special and individual types. If the soul were identical with the body, it would perish with it; if it were a distinct entity and an immutable âtman, it would not be affected by conduct and there would be no use in leading a holy life. In either case there is no need of seeking religion. Buddha's solution is, that there are not two things (1) an âtman and (2) the deeds performed by the âtman, but there is one thing—a soul-activity (karma), which operates by a continuous preservation of its deed-forms or samskâras, which are the dispositions produced by the various functions of karma. There is not a being that is born, acts, enjoys itself, suffers and dies and is reborn to die again; but simply birth, action, enjoyment, suffering, and death take place. The life-activity, the deeds, the karma, the modes of motion in all their peculiar forms, alone are real: they are preserved and nothing else. Man's soul consists of the memory-forms, or dispositions, produced by former karmas. There is no self in itself, no separate âtman; the self consists in the deed-forms, and every creature is the result of deeds.

The disciples propose to the Blessed One in the *Samyutta-Nikâya* this question:

"Reverend Sir, what are old age and death? and what is it has old age and death?"

The Blessed One replies:

"The question is not rightly put. O priest, to say: 'What are old age and death? and what is it has old age and death?' and to say: 'Old age and death are one thing, but it is another thing which has old age and death,' is to say the same thing in different ways.

"If, O priest, the dogma obtain that the soul and the body are identical, then there is no religious life; or if, O priest, the dogma obtain that the soul is one thing and the body another, then also there is no religious life. Both these extremes, O priest, have been avoided by the Tathâgata, and it is a middle doctrine he teaches: 'On birth depend old age and death.'" (*Buddhism in Translations*, p. 167.)

### PERSONALITY.

But considering the practical importance of personal effort in moral endeavor, how can the denial of the existence of a separate self as the condition of personality be useful in religion?

The answer is, that the denial of the existence of a separate self, an âtman, is not a denial of the real self such as it actually exists in man's personality. There is no chariot in itself, but there are chariots; there are no persons in themselves, but there are persons. Buddha does not intend to wipe out the personality of man, but only the false notion of the metaphysical character of personality. Not only did Buddha always endeavor to adapt his teachings to different personalities, but we find generally in Buddhism as much stress laid upon the personal relation of a disciple to the master, as by Luther, who used to say that "it is not enough for a Christian to know that Jesus Christ is the Saviour, he must experience the fact in his heart and must be able to say, 'Jesus Christ has come to save me individually.'"*

There is a similar aspiration in Buddhism, which

* "Darum ist's nicht genug, dass einer glaubt, es sei Gott, Christus habe gelitten., u. dergl., sondern er muss festiglich glauben, dass Gott ihm zur Seligkeit ein Gott sei, dass Christus für ihn gelitten habe, etc." (Quoted by Köstlin in his *Luther's Theologie.*) Similar passages are frequent in Luther's writings.

Buddhagosha, in his comments on the Dhammapada, expresses as follows:

"Now when a Supreme Buddha teaches the Doctrine, those in front and those behind, and those beyond a hundred or a thousand worlds, and those even who inhabit the abode of the Sublime Gods, exclaim: 'The Teacher is looking at *me*; The Teacher is teaching the Doctrine to *me*.' To each one it seems as if the Teacher were beholding and addressing him alone. The Buddhas, they say, resemble the moon: as the moon in the midst of the heavens appears to every living being as if over his head, so the Buddhas appear to every one as if standing in front of him." (*Buddhism in Translations*, p. 470.)

Far from being an obliteration of individuality, the denial of the âtman actually involves a liberation of individuality from an error that is liable to stunt all mental growth and hinder man's free development. Buddha takes out of life the vanity of self, which is based upon the dualism of âtman and karma as separate realities. There is no need of bothering about an âtman, but it is important to be mindful, thoughtful, and energetic in all that a man undertakes and does, for the karma is the stuff of which a man is made. One's own personal endeavor and achievements constitute one's personality, and this personality is preserved beyond death, as we read:

"But every deed a man performs
With body, or with voice, or mind,
'Tis this that he can call his own,
This with him take as he goes hence.
This is what follows after him
And like a shadow ne'er departs."*

* *Buddhism in Translations*, p. 228.

These lines have reference to the parable of the man whom his family, his friends, and his property leave when he is cited before the judge, while his good deeds alone follow him through the gate of death and plead for him. Speaking without allegory, we ought to say that the deeds, or rather the deed-forms, are the man himself.

There is no duality of a doer and his doings, a thinker and his thoughts, an enjoyer and his enjoyments, a sufferer and his sufferings, an aspirer and his aspirations. There is not an âtman that performs karma; but there is karma which, wherever incarnated in an individual group, appears as an âtman. The words doer, agent, enjoyer, etc., are mere modes of speech. The realities of soul-life consist in doings, thoughts, sufferings, enjoyments, and aspirations. Actions take place, and the peculiar form of every action is preserved as an analogous disposition to repeat that same action in the shape of memory-structures; and all living beings start life as the summed-up memory of their deeds in former existences.

### THE DEATHLESS.

There is no âtman-soul; accordingly there is no transmigration of an âtman-soul; yet there is rebirth: there is a reincarnation of the ancestral karma by a preservation and reproduction of the soul-forms transmitted from generation to generation.

Here we must make a distinction between pure forms and materialized forms. By the pure form of a right-angled triangle we mean the mathematical conception in its abstract and absolute distinctness. The relations of the angles and sides are definite conditions of unalterable rigidity. They can be formulated in theories which are readily recognized as eternal verities. The materialist who believes that material bodies alone are real, would say that pure forms are non-existent, but the mathematician knows that a right-angled triangle is a definite actuality which, whenever an occasion arises, will manifest itself with unfailing exactness. Manifestations of right-angled triangles take place in materialized forms, by which we mean some single drawing made in ink, pencil, or chalk, or a relation obtaining somehow among three points represented by the centres of stars or indicated by rays of light. The actualization of a pure form may be more or less perfect, but it always exemplifies the laws of pure form and is, so to speak, its incarnation. In this sense Plato speaks of ideas as being above time and space, and Schiller sings of the higher realm of pure forms :

> " In den höheren Regionen
> Wo die reinen Formen wohnen."

For ethical considerations man must learn to identify himself, not with the materialization of his thought and aspirations, but with their forms ; for the former are transient, the latter eternal. He must let go all attachment to the special and particular embodiment in which his soul appears. He must find his anchorage in that which cannot be destroyed but will last forever and aye. The pure forms of his soul-being must be understood as possessing his body they shape his brain, the nervous structures of his thoughts, the materialized forms of his sentiments and aspirations; they dominate his life, his energies, his everything, but not *vice versa:* his bodily incarnation does not lord it over the eternal type which in him becomes manifest. The material elements do not possess the directing faculty, for direction is a formal principle.

In this sense Christ existed since eternity as the divine Logos and became flesh in Jesus; and Buddha descended from the Tusita Heaven to earth for the purpose of being incarnated in the son of Mâya. In this same sense Buddhists speak of attaining to the Bôdhi, i. e. enlightenment or Buddhahood, which implies that the Bôdhi existed before Gautama found it. In the same sense, the right-angled triangle and its law existed before Pythagoras; he did not invent the theorem that bears his name: he discovered it. The idea of a right-angled triangle with all its essential relations dawned upon him, became incarnated in him, manifested itself in him.

But here we must pause a moment, for here lies a difficulty which has greatly embarrassed the translators of Buddhist scriptures. The Pâli word *rupa* means "form," but it is frequently used in the sense of materialized form (*rupa kayo*), not in the sense of pure form; indeed, it must sometimes be translated by body. Thus that which Plato and Schiller would call pure form is in Pâli called *arûpo*,* "that which is without *rupa*, the bodiless," commonly translated "the formless."

We read in the Buddhist scriptures that the attainment of Nirvâna is not possible unless we comprehend "the formless," which is the unmaterial, the eternal, the deathless. This deathless, this unmaterial, this "formless," or rather this eternal realm of pure form the *arúpaloco* is not an essence, not an entity, not an individual being or a personal deity; it has no special dwelling, nor is it a locality, or a heavenly abode; and yet it is the most important truth to be known.

> "There is, O disciples, something not-born, not-originated, not-made, not-formed. If, O disciples, there were not this not-born, not-originated, not-made, not-formed, there would be no escape for the born, the originated, the made, the formed." *Udâna*, VIII., 3.

The deathless is a mere nothing, if "nothing" means absence of materiality, and yet it is the most important factor of life, for it makes enlightenment possible and is the condition of salvation. In the *Majjhima Nikâya* (Sutta 26), in which Buddha declares that "the deathless has been gained," the theory is set forth that the "Nothing" is not a nonentity, but that it exists; and "of the priests who dwells in the realm of nothingness" it is said that "he has blinded Mâra, made useless the eye of Mâra, gone out of sight of the Wicked One."

* Also spelt âruppo and arûpe. The neuter of arûpo (arúpam) is used as a synonym of Nirvâna.

He who clings to bodily form, i. e., the materialized incarnation of pure form, and identifies his self with this compound of atoms, this aggregation of material elements, is not free from the illusion of selfhood; he has not found the eternal resting-place of life; the bliss of Nirvâna, the peace of his soul; he is driven round in a whirl of eternal turmoil, in the samsâra of worldly interests, in aspirations for transient goods.

He who has attained *arúpam*, the formless, surrenders with it all petulancy of self, for jealousy, spite, hatred, pride, envy, concupiscence, vainglory —all these and kindred ambitions—have lost their sense. He is energetic, but without passion; he aspires, but does not cling; he administers, but does not regard himself an owner; he acquires, but does not covet. This is expressed in the *Milindapañha*,[1] where we read:

"Said the king, 'Bhante Nāgasena, what is the difference between one who has passion and one who is free from passion?'

"'Your majesty, the one clings, the other does not cling.'

"'Bhante, what do you mean by "clings" and "does not cling"?'

"'Your majesty, the one covets, the other does not covet.'

"'Bhante, this is the way I look at the matter: both he who has passion and he who is free from passion have the same wish, that his food, whether hard or soft, should be good; neither wishes for what is bad.*

"'Your majesty, he that is not free from passion experiences

*Quoted from Henry Clarke Warren, *Buddhism in Translations*, p. 421. See also *Sacred Books of the East*, XXXV., p. 119.

both the taste of that food, and also passion due to that taste, while he who is free from passion experiences the taste of that food, but no passion due to that taste.'"

### THE MIDDLE DOCTRINE.

Buddha calls his solution of the psychological problem the middle doctrine, because it avoids both extremes of what, in the terms of the schoolmen, may be called extreme Realism and extreme Nominalism. Buddha denies that there are things in themselves of any kind. Compounds have no existence outside their parts, and man, like other things, animals, plants, chariots, worlds, etc., is a compound. There is no self in man as a separate entity. Self denotes the whole man. He who says compounds are things in themselves is mistaken, but he who denies the existence of compounds, he who proclaims the doctrine of non-existence is mistaken also. Compounds are real enough, the relation among things and their interaction are not mere illusions. While there are no things in themselves, there are forms in themselves. Buddhagosha argues in the *Visudhi-Magga*, Chap. XVIII.:

"Just as the word 'chariot' is but a mode of expression for axle, wheels, chariot-body, pole, and other constituent members, placed in a certain relation to each other, but when we come to examine the members one by one, we discover that in the absolute sense there is no chariot; and just as the word 'house' is but a mode of expression for wood and other constituents of a house, surrounding space in a certain relation, but in the absolute sense there is no house; and just as the word 'fist' is but a mode of expression for the fingers, the thumb, etc., in a certain relation; and the word 'lute' for the body of the lute, strings, etc., 'army' for elephants, horses, etc.; 'city' for fortifications, houses, gates, etc.; 'tree' fo trunk, branches, foliage, etc., in a certain relation, but when we come to examine the parts one by one, we discover that in the absolute sense there is no tree; in exactly the same way the words 'living entity' and 'âtman' are but a mode of expression for the presence of the five attachment groups, but when we come to examine the elements of being one by one, we discover that in the absolute sense there is no living entity there to form a basis for such figments as 'I am' or 'I'; in other words, that *in the absolute sense there is only name and form.* The insight of him who perceives this is called knowledge of the truth." (*Ibid.*, p. 133.)

As soon as we abandon the middle doctrine and assume the existence of a self which is supposed to be an entity that is in possession of all the parts of a compound, we must either assume that this entity after the dissolution of its parts will persist or that it will perish; and both views are erroneous because they start from a wrong premise. He who imagines that his self is immortal is mistaken and will cherish foolish ideas as to the mode and place of its future residence. But he who thinks that his self will perish is not less mistaken; he is unnecessarily afraid of death, for there is no self that can perish. Both propositions are senseless, because based on the illusions of either an extreme realism or an extreme nominalism.

He who sees things as they really are ceases to cleave to existence; he does not think that sensation or thought or any one of the aggregates is the âtman, but for that reason his personality is not wiped out.

"He ceases to attach himself to anything in the world, and being free from attachment, he is never agitated, and being never agitated, he attains to Nirvâna in his own person." (*L. c.* p. 137.)

### NOT A DOCTRINE OF ANNIHILATION.

If man is "name and form" and no self in itself, the proposition seems to suggest itself that death ends all; but the doctrine of annihilation is not countenanced by any of the orthodox Buddhists. We read in the *Samyutta Nikaya* (XXII., 85):

"Now at that time the following wicked heresy had sprung up in the mind of a priest named Yamaka: 'Thus do I understand the doctrine taught by the Blessed One, that on the dissolution of the body the priest who has lost all depravity is annihilated, perishes, and does not exist after death.'" (*L. c.*, p. 138.)

And a number of priests who had heard the report drew near and said:

"Say not so, brother Yamaka. Do not traduce the Blessed One; for it is not well to traduce the Blessed One. The Blessed One would never say that on the dissolution of the body the saint who has lost all depravity is annihilated, perishes, and does not exist after death." (*Ibid.*)

Then Shâriputra instructs Yamaka by teaching him that there is no such a being as a saint or a man in himself, for all his constituents are transitory and cannot be regarded as his âtman or enduring self; the saint is not bodily form, not sensation, not perception, not any of the predispositions, not consciousness. How then can the saint be annihilated in death? All the constituents of the saint depend upon causation, but holiness and enlightenment are the deathless state which is not touched by death. The *Visuddhi-Magga* comprises this doctrine in these four lines, which sound almost paradoxical:

> "Misery only doth exist, none miserable.
> No doer is there; naught save the deed is found.
> Nirvâna is, but not the man who seeks it.
> The Path exists, but not the traveller on it."*

And is Nirvâna non-existence? Not at all. It is the attainment of the deathless state, of immateriality, of pure form of eternal verity, of the immutable and enduring, where there is neither birth nor death, neither disease nor old age, neither affliction nor misery, neither temptation nor sin.

"'Wherein does Nirvâna consist?' And to him, whose mind was already averse to passion, the answer came: 'When the fire of lust is extinct, that is Nirvâna; when the fires of hatred and infatuation are extinct, that is Nirvâna; when pride, false belief, and all other passions and torments are extinct, that is Nirvâna.'" (*L. c.*, p. 59.)

He who attains Nirvâna continues to exist in his personal identity as pure form of a definite character, but he is without any trace of clinging to a particular incarnation. Thus he is no longer reincarnated in any special individual, and this is the sense in which Buddha has passed away and yet continues to exist in his bodiless personality, as we read in the *Milindapañha*†:

"The king said: 'Is there such a person as the Buddha, Nâgasena?'

---

*See *Sacred Books of the East*, XXXV., pp. 113–114.

† *L. c.*, p. 146.

"'Yes.'

"'Can he then, Nâgasena, be pointed out as being here and there?'

"'The Blessed One, O king, has passed away by that kind of passing away in which nothing remains which could tend to the formation of another individual. It is not possible to point out the Blessed One as being here or there.'"

### THE CONQUEST OF DEATH.

The surrender of the self-illusion with its pretensions brings us practically to the same maxim of life which St. Paul sets forth in 1 Cor., vii., 29–30:

"But this I say, brethren, the time is short: it remaineth, that both they that have wives be as though they had none.

"And they that weep, as though they wept not; and they that rejoice, as though they rejoiced not; and they that buy, as though they possessed not."

This view does not lead to the neglect of the body, but to its being subservient to higher ends and a nobler cause. The Buddha compares the body to a wound which we nurse although we do not love it. Nâgasena says:

"They who have retired from the world take care of their bodies as though they were wounds, without thereby becoming attached to them." (*Buddhism in Translations*, p. 423. Compare *Sacred Books of the East*, XXXV., p. 115.)

All vicissitudes and afflictions affect the bodily incarnation, not the eternal soul, the pure form or the arûpam, or bodiless, i. e., that which is without rupa; and thus the Samyutta Nickâya declares that the saint may be "wretched of body" but can never be "wretched of mind." The actuality of the world, the material reality of existence, the samsâra is absolutely void of permanency. All is transient and nothing endures. Therefore he who sets his heart on anything of the world or its various realizations of form, is sure to suffer; while he who has understood the emptiness of all material existence seeks refuge in Nirvâna, the domain of eternal verities which, in comparison to bodily realizations, constitute the Void, the Nothing, the existence-less. The eternal verities are immanent in all reality and condition its evolution; they are the aim and purpose of life; they are, to use Goethe's words, "the unattainable of which all actual things are but symbols." They are the nothingness of which we read in the *Majjhima Nikâya* (Sutta 26), that he who dwells in it is "out of the reach of Mâra," the Evil One.

"He has blinded Mâra, made useless the eye of Mâra, gone out of sight of the Wicked One." (*Ib.*, p. 348.)

An ancient Pâli verse (preserved in the *Udâna*, IV., 4) characterizes this condition as follows:

"The man whose mind, like to a rock,
Unmoved stands, and shaketh not;
Which no delights can e'er inflame,
Or provocations rouse to wrath—
O, whence can trouble come to him,
Who thus hath nobly trained his mind?"[1]

The belief in self, a separate soul-entity or âtman, is the most serious obstacle to the attainment of the

[1] Buddhism in Translations, p. 315.

eternal and deathless, because the thought of self infuses all creatures with fear of dissolution as well as a desire for this particular and special copy of its own eternal being. The *Visudhi-Magga* (the Book on the Path of Purity) dwells on the subject in Chapter XXI., where we read :

" To one who considers them [the constituents of being] in the light of their transitoriness, the constituents of being seem *perishable.* To one who considers them in the light of their misery, they seem *frightful.* To one who considers them in the light of their want of an Ego, they seem *empty.*

" He who considers them [the constituents of being] in the light of their transitoriness abounds in faith and obtains the *unconditioned* deliverance ; he who considers them in the light of their misery, abounds in tranquillity and obtains the *desireless* deliverance ; he who considers them in the light of their want of an Ego, abounds in knowledge and obtains the *empty* deliverance." (*Ib.*, p. 379.)

This is said to explain the stanza :

" Behold how empty is the world,
Mogharâja ! In thoughtfulness
Let one remove belief in self
And pass beyond the realm of death.
The king of death can never find
The man who thus the world beholds." *

MODERN PSYCHOLOGY.

The world has been greatly astonished in these latter years by the results reached by modern psychologists, Herbart, Fechner, Weber, Wundt, Ribot, etc., who have arrived at the conclusion that there is no soul-being, a theory which received the paradoxical name of " a psychology without a soul." The

* Ib. p. 376.

name is misleading, for the truth is that modern psychology discards the metaphysical conception of the soul only, not the soul itself. The unity of the soul has ceased to be a monad, an atomistic unity, and is recognized as a unification. The personality of a man is a peculiar idiosyncrasy of psychic forms, a system of sensations, impulses, and motor ideas, but it is not a monad, not a distinct entity, not a separate unit. In a word, there is no soul-entity, or soul-substance, or soul-substratum, that is possessed of sensations, impulses, and motor ideas; but all the sensations, impulses, and motor ideas of a man are themselves part and parcel of his soul. Mr. Hegeler expresses it by saying: "I have not ideas, but I am ideas."

The modern theory of the soul is not quite new, for it was clearly outlined by Kant, who counted the notion of a distinct ego-soul as a contradiction, or, as he termed it, one of the paralogism of pure reason. He did not exactly deny the separate existence of an ego, by which he understands apperception as a unit, viz., self-consciousness, but he proved the inconsistency of the assumption and retained the notion only on practical grounds, because he argued that the ego-conception is an idea without which ethics would fall to the ground. Theoretically he rejected the existence of an ego-soul, but for the sake of morality he retained it as a postulate of practical reason.

The ego-soul is nothing but the ancient and famed thing-in-itself in the province of psychology. Metaphysicians of the old school believe that philosophy consists in the search for the thing-in-itself, while the new positivist abandons the idea that there is a separate entity behind or within the parts of things. There is no watch-in-itself; but a peculiar combination of wheels and other mechanical contrivances, together with a dial and the movable hands on the dial, is called a watch. This is as little denial of the existence of watches as the new psychology is a psychology without a soul. Yet the enemies of the new positivism will still insist that the denial of things-in-themselves implies a philosophical nihilism.

But the new psychology is still older than Kant. As the doctrine of a separate soul prevailed in India among the Brahmans, so the denial of the existence of a separate soul was pronounced more than two thousand years ago by that school of thought which under the leadership of the great Shâkyamuni grew up in opposition to Brahmanism and became known by the name of Buddhism. Not only are the similarities that obtain between modern psychology and Buddhism striking, but we meet also with the same misconceptions and objections. The denial of the existence of a soul-entity is supposed to be a denial of the soul and also of its immortality or its reincarnation.

### PROFESSOR OLDENBERG'S VIEW.

Among the expounders of Buddhism Professor Oldenberg of Kiel ranks high. There are others that are his equal, but there is perhaps none who is his superior in scholarship. But with all his philological knowledge, the learned Professor is sadly deficient in philosophical comprehension. He appears absolutely unable to grasp the significance of the Buddhistic soul-conception, and since his book on Buddha has become a great authority, in Germany almost the sole authority, from which our reading public take their opinions on Buddhism ready-made, his misconceptions have become instilled into the minds of European and American thinkers, and it will be worth while to point out the deficiencies of his propositions.

H. Dharmapâla, the secretary of the Mâha-Bâdhi Society and editor of the Mâha-Bhâdi Journal, the official delegate of Ceylonese Buddhism to the Chicago Parliament of Religions, wrote sorrowfully to me two years ago:

> "Professor Oldenberg, the erudite scholar, has not grasped the spirit of the Dharma. He has translated carefully the Pâli words,—and that is all. A philologist may dissect the root of a Pâli word, but it does not make him know the spirit of Buddhism."

I have greatly profited by Professor Oldenberg's researches, which, considered as philological lucubrations, are very valuable, but I have, after all, felt constrained to adopt Mr. Dharmapâla's opinion. I have done so, however, not without hesitation, and not without having previously tried to reach a satisfactory explanation of his position. I shall here briefly call attention to his presentation of the Buddhist soul-conception and then point out the fallacies of his views. Professor Oldenberg says in the chapter entitled "The Soul:"

"It is not incorrect to say that Buddhism denies the existence of soul, but this must not be understood in a sense which would in any way give this thought a materialistic stamp. It might be said with equal propriety that Buddhism denies the existence of the body. The body, and in the same sense the soul also, does not exist as distinct and self-sustaining substances, but only as a complex of manifold inter-connected processes of origination and decease. Sensations, perceptions, and all those processes which make up the inner life, crowd upon one another in motley variety; in the centre of this changing plurality stands consciousness (viññâna), which, if the body be compared to a state, may be spoken of as the ruler of this state."* But consciousness is not essentially different from perceptions and sensations, the comings and goings of which it at the same time superintends and regulates; it is also a Sankhâra, and like all other Sankhâras, it is changeable and without substance."

Professor Oldenberg adds:

"We must here divest ourselves wholly of all customary modes of thinking. We are accustomed to realize our inner life as a comprehensible factor, only when we are allowed to refer its changing ingredients, every individual feeling, every distinct act of the will, to one and the same identical ego, but

* "The following passage is often repeated in the sacred texts (e.g., in the 'Sâmaññaphala Sutta'): 'This is my body, the material, framed out of the four elements, begotten by my father and mother . . . . but that is my consciousness, which clings firmly thereto, is joined to it. Like a precious stone, beautiful and valuable, octahedral, well polished, clear and pure, adorned with all perfection, to which a string is attached, blue or yellow, red or white, or a yellowish band."

this mode of thinking is fundamentally opposed to Buddhism. Here as everywhere it condemns that fixity which we are prone to give to the current of incidents that come and go by conceiving a substance, to or in which they might happen. A seeing, a hearing, a conceiving, above all a suffering, takes place: but an existence. which may be regarded as the seer, the hearer, the sufferer, is not recognized in Buddhist teaching." (*Buddha.* By Dr. Hermann Oldenberg. English Translation, p. 253.)

This is exactly the same as in modern psychology. The assumption of a soul-substance has been found to be a perfectly redundant hypothesis. The soul of man with all its various structures, or, as Buddhists would say, "sankhâras," is now conceived as a product of evolution. Life develops the various sense-organs in response to the stimuli of the surrounding world. The function of seeing which is a reaction taking place in response to the impact of the ether-waves of light, results in the appearance of eyes, the function of hearing being a reaction in response to the impact of the air-waves of sound, produces the ear, and the interaction among the senses begets thoughts. The translator of Oldenberg's book, Mr. William Hoey, is not happy in his selection of words, for he says in the passage quoted:

"Sensations, perceptions, and all the processes which make up the inner life, crowd upon one another in motley variety."

Where Oldenberg speaks of *ineinanderströmen* (streaming one into the other), the expression "motley variety" is a redundant addition, and conveys the idea that Buddhistic philosophy regards the soul as a motley crowd of processes. Oldenberg perused the manuscript before it went to press, and it is probable that he took no offence at the expression; indeed the context appears to justify the translator. We would not hold Oldenberg responsible for mistranslations, but English readers know him through the translation only, and for their benefit we feel urged to add a few words in explanation.

Far from regarding the inter-relations of thoughts and sensations as a chance conglomeration, Nagasena, the famous expositor of Buddhistic philosophy, makes the very opposite statement which in spite of its importance, is nowhere mentioned in Professor Oldenberg's work on Buddha.

We read in the *Milindapañha:*

> "It is by a process of evolution that the soul-structures (sankhâras) come to be."

And this statement is inculcated again and again, not less than seven times—a strange anticipation of the evolution theory! And then we read that these soul-faculties that originate through evolution "are not combined indiscriminately" (I. 6, *Sacred Books of the East*, XXXV., p. 87). "First is sight and then thought," for "all that happens happens through natural slope" (p. 90) "because of habit" (pp. 89 and 91) and "on account of an association" (p. 89). In the same sense modern psychologists speak of the "path of least resistance," and the principle of association is so highly appreciated that the English school calls its doctrine the "psychology of association." There is certainly no justification for such a term as "motley variety" in characterizing Buddhist psychology. On the contrary, we should be astonished at the anticipations of the most modern ideas.

Those who are accustomed to refer all psychic activity to one and the same identical ego, must, as Professor Oldenberg says, divest themselves of their customary modes of thinking; and he tries hard to do so himself, but he does not succeed.

The new psychology is, in fact, as much simpler than the old one as the Copernican system is simpler than the Ptolemaic system, but in order to appreciate this truth we must be acquainted with the facts. The geocentric astronomy appears natural to him who believes that there is an upside and a down, not only on earth, but also in the heavens; and the egocentric psychology is that childlike soul-conception which knows nothing of evolution, but assumes that a stork or other messenger brings into the world at the moment of birth a soul, we do not know whence, which soul is made the lord of the newborn baby with all his inherited tendencies. A certain amount of knowledge is necessary to comprehend the new views in both sciences, but he who has outgrown his mental swaddling clothes will not fail to abandon both the geocentric view in astronomy and the egocentric view in psychology.

### VACCHAGOTTA'S QUESTION.

Professor Oldenberg believes that not only the negation of the ego but also the negation of an eternal future must be regarded as the correct solution of the Buddhistic dialectic, and he claims that this was not openly pronounced by the Buddha because he feared to shock the hearts that quailed before the nothing. And yet Oldenberg quotes at the same time the passage of the *Samyuttaka Nikâya* in which the doctrine of annihilation is squarely denounced as a heresy. We read:

"'At this time a monk named Yamaka had adopted the following heretical notion: "I understand the doctrine taught by the Exalted One to be this, that a monk who is free from sin, when his body dissolves, is subject to annihilation, that he passes away, that he does not exist beyond death."'" (Oldenberg, *Buddha*, Engl. ed., p. 281.)

When Sâriputta convinces Yamaka that he does not even in this world appreciate the Perfect One, the monk confesses his error and he says:

"'Such, indeed, was hitherto, friend Sâriputta, the heretical view which I ignorantly entertained. But now when I hear the venerable Sâriputta expound the doctrine, the heretical view has lost its hold of me, and I have learned the doctrine.'" (*Ib.*, p. 282.)

In spite of innumerable passages which prove that Nirvâna is not annihilation, Oldenberg declares that "the doctrine that there is no ego is equivalent to the proposition: The Nirvâna is annihilation." Professor Oldenberg adds:

"But we can well understand why these thinkers, who were in a position to realize this ultimate consequence and to bear it, abandoned the erection of it as an official dogma of the Buddhist order. There were enough, and more than enough of hopes and wishes, from which he who desired to follow the Sakya's son, had to sever his heart. Why present to the weak the keen edge of the truth ; the victor's prize of the delivered is the Nothing? True, it is not permissible to put falsehood in the place of truth, but it is allowable to draw a well-meant veil over the picture of the truth, the sight of which threatens the destruction of the unprepared. What harm did it do? That which was alone of intrinsic worth and essential to excite the struggle for deliverance was maintained in unimpaired force, the certainty that deliverance is to be found only where joys and sorrows of this world have ceased. Was the emancipation of him, who knew how to free himself from everything transitory, not perfect enough? Would it become more perfect, if he were driven to acknowledge that beside the transitory there is only the Nothing?" (*Ib.*, 273, 274.)

Buddha, it is true, limited himself to that which conduces to deliverance, holiness, peace, and enlightenment, and gave no answer to questioners who were not prepared to understand his doctrine. Thus Oldenberg quotes the following passage from the *Samyuttaka Nikâya* :

"'Then the wandering monk* Vacchagotta went to where the Exalted One was staying. When he had come near him he saluted him. When, saluting him, he had interchanged friendly words with him, he sat down beside him. Sitting beside him the wandering monk Vacchagotta spake to the Exalted One, saying : "How does the matter stand, venerable Gotama, is there the ego (attâ)?"'

"When he said this, the Exalted One was silent.

"'How, then, venerable Gotama, is there not the ego?'

"* A monk of a non-Buddhistic sect. The dialogue here translated is to be found in the *Samynttaka Nikâya*, Vol. II., fol. tan.

"And still the Exalted One maintained silence. Then the wandering monk Vacchagotta rose from his seat and went away.

"But the venerable Ananda, when the wandering monk Vacchagotta had gone to a distance, soon said to the Exalted One: 'Wherefore, sire, has the Exalted One not given an answer to the questions put by the wandering monk Vacchagotta?'

"'If I, Ananda, when the wandering monk Vacchagotta asked me: "Is there the ego?" had answered: "The ego is," then that, Ananda, would have confirmed the doctrine of the Samanas and Brahmanas who believe in permanence. If I, Ananda, when the wandering monk Vacchagotta asked me: "Is there not the ego?" had answered: "The ego is not," then that, Ananda, would have confirmed the doctrine of the Samanas and Brahmanas, who believe in annihilation. If I, Ananda, when the wandering monk Vacchagotta asked me: "Is there the ego?" had answered: "The ego is," would that have served my end, Ananda, by producing in him the knowledge: all existences (dhamma) are non-ego?'

"'That it would not, sire.'

"'But if I, Ananda, when the wandering monk Vacchagotta asked me: "Is there not the ego?" had answered: "The ego is not," then that, Ananda, would only have caused the wandering monk Vacchagotta to be thrown from one bewilderment into another: "My ego, did it not exist before? but now it exists no longer."'"

Oldenberg's interpretation of this passage is as follows:

"We see: the person who has framed this dialogue has in his thought very nearly approached the consequence which leads to the negation of the ego. It may almost be said that, though probably he did not wish to express this consequence with overt consciousness, yet he has in fact expressed it. If Buddha avoids the negation of the existence of the ego, he does so in order not to shock a weak-minded hearer." (*Ib.*, 272, 273.)

Any one who understands the doctrine of modern psychology will appreciate Buddha's silence, which is amply explained by Buddha's words. Buddha refuses to answer the questions of Vacchagotta, but he gives a satisfactory explanation to Ananda.

It appears that Vacchagotta was a man who exhibited hopeless confusion concerning the fundamental notions of the Buddhist psychology. Buddha, it is true, denied the existence of an ego-soul; he denied that that something in man which says "I" can be regarded as a metaphysical soul-principle lording over all the faculties of man; but Buddha does not deny the reality of man's actual soul, his sensations and motor ideas; he does not deny the presence of consciousness, nor that there is a psychic structure in him that says "I." On the other hand, he does not teach that the soul of man (his sankhâras) will be annihilated in death. He teaches reincarnation, man's soul-structures will reappear, or rather they continue to exist after death. They are impressed upon others, and there is no annihilation; they are preserved exactly in the way in which they manifested themselves. Thus Vacchagotta's question could not be answered with a straightforward Yes or No. A simple Yes or No would under all conditions simply have increased the questioner's confusion. The question could be answered only after a discussion and complete explanation of the meaning of the term ego, which for reasons not mentioned in the dialogue the Buddha did not see fit to make. Probably he deemed it a waste of time to have a controversy with a professional controversialist and therefore refused to accept his challenge.

Suppose a carpenter's apprentice without education who understood nothing of mathematics, had approached the late Professor Gauss of Göttingen and asked him: "I understand that the Professor denies the reality of circles and lines, that he declares they are purely mental, ideal products of imagination, and quite unsubstantial? Will not the learned Professor answer my question squarely and in a straightforward manner, without reserve and without shirking the issue, Is mathematics substantial or is it not substantial?" What would Professor Gauss have said? Had he said, "mathematical figures are substantial," the apprentice would have acquired an erroneous notion regarding the nature of mathematics; but had the Professor said, "Mathematics are unsubstantial and purely ideal," the young fellow would have thought that mathematical constructions were arbitrary and imaginary like dreams. Professor Gauss would probably not have answered the question at all, for whatever he might have said, it would have been bewildering to the questioner. Now, should we say, on reading the report of such an interview, that Professor Gauss had practically taught the non-existence of mathematics? And could we presume that we understood why he avoided to draw the last conclusion of his doctrine; namely, for the reason that he did not want to shock a weak-minded hearer who still clung to the idea that there is a substance of mathematics?

Professor Oldenberg's interpretation of the passage quoted from the *Samyuttaka Nikâya* would make of the Buddha a hypocrite or a coward, for it represents him as not willing to concede the last consequence of his doctrine and without directly telling a lie as trying to make a false impression upon his interviewer. If Vacchagotta had been one of Buddha's followers, there might have been a reason for Buddha's not shocking his religious faith, but Vacchagotta belonged to a non-Buddhistic sect, and his question was not made in anxiety or with quivering lips. The context of the passage refutes Professor Oldenberg's interpretation.

Why not understand the passage as it reads? Had the Buddha said "the ego is not," Vacchagotta would imagine that the Buddha believed in annihilation, a doctrine which is unequivocally condemned in the Buddhist canon as a heresy. According to Professor Oldenberg, however, this would be the true import of the Buddhist religion. Vacchagotta, relying on the fact that his ego-consciousness was real, would say: "Did not my ego exist before? and now I am told that there is no ego." In the same way the hypothetical carpenter's apprentice in his interview with Professor Gauss would have said: "The lines which I use in measuring beams and boards are real; and yet this man who is supposed to be a great authority in mathematics tells me that mathematical lines are purely ideal!" We cannot help thinking that if Professor Oldenberg had asked the Buddha whether or not he taught the immortality of the ego, the Buddha would have given him the same answer as he did Vacchagotta: he would have remained silent.

Professor Oldenberg takes a denial of the existence of the ego-soul as a denial of the existence of the soul itself, in the same way that the carpenter's apprentice might have understood that Professor Gauss, not believing in a mathematical substance, denied the existence of mathematics altogether. Truly, to understand Buddhism, we must have an inkling of the fundamental notions of philosophy, and with all due respect for Professor Oldenberg's philological erudition, we cannot help saying that philosophical comprehension is a weakness of his which renders him unable to grasp the meaning of Buddhism.

The soul, according to Buddhism, does not consist of substance, but consists of sankhâras, which are sentient structures or forms produced by deeds, by karma, or function. A man's personality is name and form. The name may be preserved and the form may reappear in new generations. The individual dies, but its form continues by rebirth. There is no individuality in the sense of the Brahmanical âtman theory, but the individuality of a man, his name and form are for that reason real enough; and name and form are either singly, or sometimes together, preserved and reindividualized. There is a continuity in life in which the same form is preserved, and this continuous preservation of form is all that is and can be meant by sameness of personality. This is the secret (if there be any secret about it) of the Buddhist psychology.

### IS NIRVÂNA ANNIHILATION?

Professor Oldenberg's conception of Buddhism differs from mine; he says in a letter to me:

"Buddhism, in my opinion, suffers from the contradiction, historically quite conceivable, that on the one hand, it retains the old, concrete, and popular conception of a transmigration of the soul, on the other hand dissolves in its philosophy the idea of a soul as a substratum, an ego-being. This is a contradiction which will never be overcome by your attempt at sublimating the category of karma. Had Buddha not believed in a transmigration of the soul, suicide should have appeared to him as the quickest and best adapted means of making an end of suffering. A few drops of prussic acid would be a better, and at any rate a more rapid remedy than the holy eightfold path."

If this opinion of the learned Pâli Professor be tenable, the Buddha, who is generally regarded as one of the keenest thinkers that ever lived on earth, would have both denied the existence of a thing and at the same time have taught that it migrated from place to place. And we are requested to believe that the Buddha should have been guilty of such a gross contradiction! No, I would rather run the risk of doubting the infallibility of a German professor!

While Professor Oldenberg's summary solution is *prima facie* improbable, it is at the same time based upon incorrectly-stated facts. Buddhism teaches reincarnation, but it does not teach the migration of the soul. Professor Oldenberg's book, although good in many respects, is very deficient in its exposition of the Buddhist psychology, which is just the most important part of Buddhism. Oldenberg must have overlooked the passages in which the theory of soul-migration, in the sense of an ego-soul migrating from one body into another, is rejected. Buddhism denies that the soul is a substance, and in spite of Professor Oldenberg's statement to the contrary, it denies also most emphatically and unequivocally that there can be any transmigration or transportation of soul-substance. Yet Buddhism asserts the reappearance of the same soul-forms. We read in the *Questions of King Milinda*, III., 5, (*Sacred Books of the East*, XXXV., p. 111):

"Where there is no transmigration, Nâgasena, can there be rebirth?"

"Yes, there can."

"But how can that be? Give me an illustration."

"Suppose a man, O king, were to light a lamp from another lamp, can it be said that the one transmigrates from, or to, the other?"

"Certainly not."

"Just so, great king, is rebirth without transmigration."

"Give me a further illustration."

"Do you recollect, great king, having learnt, when you were a boy, some verse or other from your teacher?"

"Yes, I recollect that."

"Well, then, did that verse transmigrate from your teacher?'

"Certainly not."

"Just so, great king, is rebirth without transmigration."

"Very good, Nâgasena!"

In the Jataka tales and other popular legends expressions are frequently retained which suggest the old Brahmanical conception of a transmigration of soul, but philosophical expositions of the problem leave no doubt about the meaning of the Buddhistic idea of rebirth. At any rate, here is a plain statement in one of the most famous and authoritative Buddhist scriptures, which denies that there is any transmigration of a soul-entity; and thus Professor Oldenberg's charge of inconsistency falls to the ground, as it rests on a misstatement of the Buddhist faith.

Here is another example, adduced by Nâgasena in the *Milindapañha:*

The mango that is planted rots away in the ground, but it is reborn in the mangoes of the tree that grows from its seed. He who steals the fruit steals the property of him who sowed the mango. There is no transmigration of a mango-soul from the seed to the fruit, but there is a reconstruction of its form. Thus (as said he who came from Nazareth) the body of a man can be broken down like a temple that is destroyed, but it can and will be built up again. The life of a man does not end with death, for his soul is reincarnated again and again.

And how does this transfer of soul take place? Partly by heredity as is explained by Nâgasena in the illustration of the mango seed, partly by communication. A particular man is not a discrete individual, but a trysting-place of soul-activities, of sankhâras, which are impressed into him by example and education. Thus, a boy in school learns a verse by heart; there is no transfer of soul-substance migrating from the teacher to the pupil, but there is a reincarnation of a certain soul-form. The teacher's words are impressed into the boy; and this is called by Nâgasena "rebirth without transmigration."

Similar passages and similes in explanation of the same idea are found in the *Visudhi-Magga*, where the transfer of soul is illustrated by the reappearance of the form of a face in the mirror, of a voice in its echo, of a seal in its imprint, etc.

Professor Oldenberg knows very well that Nirvâna in the Buddhist texts is not annihilation, but deliverance from evil; and there are innumerable passages which characterize it as the state of highest bliss. Professor Oldenberg quotes several passages from various sources, which corroborate the positive conception of Nirvâna. He says:

> "Buddhist proverbs attribute in innumerable passages the possession of Nirvâna to the saint, who still treads the earth:
>
> "'The disciple who has put off lust and desire, rich in wisdom, has here on earth attained the deliverance from death, the rest, the Nirvâna, the eternal state.' Suttasangaha, fol. cû., a Brahmanical ascetic addresses to Sâriputta this question: 'Nirvâna, Nirvâna, so they say, friend Sâriputta. But what is the Nirvâna, friend?' 'The subjugation of desire, the subjugation of hatred, the subjugation of perplexity; this, O friend, is called Nirvâna.'" (*L. c.*, p. 264.)

But Nirvâna may be the *summum bonum*, because it involves the cutting off of the cause of existence, and the state of Nirvâna may become an actual annihilation at the moment of death. Yet even the final goal of saintship is not characterized as an absolute extinction. Professor Oldenberg quotes the following passages from the *Udâna* (fol. ghau):

"'There is, O disciples, a state, where there is neither earth nor water, neither light nor air, neither infinity of space, nor infinity of reason, nor absolute void, nor the co-extinction of perception and non-perception, neither this world nor that world, both sun and moon. That, O disciples, I term neither coming nor going nor standing, neither death nor birth. It is without basis, without procession, without cessation: that is the end of sorrow.

"'There is, O disciples, an unborn, unoriginated, uncreated, unformed. Were there not, O disciples, this unborn, unoriginated, uncreated, unformed, there would be no possible exit from the world of the born, originated, created, formed.'"

Professor Oldenberg adds the following comments:

"These words seem to sound as if we heard Brahmanical philosophers talking of the Brahma, the unborn, intransient which is neither great nor small, the name of which is 'No, No,' for no word can exhaust its being. Yet these expressions, when viewed in the connexion of Buddhist thought, convey something wholly different. To the Brahman the uncreated is so veritable a reality, that the reality of the created pales before it; the created derives its being and life solely from the uncreated. For the Buddhist the words 'there is an uncreated' merely signify that the created can free himself from the curse of being created (in the 'Dhammapada' it is said, v. 383): 'If thou hast learned the destruction of the sankhâra, thou knowest the uncreated'—there is a path from the world of the created out into dark endlessness. Does the path lead into a new existence? Does it lead into the Nothing? The Buddhist creed rests in delicate equipoise between the two. The longing of the heart that craves the eternal has not nothing, and yet the thought has not a something, which it might firmly grasp. Farther off the idea of the endless, the eternal could not withdraw itself from belief than it has done here, where, like a gentle flutter on the point of merging in the Nothing, it threatens to evade the gaze." (*Ib.*, p. 283, 284.)

Is there no other interpretation of the quoted passages than the one offered by Professor Oldenberg, viz., that the Buddhist faith is equivocal, and that it leaves the question undecided, either as an "unfathomable mystery," or as "resting in a delicate equipoise between the idea of a new existence and nothing"?

It would be difficult here for any man to speak authoritatively, but it appears to me the solution is not far to seek. The attainment of Nirvâna consists in enlightenment, that is to say, in a recognition of the fundamental truths of religion, which in their practical application are expressed in the noble eightfold path of righteousness. All individual craving has disappeared in the saint; he has become an incarnation of truth, not of theoretical or purely scientific notions concerning the nature of things, but of practical truth which manifests itself in a moral life. Thus Nirvâna is actually an utter annihilation of the thought of self and an embodiment of universal love and righteousness. Those eternal conditions which constitute righteousness are realized in a human heart.

If we translate Buddhist thought into Christian terms, we would say that the attainment of Nirvâna means God-incarnation, and the Buddha is the God-man. Shall we say that the eternal conditions of righteousness are a mere nothing, because they are unsubstantial? Are they non-existent because they are not concrete things, not material objects? That would certainly lead to a serious misconception of the most important facts of existenee!

Further, must God be considered as a nonentity when we learn to understand that God is not an individual being? Dwindles the Christian idea of Heaven away, because astronomy finds no place for it in the stars? There are things spiritual the existence of which does not depend upon a definite locality. The Pythagorean theorem is true, and would remain true, even if the world existed no longer. It is an eternal verity and not a mere nothing. This is illustrated in the "Questions of King Milinda," as follows:

> "The king said: 'Venerable Nâgasena, where does wisdom dwell?'
>
> "'Nowhere, O king.'
>
> "'Then, sir, there is no such thing as wisdom.'
>
> "'Where does the wind dwell, O king?'
>
> "'Not anywhere, sir.'
>
> "'So there is no such thing as wind.'
>
> "'Well answered, Nâgasena.'"

It may be difficult to the untrained to understand the paramount importance of eternal verities, but no one can deny their actual presence in life. What other meaning can there be in the words of Christ when he says: "Heaven and earth may pass away, but my words shall not pass away." The Buddha utters the same sentiment. He says:

"The Buddhas are beings whose word cannot fail; there is no deviation from truth in their speech", etc. (*Buddhist Birth Stories*, p. 18.)

The words of Buddha are not merely the sankhâras of his individual existence, but the eternal verities which shall not pass away, and he who realizes them in his soul has attained Nirvâna.

Now, I can see Professor Oldenberg smile, and hear him say, "That is what I mean; Nirvâna is, according to Buddha, the attainment of the eternal verities, and nothing else; accordingly it is tantamount to extinction. Nirvâna is not a place, and the Buddha after his death is no longer a definite individuality that can be pointed out to be here or there. *Ergo* he is dissolved into nothing." To be identical with verities that are eternal but have no dwelling-place in space is, in the opinion of many, an annihilation; for ubiquity and nullibiety are to their minds two expressions of one and the same thing. Kepler's soul has become the recognition of the three famous laws that bear his name; Ludolf is identified with the calculation of $\pi$; Newton with the formulation of the law of gravitation. They attained, each one in his own way, some special aspect of the uncreated, the eternal, the unborn. In the same way the Buddha (in the Buddhistic conception) has become the moral law which is, ever was, and shall remain forever the path of delivery from evil. Immortality is claimed for the Keplers, the Ludolfs, and Newtons, not for their names alone, because their names might be forgotten, but for their souls, for their ideas, for the verities with which they have become identical; and in the same sense, only in the broader field of religious truth, Buddhists believe in the eternal omnipresence of the Buddha. If that be nothing, then "Nothing" stands for the highest and noblest that can be thought of, and Nothing would be the divinest thing in the universe. Indeed, those invisible realities which, when recognized, are called truths, are of greater importance than concrete things and individual beings.

This is plain to every one who understands that truths are real, even though they are not substances or entities. And the same is true of the soul. To deny that volition, cognition and other mental activities are substances, or entities, or that they need a substratum or metaphysical subject in order to be real, is not a denial of their existence—it is simply the consistent consequence of the commonly acknowledged truth that they are not material.

Here lies the main difficulty in understanding Buddhism, which, whether we praise it or condemn it, must be recognized as the most philosophical of all religions. There is no use in understanding the words of the Buddhist texts, if we have no comprehension of their meaning. And how gross Professor Oldenberg's conception is, appears from his proposition that unless Buddha had been guilty of the inconsistency of believing in soul-transmigration, suicide would have been a better remedy for the evils of existence than the noble eightfold path of righteousness.

Suicide causes the dissolution of the individual; it sets an example which in the hearts of others will, according to circumstance, bear evil fruit; it causes consternation and unrest, and can therefore not lead to the cessation of suffering; under no condition could it conduce to the attainment of Nirvâna. He who imagines that but for the supposition of a transmigration of soul, suicide would be a more appropriate and safer method of reaching Nirvâna than the eightfold path of righteousness, has no inkling of the significance of Nirvâna.

Whatever error I may be guilty of in my own representations of Buddhism, be it in essays that I have written or in the *Gospel of Buddha*, this much is sure, that Professor Oldenberg has misunderstood its most salient doctrines, those on the nature of the soul and of Nirvâna. Being a professor who has studied the southern canon of Buddhism in its original documents, he is by many people looked upon as the greatest living authority on the subject, and he can therefore not fail to propagate his misconceptions. Misconceptions in all fields of thought are unavoidable, but if they originate in men who are called upon to be the channels of our information the result will be sad.

Professor Oldenberg is a good scholar, and, I repeat, I gladly acknowledge my indebtedness to him as a philologist; he may also be a good historian, but he has shown himself to be incompetent as an interpreter of Buddhism. His expositions remind us of the parable of the hardwood,* that is related in the *Majjhimanikâyo*, where we read:

"It is exactly, O monks, as if a man who demands hardwood, seeks for hardwood, and looks out for hardwood, climbs over the hardwood of a big hardwood tree, over the greenwood, over the bark, to the boughs and cuts off a twig, taking it along with the idea 'that is hardwood.' Suppose that a clear-sighted man observes him, saying: 'This good man really knows neither hardwood, nor greenwood, nor bark, nor boughs, nor foliage, therefore this good man who demands hardwood, seeks for hardwood, looks out for hardwood, climbs straightway over the hardwood of a large hardwood tree, over the greenwood, over the bark, and cuts off a twig in the opinion that it is hardwood. But the hardwood which he will get from the hardwood of the twig will not serve his purpose."

Professor Oldenberg has devoted his life to the decipherment of Sanskrit and Pâli, but he has failed to comprehend the significance of Buddhism. He has climbed over the hardwood of the doctrine of the Buddha without comprehending either its import or possible usefulness, and, presenting us with the foliage of externalities, assures us that this is the hardwood of Buddhism.

## CONCLUSION.

Buddhism is decidedly not nihilism, and Nirvâna does not mean annihilation. Buddhism in its purest form is, more than any other religion, stated in philosophical terms, which, the more positively phil-

* See Karl Eugen Neumann, *Die Reden Gotamo Buddho's*, p. 304-325.

osophical they are, will naturally appear to unphilosophical minds as mere negations.

Christians find it difficult to comprehend Buddhism, but the fact remains that what Christianity has been to Western peoples, Buddhism was to the nations of the East; and all the dissimilarities will in the end only serve to render the similarities that obtain between them the more remarkable.

While we are not blind to the great preferences of Christianity, we must grant that Buddhism is a truly cosmopolitan religion. Buddhism can comprehend other religions and interpret their mythologies, but no mythology is wide enough to comprehend Buddhism. Buddhism is, as it were, religious mythology explained in scientific terms; it is the esoteric secret of all exoteric doctrines. It is the skeleton key which in its abstract simplicity fits all locks.

This is the reason why Buddhism can adapt itself to almost any condition and can satisfy the spiritual needs of great and small, high and low, of the learned as well as the uncultured. It offers food for thought to the philosopher, comfort to the afflicted, and affords a stay to those that struggle. It is a guide through the temptations of life and a lesson to those in danger of straying from the right path. And yet it demands no belief in the impossible; it dispenses with miracles, it assumes no authority except the illumination of a right comprehension of the facts of existence.

# THE PSYCHOLOGICAL PROBLEM.

## THE ATMAN.

BRAHMANISM and Buddhism form a strong contrast, which becomes most apparent in the conception of the soul. Brahmanism is a religion of postulates, the basic doctrine of which must be taken on faith, while Buddhism is a religion of facts, rejecting altogether assumptions of any kind. Brahmanism teaches the existence of an Atman, or a self-soul; Buddhism rejects the theory of the existence of an Atman.

What is the Atman?

About two thousand five hundred years ago the Indian mind was engaged with the problem "What am I?" and the documents which still reveal to us the lines of argument and the chief results of these investigations are called the Upanishads. The Brahman thinker considering all the various ingredients of his make-up comes to the conclusion that none of them constitutes his Self, and now, instead of arguing that his Self is the organized totality of all his parts, he comes to the conclusion that Self is a separate being in itself.

The self or Atman was regarded as that something which says, "I am," and remains the same in all changes. It is called the Unconditioned, the Absolute, the Eternal, the Immortal.

What is this Self? Is it our body? No! Our body is subject to change; it is born, grows, then it decays, and, at last, it will die. The body is not the Self.

Is our mind the Self? The same answer. Our mind is not unconditioned; our mental activity is subject to change. Therefore, our mind is not the Self.

Perhaps our emotions are the Self? But how can they be the Self, for they come and go and are as variable as the body and the mind.

Body, mind, and the emotional soul (so the Brahmans say) are the vestures only of the Self; they are the husks or sheaths which envelope and hide it. The Self gives reality to, and is in possession of, body, mind, and soul. The self is the mysterious "ûkâsa," or quintessence of being, without which reality would not exist. We read:

> "This immutable one is the unseen seer, the unheard hearer, the unthought thinker, the unknown knower." *

We read in the Chândogya Upanishad:

> "The body is mortal and always held by death. It is the abode of that Self which is immortal and without body." (*Sacred Books of the East*, Vol. 1., pp. 140–141.)

The Self is supposed to be the "person" (purusha=person or soul) who is the agent in all the or-

* Dvivedi, *The Imitation of S'ankara*, p. 15.

gans. The Self is the seer in the eye, the smeller in the nose, the thinker of the thoughts. Thus Prajâpati, the Lord of Creation, instructs Indra on the nature of the self:

"Now where the sight has entered into the void (the pupil of the eye), there is the person of the eye, the eye itself is the instrument of seeing. He who knows, let me smell this, he is the Self, the nose is the instrument of smelling. He who knows, let me say this, he is the Self, the tongue is the instrument of saying. He who knows, let me hear this, he is the Self, the ear is the instrument of hearing.

"He who knows, let me think this, he is the self, the mind is his divine eye. He, the Self, seeing these pleasures (which to others are hidden like a buried treasure of gold) through his divine eye, i. e., the mind, rejoices.

"The Devas who are in the world of Brahman meditate on that self (as taught by Prajâpati to Indra, and by Indra to the Devas). Therefore all worlds belong to them, and all desires. He who knows that Self and understands it, obtains all worlds and all desires. Thus said Prajâpati, yea, thus said Prajâpati." (*Sacred Books of the East*, Vol. I., p. 142.)

Here the Self is defined as the consciousness of the ego-idea. The Self is said to be "he who knows, 'Let me smell, hear, think, or do this.'" The notion of Self is founded upon the fact that there is something in us which says "I am," and the question rises whether or not we are justified in regarding the consciousness as the Self, and the Self as an independent being.

What is the reality that corresponds to the pro-am "I?"

The word "I" is a central and therefore very important idea among many other ideas which constitute man's soul. The brain-structure in which this little word "I" resides is situated, together with all speech, in the island of Rolando, on the left hemisphere of the brain; and if it is conscious, we speak of this condition as ego-consciousness or self-consciousness. Its great prominence among other ideas is due to its significance which comprises nothing more nor less than the whole personality of the speaker. It may now mean the speaker's sentiments, now his body, now one of his limbs, now his thoughts, now his past history, now the potentialities of his future.

Considered by itself without the contents of its meaning, the pronoun "I" (frequently called the "ego" by philosophers) is as empty as a hollow water bubble; if devoid of the realities which it comprises in its meaning, it is a mere abstract; it is a cipher by which the speaker denotes himself. If regarded as a thing in itself, the word is without sense; it is like a circle without center and periphery; like a cart without wheels, box, and beam; like a tree without roots, stem, and branches. To reify or hypostatize it as a being in itself is a logical fallacy; and to build upon this fallacy a metaphysical system is a grave error, which naturally leads to the most fantastical illusions. We might as well hypostatize any and all other words or abstractions and regard them as real entities and things in themselves. In this way mythology has peopled our imagination with all kinds of chimeras, fairies, ogres, gods, and devils.

It is interesting to know the arguments by which the unity of animated life which manifests itself in consciousness was identified with prâna, which means breath, vital principle or the conscious animation of the body. Prajâpati explains that that is the true Self which when leaving the body renders the body most wretched. And this is to be honored like "Uktha," the divine hymn, the embodiment of divine revelation. Thus all the constituents of man, conceived as Devas, made the experiment. We read in the Aitareya-Âranyaka:

"'Well,' they said, 'let us all go out from this body; then on whose departure this body shall fall, he shall be the uktha among us.'

"Speech went out, yet the body without speaking remained, eating and drinking.

"Sight went out, yet the body without seeing remained, eating and drinking.

"Hearing went out, yet the body without hearing remained, eating and drinking.

"Mind went out, yet the body, as if blinking, remained, eating and drinking.

"Breath went out, then when breath was gone out, the body fell. . . .

"They strove again, saying: 'I am the uktha, I am the uktha.' 'Well,' they said, 'let us enter that body again; then on whose entrance this body shall rise again, he shall be the uktha among us.'

"Speech entered, but the body lay still. Sight entered, but the body lay still. Hearing entered, but the body lay still. Mind entered, but the body lay still. Breath entered, and when breath had entered, the body rose, and it became the uktha.

"Therefore breath alone is the uktha.

"Let people know that breath is the uktha indeed.

"The Devas (the other senses) said to breath: 'Thou art the uktha, thou art all this, we are thine, thou art ours'." (*Sacred Books of the East*, Vol. I., pp. 206–207.)

We can trace in the Upanishads the logical arguments on which the Indian mind arrived at the idea of an independent Self, as the breath or spirit of man which at the moment of death was supposed to leave the body and to continue in an independent existence as an immortal being. Breath became identified with consciousness and was supposed to be the Self and is called Sattya, i. e., the true (p. 209). It is the mover of movements and the agent of actions. It is that by which we obtain strength, and its recognition is the object of all knowledge. In Shankara's philosophy the Self plays the part of Kant's thing in itself. The Self is described to us in the Talavakâra-Upanishad (*Sacred Books of the East*, I., p. 147):

"It is the ear of the ear, the mind of the mind, the speech of speech, the breath of breath, and the eye of the eye. When freed (from the senses) the wise, on departing from this world, become immortal."

And it is by recognizing the Self that "the wise become immortal when they have departed from this world" (*ib.*, p. 149).

The Self was identified with God, the Creator. Brahman was said to be the Self; and "in the beginning there was only Self. He was alone; and there was nothing else whatsoever." (Aitareya-

Âranyeka, Vol. I., p. 1.) Having created worlds and the various deities, Agni (fire), Vâyu (air), Âditya (sun), the Dis (regions), Kandramas (moon), and the rest, the Self created man, and all the gods entered into man to ensoul him. They endowed him with breath, sight, touch, speech, digestion, and other functions. At last the Self entered through the suture of the cranium. We read in the Aitareya Aranyaka:*

"And then the Self thought: 'If speech names, if scent smells, if the eye sees, if the ear hears, if the skin feels, if the mind thinks, if the off-breathing digests, if the organ discharges, then what am I?'

"Then opening the suture of the skull, he got in by that door.

"That door is called the Vidriti (tearing asunder), the Nândana (the place of bliss).

"There are three dwelling-places for him, three dreams; this dwelling-place (the eye), this dwelling-place (the throat), this dwelling-place (the heart).

"When born (when the Highest Self had entered the body) he looked through all things, in order to see whether anything wished to proclaim here another (Self). He saw this person only (himself) as the widely spread Brahman. 'I saw it,' thus he said:

"Therefore he was (named) 'Idam-dra' (seeing this).

"Being Idamdra by name, they call him Indra mysteriously. For the Devas love mystery, yea, they love mystery."

Of such importance did the Hindu thinkers regard the conception of Self, which as an independent spiritual being was compared to "a bank or boundary, so that these worlds may not be confounded," that they made the belief in its existence

* *Sacred Books of the East*, Vol. I., p. 242.

an article of faith. Knowledge of the Self was supposed to be a divine revelation which would not have obtained except by the supernatural existence of the gods, of Prajâpati, of Brahma, of the Lord. The Self is mysterious in its nature. It cannot be discovered either by sense-experience or by scientific investigation; for:

"The eye has no access there, nor has speech nor mind; we do not know the Self, nor the method whereby we can impart It. It is other than the known as well as the unknown; so indeed do we hear from the sages of old who explained It thus to us."*

The existence of Self must be believed. We read in the Ch'ândogya Upanishad (*Sacred Books of the East*, I., page 122):

"When one believes, then one perceives. One who does not believe, does not perceive. Only he who believes, perceives."

On the belief in the existence of the Self man's eternal salvation was supposed to depend. We read (*Sacred Books of the East*, Vol. I., p. 124):

"To him who sees, perceives, and understands this, the spirit (prâna) springs from the Self, hope springs from the Self, memory springs from the Self; so do ether, fire, water, appearance and disappearance, food, power, understanding, reflexion, consideration, will, mind, speech, names, sacred hymns, and sacrifices—aye, all this springs from the Self."

"There is this verse, 'He who sees this, does not see death, nor illness, nor pain; he who sees this, sees everything, and obtains everything everywhere.'

* Dvivedi, *l. l.*, p. 6.

"He who sees, perceives, and understands this, loves the Self, delights in the Self, revels in the Self, rejoices in the Self —he becomes a Svarâj (an autocrat or self-ruler); he is lord and master in all the worlds."

There are various complicated systems elaborated from the metaphysics of the conception of the Self. Most of the Indian philosophers identify the Self with Brahma, so that there is really only one Self which manifests itself in many various Selves; and since the Self alone is real, the material universe is conceived as mere appearance, as sham, as an illusion of the senses. This is the doctrine of the Vedânta School, the greatest representative of which is Shankara, a thinker of unusual power and of great influence.

The Vedânta philosophy is called *advaita*, or the non-duality doctrine, as opposed to the dualism of the Samkhya School, whose founder taught that there are innumerable Selves uncreated and indestructible, among whom many, by the error of not distinguishing between Self and Body, got entangled into this material world of suffering, from which they can be ransomed only by the recognition of the true nature of the Self.

Whatever view we may take, one thing is certain, that the assumption of an independent metaphysical Self, involves us in contradictions and vagaries wherever we turn and however wisely we may attempt to avoid its consequences.

* * * * *

In opposition to these speculations, Buddha denied

the existence of an independent Self as the soul of man. While the Brahmans spoke of the Self in a dualistic sense, "as of a razor that might be fitted in a razor-case," or "as a fire that might be lit in a fire-place," Buddha propounded a consistent Monism in which he radically ignored all metaphysical assumptions and philosophical postulates, founding his religion on a consideration of the pure facts of experience. While the Brahmans declared that the Self is immortal and immutable, "that it is not increased by a good action, or decreased by a bad action," Buddha taught that there was no use in trying to improve the immutable; but he found it imperative to improve man; and man's nature, according to Buddha, consists of karma, i. e., of actions, or to use a term of natural science, of functions. Man is the product of the life and thought functions of former existences, and his own karma continues as a living factor in the generations to come.

In Brahmanism facts are nothing, and idea, that is to say theory, is everything. In Buddhism theory is nothing, and facts are everything. Theory has sense only as a comprehensive formulation of facts.*

The Self of the Brahmans is Kant's thing-in-itself applied to religion. It is the thing-in-itself of man's soul. It is the hypostatization of the abstraction of self-consciousness, which is carried so far as to deify that feature of existence which is common to all beings and to regard the particular forms which they assume as unessential. From this standpoint all

*See Dvivedi, *l. l.*, Introduction, p. xix.

differences disappear, and, as the Bhagavadgita declares, "a Brahman full of learning and virtue, a cow, an elephant, a dog, and one of low caste," all are on the same level. Shankara, speaking of "the nightmare of separateness," says:

> "He who has the firm conviction 'I am this consciousness,' not the form it takes, let him be a Brâhmana or a Chândâla, my mind points to him as the real Master." *

Buddha would on the contrary insist that the form in which consciousness appears is the man himself; that that particular form functioning in a particular way is that particular man; but that consciousness in itself, a consciousness which has no particular form and is consciousness in general, is a mere fiction, an empty abstraction, and a thought as "hollow as a water-bubble," and as "hollow as a plantain tree."

Shankara was an adversary of Buddhism, and the report goes that he had instigated the people to massacre the Buddhists without mercy. This report may have been untrue, but this much is certain, that Shankara was the most energetic reformer of Brahmanism at the time when Buddhism began to lose its hold on the Hindu mind. While Shankara rejected Buddha's philosophy, he adopted those moral truths of his doctrines which had most deeply impressed the people of India, universal love, compassion with the suffering, and the solidarity of all life. And here this theory of the Self merges into Pan-

* *The Imitation of S'ankara*, p. 181.

theism. He sees with the poet of the Bhagavadgita "all beings in Self, and Self in all beings." Feeling the thrill of omneity in his heart, Shankara says:

"I am all bliss, the bliss all eternal consciousness. Death I fear not, caste I respect not, father, mother, nay even birth, I know not, relatives, friends, I recognize not, teacher and pupil I own not; — I am all bliss, the bliss all eternal consciousness." *

While Shankara has become the undisputed leader of Hindu thought, whose sway reaches down to the present time, we must not omit to mention another less prominent school, founded by Râmânuja, which has worked out the doctrine of the Self in a form that peculiarly and closely resembles the soul-conception of modern Christianity. Râmânuja believes in a triad of existences: (1) the Highest Self, who is Para-Brahman, or Îshvara, or Vishnu, the Creator and Lord; (2) innumerable Selves of human beings, who possess separate and distinct existences; and (3) the not-self of the inanimate world. Râmânuja's moral ideal for human Selves consists in the attainment of a union with the Highest Self, in which, however, their separate identities and their individual consciousnesses are not lost.

* * * * *

The contrast between a religion based upon a belief in postulates and a religion based upon facts has not as yet disappeared. The dogmatic Christianity of the present day is a revival of the metaphysics of the Upanishads, and some representative Christian

* *The Imitation of S'ankara*, pp. 157–158 and 156.

authors remind us very much of the logic and modes of thought of the old Brahmans. Thus Mr. Gladstone, in his article on "The Future Life," says:

"The power of death to destroy living beings is conditioned by their being compounded. For as consciousness is indivisible, so it should seem is the conscious being in which it resides. And, if this be so, it follows that, the body extraneous and foreign to the true self, no presumption can arise out of the dissolution of the body against the continued existence of the true self.

"As we lose limbs, organs of sense, and yet the true self continues; and as animal bodies are always in a state of flux, with no corresponding loss or gain of the true self, we again infer the distinctness of that true self from the body, and its independence at the time of death."

If this passage, which contains the gist of Mr. Gladstone's argument in favor of an immortality in another world of immaterial existence, appeared in one of the Upanishads, it could not be regarded as out of place there, so closely does it resemble the line of thought set forth by Brahman sages. But the objection that Buddha made against the assumption of an independent Self holds good with the same force against Christian metaphysics as against Brahmanical speculations.

If modern psychology has accomplished anything beyond the shadow of doubt, it is this, that consciousness is not an indivisible unity, but a unification, a systematization or a focussing of feelings. These feelings, when not centralized, as in dreams or swoons, continue in a condition that is commonly called subconscious. The province of subconscious activity in a man's soul is very large, by far larger than the narrow circle that under the stress of attention appears on the surface of consciousness.

* * * * *

But is this not a dreary doctrine as it denies the existence of the Soul? Those readers who have followed us in our exposition on the nature of the Soul know that the Buddhist doctrine is neither dreary, nor nihilistic, nor does it deny the existence of the Soul. It only denies the assumption of the existence of a metaphysical Self, of an Atman, an independent ego-being, and proves that the Soul is larger than the ego. The rescission of that artificial wall raised up round the conception of our Self opens the vistas of eternity, both in the past and the future; it shows the connection in which our Soul stands with the whole evolution of life upon earth and impresses us with the importance of our deeds which will continue for good or evil in after-life.*

"Not from the blank Inane emerged the soul:
A sacred treasury it is of dreams
And deeds that built the present from the past,
Adding thereto its own experiences.
Ancestral lives are seeing in mine eyes,
Their hearing listeneth within mine ears,
And in my hand their strength is plied again.
Speech came, a rich consignment from the past,
Each word aglow with wondrous spirit life,
Thus building up my soul of myriad souls.

"I call that something 'I' which seems my soul;
Yet more the spirit is than ego holds.

---

* *De Rerum Natura*, pp. 7–8.

For lo! this ego, where shall it be sought?
I'm wont to say 'I see;' yet 'tis the eye
That sees, and seeing, kind'leth in the thought
The beaming images of memory.
'I hear' we say: Hearing is of the ear;
And where the caught word stirs, there chords resound
Of slumb'ring sentiment; and echoes wake
Of sounds that long ago to silence lapsed.
Not dead, perfected only, is the past;
And ever from the darkness of the grave
It rises to rejuvenated life.

"The 'I' is but a name to clothe withal
The clustered mass that now my being forms.
Take not the symbol for reality—
The transient for th' eterne. Mine ego, lo!
'Tis but my spirit's scintillating play
This fluctuant moment of eternities
That now are crossing where my heart's blood beats.
I was not, am, and soon will pass. But never
My soul shall cease; the breeding ages aye
Shall know its life. All that the past bequeathed,
And all that life hath added unto me,
This shall endure in immortality."

## GOETHE A BUDDHIST.*

BUDDHISM is commonly regarded as a religion, which, though it may be adapted to the passive

* The greater number of Goethe's poems quoted in this article are not commonly known in English-speaking countries, or at least have never as yet been translated into English. The translations offered here (with the exception of three bearing the signatures of Bayard Taylor, J. S. Dwight, and Edgar Alfred Bowring) are by the author.

nations of Asia, could never have exercised any lasting influence upon the energetic races of the West. But this is true only if Buddhism is identified with that quietism which makes of indolence the cardinal virtue of life. Nothing, however, is further removed from the Tathagata's teachings than passive indifference; and the truth is that some of the greatest geniuses of Europe have spontaneously developed the essential doctrines of the venerable sage of the Shâkya, in whom Buddhists take refuge.

One of the most striking examples of Buddhistic modes of thought in a Western mind, incredible though it may appear to those who persistently misunderstand the spirit of Buddhism, is the great German poet Wolfgang Goethe, the Darwinist before Darwin, the prophet of monism and positivism, the naturalist among bards and the bard among naturalists. Goethe, unlike Auguste Comte the founder of the French positivism, did not believe in unknowable causes behind phenomena. He proclaimed the principle of genuine positivism, saying: *

> "The highest would be to understand that all facts are themselves theory. The azure color of the sky reveals to us the fundamental law of chromatics. We must not seek anything behind phenomena; for they themselves are our lesson."
>
> "Das Höchste wäre: zu begreifen, dass alles Factische schon Theorie ist. Die Bläue des Himmels offenbart uns das Grundgesetz der Chromatik. Man suche nur nichts hinter den Phänomenen: sie selbst sind die Lehre."

This principle implies the denial of all things in

* *Sprüche in Prosa*, Edition Cotta, Vol. XIII., p. 274.

themselves supposed to reside in man's soul as well as in the world as a whole; and this truth is expressed by Buddha in the sentence: "There is no âtman." We shall prove our proposition that, in this sense, Goethe was a Buddhist, by quoting several of his poems which prove that he espoused the doctrine of Karma as well as the Buddhist psychology, which knows nothing of an âtman or separate ego-self but regards the soul of man as a complex product of many ingredients constituting our Karma inherited from former existences and destined to continue after death according to our deeds done during life.

Goethe analyzes himself in the following poem:

"From father my inheritance
 Is stature and conduct steady;
From mother my glee, that love of romance,
 And a tongue that's ever ready.

My grandpa was fond of ladies fair,
 Which still my soul is haunting.
My grandma jewels loved to wear,
 Like her I'm given to vaunting.

Now since this complex can't but be
 The sum of all these features,
What is original in me
 Or other human creatures?"

"Vom Vater hab ich die Statur,
Des Lebens ernstes Führen,
Von Mütterchen die Frohnatur
Und Lust zu fabuliren.

Urahnherr war der Schönsten hold,
Das spukt so hin und wieder;
Urahnfrau liebte Schmuck und Gold,
Das zuckt wohl durch die Glieder.

Sind nun die Elemente nicht
Aus dem Complex zu trennen,
Was ist denn an dem ganzen Wicht
Original zu nennen?"

The question "What am I?" is answered by Goethe: I am a commonwealth of inherited tendencies and ideas.

Man is inclined to look upon his own sweet self as a distinct and separate being which is something quite original and a thing in itself, analogous to the metaphysical things in themselves of Kantian philosophy. But this notion of oneself is an error; it is what Buddhists call "the illusion of the thought 'I am.'" The central idea of Buddhism is the doctrine that enlightenment dispels the ego-illusion, and Goethe says tersely:

"'Cognize thyself,' 'tis said. How does self-knowledge pay?
When I cognize myself, *I* must at once away."

"Erkenne dich! —Was hab ich da für Lohn?
Erkenn' ich mich, so muss ich gleich davon."

Goethe was a man of great self-assertion and it is apparent that he does not mean self-annihilation or resignation. Goethe does not mean to say that he himself (Goethe or Goethe's soul) does not exist. He means that that vanity of self which imagines that a man's self consists in an independent and quite original being which is exclusively a thing of its own is an illusion that is dispelled by self-knowledge.

"I" am not a separate ego-consciousness that is in possession of a soul with all its impulses, thoughts, and aspirations. Rather the reverse is true. My soul, consisting of definite soul-structures, is in possession of an ego consciousness; and my entire soul is meant when I say "I." In this sense every one can say of himself, "I existed long before I was born." To be sure I did not exist in this exact combination of soul-elements; but the soul-elements of my Karma existed.

Such is the Buddhistic doctrine, and such is Goethe's view of the soul. The words which constitute our thought, the most essential part of ourselves, were first uttered millenniums ago, and have been handed down with imperceptible changes in pronunciation, grammar, and construction until they have become again incarnated in the system of our mind. But it is not our language alone that existed before us, but also our habits of daily life, our modes of living, our loves and hates, our morals, our hopes, and our aspirations. Goethe says:

> "When eagerly a child looks round,
> In his father's house his shelter is found.
> His ear, beginning to understand,
> Imbibes the speech of his native land.
>
> Whatever his own experiences are,
> He hears of other things afar.

Example affects him ; he grows strong and steady
Yet finds the world complete and ready.

This is prized, and that praised with much ado ;
He wishes to be somebody too.
How can he work and woo, how fight and frown?
For everything has been written down.

Nay, worse, it has appeared in print,
The youth is baffled but takes the hint.
It dawns on him, now, more and more
He is what others have been before."

"Wenn Kindesblick begierig schaut,
Er findet des Vaters Haus gebaut ;
Und wenn das Ohr sich erst vertraut,
Ihm tönt der Muttersprache Laut ;
Gewahrt er diess und jenes nah,
Man fabelt ihm, was fern geschah,
Umsittigt ihn, wächst er heran :
Er findet eben alles gethan ;
Man rühmt ihm diess, man preist ihm das :
Er wäre gar gern auch etwas.
Wie er soll wirken, schaffen, lieben,
Das steht ja alles schon geschrieben
Und, was noch schlimmer ist, gedruckt.
Da steht der junge Mensch verduckt
Und endlich wird ihm offenbar :
Er sei nur was ein andrer war."

The idea that we are an individual in the literal sense of the word, i. e., an indivisible soul-being; a genuine unity but not a unification ; a kind of spirit-monad, seems at first sight to flatter our vanity, because it renders us independent of our own past that produced us, and ignores the debt we owe to our spiritual and physical ancestry, giving us the appearance of originality. With a good deal of humor Goethe describes this craving of our natural vanity in these lines:

> " Would from tradition break away,
> Original I'd be!
> Yet the feat so grand, to my dismay,
> Greatly discomfits me.
> The honor of being an autochthon *
> Would be a great ambition,
> But strange enough, I have to own,
> I am myself tradition."

> " Gern wär ich Ueberliefrung los
> Und ganz original;
> Doch ist das Unternehmen gross
> Und führt in manche Qual.
> Als Autochthone rechnet' ich
> Es mir zur höchsten Ehre,
> Wenn ich nicht gar zu wunderlich
> Selbst Ueberliefrung wäre."

The two last lines express in simple terms the substance of both the ancient Buddhist doctrine of Karma and modern psychology. We do not have our thoughts, habits, and aspirations, but we are they. That which existed before us and is being handed down from generation to generation, is our own pre-existence. We do not receive the tradition of the past, but we ourselves are this tradition as it has been shaped by the Karma of the past.

This conception of the soul seems to lead to a

* From *αὐτός*, self, and *χθών*, earth, meaning " sprung from the earth, an aboriginal inhabitant"; here, " unconditioned by history," or " absolutely original."

splitting up of our existence into as many personalities as receive the soul-seeds of our Karma. But the splitting up is not an absorption into a vague and indefinite half-existence, but rather a duplication and multiplication of our soul in the way a pattern is reproduced, or as a book that is printed in many copies may sow the seed of the author's thought in its entirety in the hearts of innumerable readers. There is a splitting up, but no division; there is a scattering of our spiritual treasures, but everywhere the soul remains entire, both in its inner sentiments and outer forms. Says Goethe:

> "Life I never can divide,
> Inner and outer together you see.
> Whole to all I must abide,
> Otherwise I cannot be.
> Always I have only writ
> What I feel and mean to say.
> Thus, my friends, although I split,
> Yet remain I one alway."

> "Theilen kann ich nicht das Leben,
> Nicht das Innen noch das Aussen,
> Allen muss das Ganze geben,
> Um mit euch und mir zu hausen,
> Immer hab ich nur geschrieben
> Wie ich fühle, wie ich's meine,
> Und so spalt ich mich, ihr Lieben,
> Und bin immerfort der Eine."

This conception of our own being is of practical importance, for it teaches us to think with reverence of the past, and to contemplate with earnestness the future. Our existence is not limited to the span of the present life; it is not limited by birth and death; it began with the appearance of life upon earth; nay, it is older than that even; for it lay hidden in the conditions of organized life, whatever they may have been; and we shall continue to live so long as mankind will flourish on earth, nay, even longer; for wherever the same soul-structures rise, there our soul will be formed again and rise anew into being. In a word, our soul is illimited, in the past as well as in the future. Eternity lies behind us and also before us.

Goethe believes in immortality. He says:

> "'Hast immortality in mind
> Wilt thou the reasons give?'
> —The most important reason is,
> We can't without it live."

> "'Du hast Unsterblichkeit im Sinn;
> Kannst du uns deine Gründe nennen?'
> Gar wohl! Der Hauptgrund liegt darin,
> Dass wir sie nicht entbehren können."

Goethe does not believe that immortality involves the belief in a Utopian heaven, and, like Buddha, he urges that if such a heaven existed, as many Christians imagine it to be, it would not be a place of salvation, but a mere transfiguration of the trivialities of this world. Thus Goethe prefers to be counted among the Sadducees, of whom the Scriptures say, they hold that there is no resurrection from the dead. Goethe says:

"A Sadducee I'll be fore'er,
For it would drive me to despair,
If the Philistines who now cramp me
Would cripple my eternity.
'Twould be the same old fiddle-faddle,
In heaven we'd have celestial twaddle."

"Ein Sadducäer will ich bleiben!—
Das könnte mich zur Verzweiflung treiben,
Dass von dem Volk, das hier mich bedrängt,
Auch würde die Ewigkeit eingeengt:
Das wär doch nur der alte Patsch,
Droben gäb's nur verklärten Klatsch."

Immortality is not an intrinsic condition of our soul, but can only be the result of our exertions. We do not possess immortality, but we must earn it. As Christ expresses it, we must lay up treasures which neither moth nor rust doth corrupt and where the thieves do not break through or steal. We are tradition and we live on as tradition. Our own immortalization is the purpose of our life. Goethe says:

"Drop all of transciency
Whate'er be its claim,
Ourselves to immortalize,
That is our aim."

"Nichts vom Vergänglichen,
Wie's auch geschah!
Uns zu verewigen
Sind wir ja da."

The Egyptian method of immortalizing the bodies of the dead by embalming and mummifying, and of building pyramids is erroneous; rather let the tradition of which we consist and which we impart to others be of the right kind. The greatest treasures we can give to others are we ourselves, our souls, the truths which we have discovered, our hopes, our loves, our ideals. Goethe says:

> "It matters not, I ween,
> Where worms our friends consume,
> Beneath the turf so green,
> Or 'neath the marble tomb.
> Remember ye who live,
> Though frowns the fleeting day,
> That to your friends you give
> What never will decay."
> —*Translated by Edgar Alfred Bowring.*

> "Und wo die Freunde faulen,
> Das ist ganz einerlei,
> Ob unter Marmor-Saulen
> Oder im Rasen frei.
> Der Lebende bedenke,
> Wenn auch der Tag ihm mault,
> Dass er den Freunden schenke
> Was nie und nimmer fault."

Goethe's idea of salvation, as exemplified in Faust, is self-salvation through our own deeds. He says:

> "Yes! to this thought I hold with firm persistence;
> The last result of wisdom stamps it true:
> He only earns his freedom and existence,
> Who daily conquers them anew.
> Then dared I hail the Moment fleeing:
> 'Ah, still delay—thou art so fair!'

The traces cannot, of mine earthly being,
In æons perish,—they are there!"
—*Translated by Bayard Taylor.*

"Ja! diesem Sinne bin ich ganz ergeben,
Das ist der Weisheit letzter Schluss:
Nur der verdient sich Freiheit wie das Leben,
Der täglich sie erobern muss.
Zum Augenblicke dürft ich sagen:
Verweile doch, du bist so schön!
Es kann die Spur von meinen Erdentagen
Nicht in Aeonen untergehn.—"

Life possesses no intrinsic value: the worth of a man depends entirely upon himself. Says Goethe:

"Thy worth wouldst thou have recognized?
Give to the world a worth that's prized!"

"Willst du dich deines Werthes freuen,
So musst der Welt du Werth verleihen."

The Buddhist's Nirvâna is the obliteration of the ego-illusion; it is the annihilation of the error of selfhood, but not annihilation of man's soul or of the world. Nirvâna is not death, but life; it is the right way of living, to be obtained by the conquest of all the passions that becloud the mind. Nirvâna is the rest in activity, the tranquillity of a man who has risen above himself and has learned to view life in its eternal aspects. True rest is not quietism, but a well-balanced activity. It is a surrender of self in exchange for the illimitable life of the evolution of truth. It is in our life and life aspirations the entire omission of the thought of self, of the conceit

"Mark all the world, 'tis I who do this"; and the surrender of all egotistic petulancy is not (as the egotistic imagine) a resignation, but it is bliss. Says Goethe, in his poem "*Eins und Alles*":

"Into the limitless to sink,
No one, I trow, will ever blink,
For there all sorrow we dismiss.
Instead of cravings and wants untold,
Fatiguing demands and duties cold,
Surrender of one's self is bliss."

"Im Grenzenlosen sich zu finden,
Wird gern der Einzelne verschwinden,
Da löst sich aller Ueberdruss:
Statt heissem Wünschen, wildem Wollen,
Statt läst, gem Fordern, strengem Sollen,
Sich aufzugeben ist Genuss."

Contemplation and retirement have their charms and are preferable to the turmoil of a worldly life, and Goethe appreciated the sweetness of seclusion. He said in his "Song to the Moon":

"Happy he who, hating none,
Leaves the world's dull noise,
And, with trusty friends alone,
Quietly enjoys

"What, forever unexpressed,
Hid from common sight,
Through the mazes of the breast
Softly steals by night!"

—*Translated by J. S. Dwight.*

"Selig, wer sich vor der Welt
Ohne Hass verschliesst,
Einen Freund am Busen hält
Und mit dem geniesst,

"Was, von Menschen nicht gewusst,
Oder nicht gedacht,
Durch das Labyrinth der Brust
Wandelt in der Nacht."

Such being Goethe's view of the soul and the aspirations of man, as expressed in his own verses, we shall find it natural that his God-conception is more like Amitâbha than like Zeus or Yahveh. Goethe's God is not an individual being; not a person. He says:

"Why do you scoff and scout
About the All and One?
The professor's a person, no doubt,
God is none."

"Was soll mir euer Hohn
Ueber das All und Eine?
Der Professor ist eine Person,
Gott ist keine."

Nor does Goethe expect help from heaven; he has learned to rely on himself. He makes Prometheus say:

"When in my childhood
I knew not where to turn,
My seeking eyes strayed sunward,
As though there were in heaven
An ear to listen to my prayer,
A heart like mine,
To feel for my distress compassion.

"Who helped me
Against the Titan's insolence?
And who delivered me from death?
Didst thou not rescue thee, thyself,
My holy, glowing heart,
In goodness and in youth
Aglow with gratitude, deceived,
For the slumb'ring God above!"

"Da ich ein Kind war,
Nicht wusste, wo aus noch ein,
Kehrt' ich mein verirrtes Auge
Zur Sonne, als wenn drüber wär'
Ein Ohr, zu hören meine Klage,
Ein Herz, wie meins,
Sich des Bedrängten zu erbarmen.

"Wer half mir
Wider der Titanen Uebermut?
Wer rettete vom Tode mich,
Von Sklaverei?
Hast du nicht alles selbst vollendet,
Heilig glühend Herz?
Und glühtest jung und gut,
Betrogen, Rettungsdank
Dem Schlafenden da droben!"

Goethe's God is the eternal in the transient, the immutable in the change and the rest that the thoughtful will discover in the ever agitated evolution of circling worlds: God, in a word, is the cosmic Nirvâna, the rest in unrest, the peace in strife, and the bliss that is attained in the tribulations of noble aspirations. Goethe says:

"When in the infinite appeareth
The same eternal repetition,
When in harmonious coalition

A mighty dome its structure reareth ;
  A rapture thrills through all existence
All stars, or great or small are blessed,
  Yet all the strife and all resistance
In God, the Lord's eternal rest."

"Wenn im Unendlichen dasselbe
  Sich wiederholend ewig fliesst,
Das tausendfältige Gewölbe
  Sich kräftig in einander schliesst,
Strömt Lebenslust aus allen Dingen,
  Dem kleinsten wie dem grössten Stern,
Und alles Drängen, alles Ringen
  Ist ewige Ruh in Gott dem Herrn."

Whatever Buddha's doctrines may have been, this much is sure, that the principle of Buddhism is the same as the principle of the Religion of Science; for Buddhism is the religion of enlightenment, and enlightenment means a perfect comprehension of the significance of life in matters of religion. On this point, too, Goethe expressed himself in unequivocal terms. He equals in breadth Buddhism, and thus did not reject the Christian religion, but only refused to be limited by the narrowness of its dogmatism. Goethe accepted the truths which Christianity had given to the world; and mark the reason why he accepts them: Because they cannot be claimed as the exclusive possession of a sect, but are the heirloom of all mankind, therefore, he contends, the "scientist" has a right to them; and identifying his right with that of the scientist, Goethe claims them for himself.

Addressing the Christian believers, Goethe says:

> "Ye faithful, do not claim that your confession
> Be truth alone; for we have faith like you.
> Science can't be deprived of the possession
> Belonging to the world, and to me too."

> "Ihr Gläubigen! rühmt nur nicht euern Glauben
> Als einzigen: wir glauben auch wie ihr;
> Der Forscher lässt sich keineswegs berauben
> Des Erbtheils, aller Welt gegönnt—und mir."

How near Goethe, the scientist (*Forscher*), comes in these lines to calling his faith "the religion of science"!

The fact that Goethe's conception of the soul is in perfect agreement with Buddha's teachings, is the more remarkable as Goethe was not familiar even with the mere outlines of the Buddhistic Abhidhârma.

There are many similar agreements that can be traced between Buddhism and the tenets of modern science, especially psychology; and this is not at all surprising, for Buddhism is a religion which recognizes no other revelation except the truth that can be proved by science. Buddha teaches his disciples to contemplate the facts of life without distorting them by postulates or metaphysical assumptions. His religion is the most radical freethought, that blinks no consequences nor allows any one to be misguided by phantasms of the heart; yet at the same time, it is the most earnest devotion to truth, for the salient feature of Buddhism has always been that the surrender of the ego-illusion does not remain a mere theory but becomes a maxim of conduct, which induces Buddha's followers to renounce all egotism, to exert themselves in brotherly love and purity of heart, to devote themselves to the welfare of their fellow-creatures, and, above all, to serve the needs of those who toil and suffer.

Christ taught by example, and in pithy aphorisms and parables, an ethics which closely agrees with Buddhistic ethics; but he taught no philosophy and no systematic religious dogma. Christ's ethics exhibits a broad humanitarianism, and the figure of Christ stands before us as the *ecce homo*—the Son of man, the representative of mankind. The church that developed from the moral movement started by Christ has supplemented the theoretical doctrines which Christ had neglected to teach, but unfortunately the dogmatists of the church replaced the broad *ecce homo* by a narrow *ecce ego;* and thus the assumptions of the ego-psychology have become officially recognized as Christian dogmas. Yet I venture to say that those two masters in the world of thought, Buddha and Goethe, are nearer to the spirit of Christ than those who bear his name and call themselves his disciples. If Christian dogmatists would begin to listen to the teachings of science, they might at last be converted to the ethics of their master.

## ADVANTAGES OF SELF-RESIGNATION.

Both Buddhism and Christianity inculcate in strong terms an ethics of self-resignation, and the Religion of Science joins them, if not always in the letter, certainly in the spirit of their teachings. It would not be advisable to turn the right cheek to him who smites you on the left cheek, but it is not only moral but also wise to drop in all affairs of life the motive of selfishness.

The surrender of the thought "I am," appears at first sight very impracticable, and we hear much of the importance of personal ambition and even vanity as a spring prompting people to great achievements. But when we inquire into the cause of the success of any man, we find it—whatever be his ultimate motives—invariably based upon direct application to the work to be performed, joined to an utter neglect of all personal preferences, pleasures, or considerations.

### NAPOLEON'S CAREER.

Take, for instance, that greatest of all egotists, Napoleon Bonaparte, who would deserve the name the Great if his greatness were not dwarfed by the puniness of his motives. Napoleon pursued his ambitious purpose, which was the acquisition of power, without consulting his personal welfare. He exposed his life courageously to the bullets of the Austrians on the bridge at Lodi, and faced death unflinchingly in many bloody battles. And in establishing his power he looked out for the needs of the people. Whatever wrongs he may have done, his sins are by far outnumbered by the blessings which for the consolidation of his power he conferred upon mankind. The reformation alone of the laws, which was carried out in the *Code Napoléon*, amply atoned for the tyranny which he exercised for a number of years over Europe. He further abolished a number of mediæval institutions which the legitimate rulers would never have dared to touch from fear that the principle of legitimacy might thereby be weakened. The biographies of Napoleon are mostly narratives of his life from a partisan standpoint; an objective appreciation of his greatness can only be written by him who is able to trace the services which Napoleon rendered mankind by administering to the demands of the time and devoting his influence to the practical and correct solution of burning questions without consulting his own self. Napoleon was personally vain, but he suppressed his vanity; he loved women, but he knew it, and watched himself in the presence of beautiful women. He offended the young Queen of Prussia, because he was afraid of her beauty and feared her influence over himself. He grew careless only when he imagined that he had won the world, and the keen-eyed Czar of Russia duped him in the conference at Erfurt by the baldest flattery. Pretending to admire him, the Czar said about the French Emperor, "If I were a woman, I would fall in love with him," and took care that this remark should be reported. The idea that the Czar was dazzled with the brilliancy of his genius blinded Napoleon to the extent that he thought the Czar would never dare to resist his armies, and, when the war with Russia broke out, he expected to overawe him with rapid victories. The vanity in which Napoleon indulged proved fatal to his career. It marks the turning point in the curve of his life with which its descent begins.

The partial success of criminals is mostly, if not always, due to self-control and to a temporary suppression of the thought of self.

### OMAR KHAYYAM.

Even he who in this world of sorrow would live for pleasure can do so only by a resolute resignation of his selfhood. He must harden his heart, and be indifferent about his personal fate and the transiency of the pleasures he loves. This is best illustrated in the Rubaiyat of Omar Khayyam, the poet of wine and love. He sings:

"There was the Door to which I found no key;
There was the Veil through which I could not see:
Some little talk awhile of ME and THEE
There was,—and then no more of THEE and ME.

"And if the wine you drink, the lip you press,
End in what All begins and ends in,—yes;
Think then you are TO-DAY what YESTERDAY
You were,—TO-MORROW you shall not be less.

"Waste not your hour, nor in the vain pursuit
Of this and that endeavor and dispute;
Better be jocund with the fruitful grape
Than sadder after none or bitter fruit.

"Ah, make the most of what we yet may spend,
Before we, too, into the dust descend;

Dust into dust, and under dust to lie,
Sans wine, sans song, sans singer, and sans end."

He who identifies himself with his bodily incarnation sees his future in the dust of his remains; but even then in order to enjoy pleasure he must resign himself and take the fleeting moment, laughing to scorn the fate that awaits him.

Omar Khayyam's verses are beautiful in themselves as they stand in Fitzgerald's translation, but their philosophical meaning is brought out with great force in Vedder's illustrations.

### GOETHE'S TRUST IN NOTHINGNESS.

A similar idea, only expressed with greater force and showing more manliness, is expressed by Goethe in his *Vanitas Vanitatum Vanitas.* The hero of the poem is an old, one-legged soldier who is the merriest comrade in the jovial circle of carousers. He says: *

" My trust in nothing now is placed,
    Hurrah!
So in the world true joy I taste,
    Hurrah!
Then he who would be a comrade of mine
Must clink his glass, and in chorus combine
And drink his cup of wine.

" I placed my trust in gold and wealth,
    Hurrah!
But then I lost all joy and health,
    Lack-a-day!

* A revised version of Edgar Alfred Bowring's translation.

Both here and there the money roll'd,
And when I had it here, behold,
There disappeared the gold!

"I placed my trust in women next,
Hurrah!
But there in truth was I sorely vex'd,
Lack-a-day!
The False another lover sought,
The True with tediousness was fraught,
The Blest could not be bought.

"I trusted in travel and started to roam,
Hurrah!
Cast off the habits of my home,
Lack-a-day!
But not a single thing seem'd good,
The beds were bad, and strange the food,
And I not understood.

"In honor trusted I and fame,
Hurrah!
Another put me straight to shame,
Lack-a-day!
And when I had achieved advance
The people looked at me askance,
With none I had a chance.

"I placed my trust in war and fight,
Hurrah!
We gain'd full many a victory bright,
Hurrah!
Into the foeman's land we cross'd,
Alas, though, at our triumph's cost!
For there a leg I lost.

"In nothing now my trust shall be,
Hurrah!
And all the world belongs to me,
Hurrah!

And as we end our feast and strain,
The cup we'll to the bottom drain;
Let nowhere dregs remain!"

Goethe's poem appears at first sight frivolous, but its apparent levity conceals a rare moral courage, which was a trait of the poet's own character.

### SELFHOOD AN ILLUSION.

Self-resignation is the indispensable condition of success, but as soon as self-resignation becomes complete, when it rests upon a clear conception of the non-existence of a separate self and utter futility, nay, vanity of selfhood, it therewith ceases to be a resignation, and becomes an exaltation.

It is no longer a submission of one's own personality under a higher authority, but it is the rescission of the limits of one's own being and a vindication of one's own personality as limitless in both time and space. It becomes, to use the language of Tauler and Jacob Böhme, a perfect union with God and makes man feel the thrill of the divine spirit that begot his soul. This state is no more a surrender, it is the acquisition of enlightenment with all its bliss. It is ecstasy; not a fitful rapture but a calm serenity of imperturbable peace. It is no longer an abdication of selfhood, it has become a conquest of death.

Selfishness would be the right policy in life if we were genuine and true selves, but we are not.

When the awakening consciousness begins to illumine all those functions of sense and thought activity which are the product of an ancestral karma, which is the pre-natal history that produced us, everything appears so new that the illusion of an âtman, a self-individuality, is quite natural, and the thoughtless are fain to join in the declamations of Wagner, the overbearing disciple of Faust, when he says:

"This is Youth's noblest calling and most fit!
The world was not, ere I created it;
The sun I drew from out the Orient sea;
The moon began her changeful course with me;
The Day put on his shining robes, to greet me;
The Earth grew green, and burst in flower to meet me;
And when I beckoned, from the primal night
The stars unveiled their splendors to my sight,
Who, save myself, to you deliverance brought
From commonplaces of restricted thought?
I, proud and free, even as dictates my mind,
Follow with joy the inward light I find,
And speed along in mine own ecstasy,
Darkness behind, the Glory leading me!"

It is not "the inward light" that gives us reliable information, but the facts of experience. The revelation of truth comes in to us from without, and "the light within" is only a reflection of the All, whose image we are. A man who, like Wagner, imagines in his self-conceit that he only made the sun to rise in the world, is not likely to perform useful work. He clings to the separateness of his present embodiment as his true self, and loses sight of the actual constituents of his being. He will try to acquire fame, but will not perform the work that would entitle him to it. He identifies himself with the abstract and empty idea of his being, of himself, and forgets over it the realities of which it consists. He may accomplish his ends, and what would in that case be the result? His name, not his real soul, would continue to live and be linked with the achievements of others. His name! And what is his name? A mere word!

The instance of the preservation of the thought of one man under the name of another is sufficiently instructive to deserve discussion of one flagrant instance, as which we select the case of Hooke against Newton.

### HOOKE OR NEWTON.

We do not intend to decide the priority claims of Hooke *versus* Newton in the formulation of the law of gravitation as expressed by the inverse square of the distance, because an exhaustive presentation of the case is no easy matter and would take more space than we can spare.

Hooke's claim may be considered as well established, but he must probably blame mainly himself for the ill-treatment he met at the hands of his contemporaries. He was a man who "originated much but perfected little," he was at the same time "irritable in his temper," which rendered him among his acquaintances unpopular. Add to this his penurious appearance, his crooked figure, shrunken limbs, dishevelled hair, his solitary life, and miserly habits!

Yet, this unattractive abode harbored the inventiveness of a genius and the keenness of a great discoverer. He was instrumental in inventing the air-pump; it was he who proposed to regulate watch movements by balance springs; he urged the advantage of telescopic sight over plain sight in surveying; he propounded valuable theories about the composition of the air, which "foreshadowed the discoveries of Priestley." Next to Tycho Brahe he has the best claim to being regarded as the inventor of the sextant. He stated the law of tension and force in the terse formula *ut tensio sic vis*, which is still called "Hooke's law." (See *Encyclopædia Britannica*, III., 64; V., 461; VII., 803; XXII., 595; and XVII., 442.)

The *Encyclopædia Britannica* contains a notice of Hooke's claims, from which we extract the following passage:

"Hooke was offended because Sir John did not mention what he had told him of his own discovery. Halley only communicated to Newton the fact 'that Hooke had some pretensions to the invention of the rule for the decrease of gravity being reciprocally as the squares of the distances from the centre,' acknowledging at the same time that, though Newton had the notion from him, 'yet the demonstration of the curves generated thereby belonged wholly to Newton.' 'How much of this,' Halley adds, 'is so, you know best, so likewise what you have to do in this matter; only Mr. Hooke seems to expect you should make some mention of him in the preface, which 'tis possible you may see reason to prefix. I must beg your pardon that 'tis I that send you this ungrateful account; but I thought it my duty to let you know it, so that you might act accordingly, being in myself fully satisfied that nothing but the greatest candor imaginable is to be expected from a person who has of all men the least need to borrow reputation.'

"In thus appealing to Newton's candor, Halley obviously wished that some acknowledgment of Hooke should be made. He knew indeed that before Newton had announced the inverse law, Hooke and Wren and himself had spoken of it and discussed it, and therefore justice demanded that, though none of them had given demonstration of the law, Hooke especially should receive credit for having maintained it as a truth of which he was seeking the demonstration."

Newton at last consented to insert this concession as an addition to his fourth proposition:

"The inverse law of gravity holds in all celestial motions, as was discovered also independently by my countrymen Wren, Hooke, and Halley."

Newton claims that he had thought of the solution sixteen years before he began to work it out in his *Principia*, but had rejected the idea on account of the objections which were solved only by the discovery of the flattened condition of the poles. Schopenhauer says: "No man who has found a new theory will on account of some slight obstacle reject and forget it for sixteen years. That is not the treatment which we give to the children of our own thought, but to step-children or foundlings. As to our own theories, we are in the habit of trying them over and over again, until we find some ground on which they can be justified. Poor Hooke," adds Schopenhauer, "he had the same fate as Columbus. America is the name of the continent which he discovered, and we speak of Newton's law of gravitation."

If Newton had been the great thinker and discoverer which he is reputed to be, it would indeed be strange that he was proud of the silly commentary he had written on the Revelation of St. John.

Now, suppose we accept the view of Schopenhauer concerning the priority claims of Hooke, does not Hooke's thought live on, whether or not the honor of priority is attributed to Newton? Is it not simply as though Hooke had written under the *nom de plume* of Isaac Newton? It is, after all, his actual soul that marches down triumphantly with the mark of truth through the ages and is reincarnated in many thousands of scientists. The actual soul of a man, which alone can properly be called his own, is not his name, but consists in the thought-forms, sentiment forms, and deed-forms which originate in him. They are characteristic of him as the peculiar product of an interaction among those other soul-forms of his which constitute his inheritance from former ages.

He who seeks his self and is anxious to preserve it in its separateness, will surely fail, for his present individuality will at last be dissolved in death. He who attempts to immortalize his name, may or may not succeed. A name, the combination of letters in the mouth of posterity, is in itself an empty thing, and for that reason it is sometimes more lasting than our bodily organization. But he who endeavors to be an incarnation of the truth, and nothing else besides, is sure to succeed ; he will not be hampered by other considerations ; he has attained immortality, and his soul in its peculiar personal idiosyncrasy will be, and will forever remain, a most valuable presence, a never-failing blessing, in the advancing and growing spirit of the human race.

## THE BASIC CONCEPTS OF BUDDHISM.

BUDDHISM is generally characterized as a religion without a belief in God and the human soul, without the hope of a future existence, pessimistic and desolate, looking upon life as an ocean of suffering, quietistic in ethics, and finding comfort only in the expectation of a final extinction in nothingness. Now, it is true that Buddhists, with the exception of some less important heretical sects, do not believe in a personal God; but, while on the one hand, there are many faithful Christians who look upon the theistic dogma merely as the symbolical expression of a deeper truth, on the other hand, the Buddhists believe not only in the Sambhôga Kâya which is an equivalent of the Christian God-idea, but even in a trinity of Sambhôga Kâya, Nirmâna Kâya, and Dharma Kâya, bearing a close resemblance to the Christian conception of Father, Son, and Holy Ghost. Further, it is undeniable that Buddhists do not believe in the âtman or Self which is the Brahman philosophers' definition of soul, but they do not deny the existence of mind and the continuance of man's spiritual existence after death. Men trained in Western modes of thought, however, are so accustomed to their own terminology that Eastern thinkers, when using expressions denying the allegoric terms of Christian thought, are suspected of negativism. Even Western thinkers who have ceased to be believers in Christianity fail to see the positive aspect of the Buddhist world-conception, and we are again and again confronted with the refrain: If Buddha's doctrine is not nihilism, it practically amounts to nihilism.

Benfey says in the preface to his translation of the "Pantscha Tantra":

"The very bloom of the intellectual life of India (whether it found expression it Brahmanical or Buddhist works) proceeded substantially from Buddhism, and is contemporaneous with the epoch in which Buddhism flourished;—that is to say, from the third century before Christ to the sixth century after Christ. Taking its stand upon that principle, said to have been proclaimed by Buddhism in its earliest years, 'that only *that* teaching of the Buddha's is true which contraveneth not sound reason,' * the autonomy of man's Intellect was, we may fairly say, effectively acknowledged; the whole relation between the realms of the knowable and of the unknowable was subjected to its control; and notwithstanding that the actual reasoning powers, to which the ultimate appeal was thus given, were in fact then not altogether sound, yet the way was pointed out by which Reason could, under more favorable circumstances, begin to liberate itself from its failings. We are already learning to value, in the philosophical endeavors of Buddhism, the labors, sometimes indeed quaint, but aiming at thoroughness and worthy of the highest respect, of its severe earnestness in inquiry. From the prevailing tone of our work, and still more so from the probable Buddhist origin of those other Indian story-books which have hitherto become known to us, it is clear that, side by side with Buddhistic earnestness, the merry

* Wassiliew, *Der Buddhismus*, etc., p. 68.

jests of light, and even frivolous poetry and conversation, preserved the cheerfulness of life."

This description does not show Buddhism in a gloomy light, and it is different from what people usually imagine it to be.

In spite of the innumerable exuberances of modern Buddhism, its power and possibilities are still great, mainly because it enjoins on its devotees the free exercise of their reasoning powers. Among all religious men Buddhists more than others appear to be at the same time full of religious zeal and also open to conviction.

We read in M. Huc's *Travels in Tartary, Thibet and China* (II., p. 189) that the Regent of Lhasa incessantly repeated to the French missionaries:

"'Your religion is like our own, the truths are the same; we differ only in the explanation. Amid all that you have seen and heard in Tartary and Thibet you must have found much to condemn; but you are to remember that many errors and superstitions that you may have observed, have been introduced by ignorant Lamas, but are rejected by intelligent Buddhists.' He admitted between us and himself only two points where there was disagreement—the origin of the world and the transmigration of souls. 'Let us examine them both together,' said he to them again, 'with care and sincerity; if yours is the best, we will accept it; how could we refuse you? If, on the other hand, ours is best, I doubt not you will be alike reasonable, and follow that.'"

Now it is strange that in those two points which constitute the main differences between Buddhism and Christianity, viz., creation and the nature of the soul, modern science, represented exclusively by scientists educated in Christian schools and with a Christian tradition of two millenniums, will certainly side with Buddhism. There is scarcely any one among our scientists who would be willing to endorse a creation out of nothing, and among our prominent psychologists few only will be found who adhere to the dualistic soul-conception which assumes the existence of a psychic agent behind the facts of soul-life. Nevertheless our popular conception of a Creator-God and an ego-soul are so deeply rooted in the minds of our people that, as a rule, they still consider these two ideas as the indispensable foundations of all religion.

We intend here briefly to review the fundamental conceptions of Buddhism, and hope to prove that although its doctrines of the soul and of Nirvâna may to Western minds appear to be the equivalent of nihilism, they certainly are not nihilism if we take the trouble to look at them from the Buddhist standpoint. And far from being pessimistic in the Western sense of pessimism, the Buddhist possesses a cheerful disposition which in this world of tribulation lifts him above pain and suffering.

## KARMA.

Soul was identified by Brahmanical philosophers, as we have learned in a previous article, with the âtman, the self, the ego, or the ego-consciousness, viz., that something in man which says "I." This âtman was conceived as a metaphysical entity behind man's sensations, thoughts, and other activities. Not the eye sees, they said, but the seer in the eye; not the ear hears, but the hearer in the ear; not the tongue tastes, but the taster in the tongue; not the nose smells, but the smeller in the nose; not the mind thinks, but the thinker in the mind; not the feet walk and the hands act, but the actor in the hands and the feet. The mysterious being in man which says "I am this person, I possess eyes, ears, nose, tongue, hands and feet, I see, hear, smell, taste, feel the contact of bodies, walk and act," is said to be the agent of man's activity. This "I" or the ego of the soul, the agent of man's activity, is called the âtman or self; and in so far as the existence of the âtman is denied by Buddha, Buddhism teaches that there is no soul.

When Buddhists speak of the soul, they mean the Brahmanical âtman. When they mean what we would call soul, they speak of mind; and Buddhism, far from denying the existence of mind, only replaces the dualistic conception of Brahmanical philosophy by a monistic soul-theory, which in the course of time naturally developed the doctrine that there is nothing but mind.

The phrase "there is nothing but mind," reminds us of Clifford's dictum: Everything that exists is mind-stuff; and it may be explained as follows: All outside things appear to us as matter moving in space; so we appear to other beings as matter moving in space; we appear to be body to our own and to other people's senses; but in ourselves we feel our existence as that which we call mind or soul. Body is that as which mind or soul appears. Our body consisting of the same material as the things of the surrounding world and having originated therefrom, we conclude that all the world consists of the same material. All that which appears to us as matter can, if it but assume the proper form, become such minds or souls as we are; in a word: all existence is spiritual, or more exactly speaking, psychical.*

The psychology of Buddhism is briefly laid down in the first verse of the Dhammapada:

> "All that we are, is the result of what we have thought: it is founded on our thoughts, it is made up of our thoughts."

This shows that Buddhism does not deny the ex-

* In a partial accommodation to the translators' usage of terms, who, as a rule, render *âtman* by "soul" and that which we would call "soul," i. e., the totality of our thoughts, sensations, and aspirations by "mind," we speak here of "soul or mind." Otherwise, and according to a stricter usage of terms, we propose to make a distinction. When speaking of "soul," we mean mainly the feeling or sentient element of man's existence; when of mind, we think mainly of the intellectual and rational features with which the various feelings are endowed. Thus it would have been more proper for Clifford to say "soul-stuff" instead of "mind-stuff;" and the Buddhist doctrine, "everything is mind," should be expressed in the sentence: "Every reality which appears to sentient beings as objective, is in itself subjective; we call it matter, but it is in itself potential feeling; it can become sentient, it is soul, or better, soul-stuff." For details as to definitions of "soul" and "mind" see *Primer of Philosophy*, p. 193.

istence of the soul, if by soul is meant man's ideas, aspirations, and mental activities. Buddhists declare that man's soul is not an indissoluble unit, not a metaphysical self, but a compound. Man's physical and spiritual being consists of sa*m*skâras,* i. e., of certain forms and formative faculties which, according to the law of Karma, are preserved and thus condition the continuity of his existence in the whirl of constant changes. Oldenberg translates the word samskâra by *Gestaltung*, and says in explanation of the term p. 242, Engl. Transl.):

"We might translate Sa*m*khâra directly by 'actions' if we understand this word in the wide sense in which it includes also, at the same time, the internal actions, the will and the wish."

Samskâra denotes soul structure, manifesting itself in functions as the formative element which shapes our existence and destiny. Oldenberg continues:

"Buddhism teaches: 'My action is my possession, my action is my inheritance, my action is the womb which bears me, my action is the race to which I am akin, my action is my refuge.' (Anguttara Nikâya, Pañcaka Nipâta.) What appears to man to be his body is in truth 'the action of his past state which then assuming a form, realised through his endeavor, has become endowed with a tangible existence.'"

The Jewish-Christian world-conception represents us as the creatures of God. We are like vessels in the potter's hand; some of us are made for noble

* "Samskára" is Sanskrit, "Sa*n*khâra" or "Sa*m*khâra" is Pâli.

purposes, others as vessels of impurity. Buddhists look upon our character and fate as the result of our own doings in our present and innumerable past existences. In this sense the Dhammapada * says:

> "By oneself the evil is done; by oneself one suffers.
> By oneself evil is left undone; by oneself one is purified.
> Purity and impurity belong to oneself, no one can purify another.
> You yourself must make an effort. The Buddhas are only preachers.
> The way was preached by me when I understood the removal of the thorn in the flesh."

According to Buddhist doctrines, the souls of men continue to exist as they are impressed upon other generations by heredity and education. A man remains the same from yesterday until to-day, and from to-day until to-morrow, in so far as he consists of the same sa*m*skâras; his character remains the same, exactly as a light burning several hours remains the same light, although the flame is always fed by other particles of oil.† The man of the same character as you, is the same as you, in somewhat the same sense as two triangles of equal angles and sides are congruent. This is tersely expressed in the saying *Tat twam asi*, "That art thou," which Schopenhauer makes the corner-stone of ethics, for this view of the soul, in which one recognizes oneself in others, removes all motives of selfishness.

* *Sacred Books of the East*, Vol. X, pp. 46 and 67.

† This simile is used in *The Questions of Milinda.*

There are two isolated passages in the Dhammapada which apparently are a contradiction of Buddha's doctrine of the illusion of self. We read in verse 160: "Self is the lord of self. Who else could be the lord"; and in verse 323: "A man who controls himself enters the untrodden land through his own self-controlled self." Prof. Max Müller, who is himself a champion of the âtman doctrine, makes the most of these passages, in proving that Buddha might have taught the existence of self. But his proposition is improbable in the face of so many other unequivocal statements. Moreover, the general meaning of the quoted sentences is unmistakable. There is no reference to the existence of a self in the sense of the Brahmanical âtman. The author of these passages—whether Buddha himself, or a Buddhist, or, what is not improbable, some thinker older than Buddha—simply means that "by self-control alone man can attain salvation," but we have no right to interpret the words in a sense which would antagonize one of the cardinal doctrines of Buddhism. We must bear in mind that Buddha does not deny the existence of the idea of self in man. He only denies the existence of a soul-substratum such as was assumed under the name of self by the most prominent philosophers of his time. Buddha does not deny that there is an ego-consciousness in the soul. He only rejects the assumption that our ego-consciousness is the doer of our acts and the thinker of our thoughts, or a kind of thing-in-itself behind our existence.

There are many words which are used in various applications, implying radically different or even contradictory meanings, and the word "self" is in this respect no exception. Generally speaking, self is that idea in a man's mind which represents the totality of his existence, his bodily form, his senses and their activities, his thoughts, his emotions, his likes and dislikes, his aspirations and hopes. Far from proposing to exterminate self in this sense, Buddha's religion preaches the elevation and sanctification of every one's self, so much so that Oldenberg characterizes the ethics of Buddhism as self-culture and self-discipline ("sittliche Arbeit an sich selbst"), as expressed in verse 239 of the Dhammapada:

> "Let a wise man blow off the impurities of his self as a smith blows off the impurities of silver, one by one, little by little, and from time to time."

When Buddhists speak of the illusion of self, denouncing the idea of self as the main cause of all evil, they mean that erroneous notion which not only hypostatizes the idea of self into an independent being, but even makes of it the metaphysical agent of all our activities. The adoption of this metaphysical self-conception is said to warp all our thoughts and to dim our spiritual vision; it makes us neglect the true substance of our soul for a mere shadow.

Buddha, while denying the Brahmanical theory of the âtman, offered a new solution of the problem of the soul. Says Rhys Davids in his "Hibbert Lectures," p. 29:

"The distinguishing characteristic of Buddhism was that it started a new line, that it looked upon the deepest questions men have to solve from an entirely different standpoint. It swept away from the field of its vision the whole of the great soul-theory which had hitherto so completely filled and dominated the minds of the superstitious and the thoughtful alike. For the first time in the history of the world, it proclaimed a salvation which each man could gain for himself and by himself, in this world, during this life, without even the least reference to God, or to gods, either great or small. Like the Upanishads, it placed the first importance on knowledge; but it was no longer a knowledge of God, it was a clear perception of the real nature, as they supposed it to be, of men and things. And it added to the necessity of knowledge, the necessity of purity, of courtesy, of uprightness, of peace, and of a universal love far-reaching, grown great and beyond measure."

While Self, that hypothetical agent behind the soul, thus disappears in the teachings of Buddhism, the conception soul or mind is not abolished and the idea of soul-transmigration gains a new importance. The pre-Buddhistic notion of a soul flitting about and seeking a new abode in another body was given up by Shâkyamuni for the more correct idea of a transfer of the Sa*m*skâras according to the law of Karma. Buddhism recognizes the law of Karma as irrefragable and bases upon it the unfailing justice of the moral law.

Concerning the migration of souls underlying the moral of the Jâtaka-tales in the "Buddhist Birth Stories," Prof. Rhys Davids says in the preface to his translation, p. lxxv:

"The reader must of course avoid the mistake of importing Christian ideas into this Conclusion by supposing that the identity of the persons in the two stories is owing to the passage of a 'soul' from the one to the other. Buddhism does not teach the Transmigration of Souls.* Its doctrine would be better summarised as the Transmigration of Character; for it is entirely independent of the early and widely-prevalent notion of the existence within each human body of a distinct soul, or ghost, or spirit."

The same author says in his manual of "Buddhism." p. 104:

"As one generation dies and gives way to another — the heir of the consequences of all its virtues and all its vices, the exact result of pre-existing causes; so each individual in the long chain of life inherits all, of good or evil, which all its predecessors have done or been; and takes up the struggle towards enlightenment precisely there, where they have left it."

Speaking of Karma, Professor Davids explains the nature of Buddhism as follows:

"Most forms of Paganism, past and present, teach men to seek for some sort of happiness here. Most other forms of belief say that this is folly, but the faithful and the holy shall find happiness hereafter, in a better world beyond. Buddhism maintains that the one hope is as hollow as the other; that the consciousness of self is a delusion; that the organized being, sentient existence, since it is not infinite, is bound up inextricably with ignorance, and therefore with sin, and therefore with sorrow. 'Drop then this petty foolish longing for personal happiness,' Buddhism would say! 'Here it comes of ignorance, and leads to sin, which leads to sorrow,' and there the conditions of existence are the same, and each new birth will leave you ignorant and finite still. There is nothing eternal; the very cosmos itself is passing away; nothing is, everything becomes; and all that you see and feel, bodily or mentally, of yourself will pass away like everything else;

---

* I. e., of âtmans.

*there will only remain the accumulated result of all your actions, words, and thoughts.** Be pure then, and kind, not lazy in thought. Be awake, shake off your delusions, and enter resolutely on the "Path" which will lead you away from these restless, tossing waves of the ocean of life;—the Path to the Joy and Rest of the Nirvâna of Wisdom and Goodness and Peace!'"

Rhys Davids says: "There will only remain the accumulated result of all your actions, words, and thoughts." True; but why does he say "only"? The accumulated result of your actions (viz., your sa*m*skâras) *are* your own being. They constitute your mind so long as you live, and there is no self behind them, no ego, no âtman, no metaphysical soul-monad. Thus it appears that, according to Buddhist notions, we ourselves continue in the accumulated results of our actions. Since Prof. Rhys Davids fails to bear in mind that our Sa*m*skâras are we ourselves, it is perhaps natural that he, although one of the profoundest of Buddhist scholars, does not, in spite of his perfect knewledge of facts, appreciate the importance of the Buddhistic conception of Karma and the migration of soul. I do not say that he misunderstands this part of the Buddhist doctrine; but I say that he does not appreciate it. He continues the passage just quoted:

"Strange is it and instructive that all this should have seemed not unattractive these 2,300 years and more to many despairing and earnest hearts—that they should have trusted themselves to the so seeming stately bridge which Buddhism

---

*Italics are ours.

has tried to build over the river of the mysteries and sorrows of life. They have been charmed and awed perhaps by the delicate or noble beauty of some of the several stones of which the arch is built; they have seen that the whole rests on a more or less solid foundation of fact; that on one side of the keystone is the necessity of justice, on the other the law of causality."

Then, he adds:

"But they have failed to see that the very keystone itself, the link between one life and another, is a mere word—this wonderful hypothesis, this airy nothing, this imaginary cause beyond the reach of reason—the individualized and individualising force of Karma.

Prof. Rhys Davids adds in a foot-note:

"Individualized, in so far as the result of a man's actions is concentrated in the formation of a second sentient being; individualizing, in so far as it is the force by which different beings become one individual. In other respects the force of Karma is real enough."

Modern science teaches that it is function which creates the organ, and, *vice versa*, the organ is but the visible result of innumerable former functions. This may be considered as a modern restatement of the Buddhist doctrine of the Sa*m*khâras. All the seeings of ancestral eyes continue to live in our eyes. Our ancestors are not dead; they are still here in us; and by ancestors the–Buddhist understands not only progenitors, but also those who formed our soul Shâkyamuni says to his father, that not he and his fathers, the Kings of the Shâkya, but the Buddhas of former ages were his ancestry.

In the name of Buddhism, I venture to make a reply to Prof. Rhys Davids: Buddhism has torn down the imaginary fence which separates man's self from other selves. He who fails to see the link between one life and another, or speaks of it as an "airy nothing," still holds to the illusion of self. He who abandons the idea of self must recognise the sameness of two souls consisting of the same Sa*m*skâras. Otherwise we ought to deny also the sameness of the "I" of to-day and of yesterday. That which constitutes the identity of person in one and the same individual is only the continuity and the sameness of his character. The "I" of to-day has to take all the consequences of the actions which the "I" of yesterday performed. Thus the individualized Karma of future times will reap all that which the individualizing Karma of the present time sows.

And, strange enough, this Buddhistic conception of the soul is quite in harmony with the views of the most prominent psychologists of Europe.

Since this remark on Prof. Rhys Davids was written and published in the April number of *The Monist* for 1894, he has apparently changed his view of the subject and I would have cancelled the whole passage in which I take exception to his statement, did not his former and more popular book remain before the public and continue to exercise a powerful influence; for he is (and justly so) deemed a great authority on Buddhism. In his latest publication Prof. Rhys Davids, touching upon the same problem, sums the case up in these words:

" A man thinks he began to be a few years—twenty, forty sixty years—ago. There is some truth in that; but in a much larger, deeper, truer sense he has been (in the causes of which he is the result) for countless ages in the past; and those same causes (of which he is the temporary effect) will continue in other like temporary forms through countless ages yet to come.

" There is no such thing as an individuality which is permanent; even were a permanent individuality to be possible, it would not be desirable, for it is not desirable to be separate. The effort to keep oneself separate may succeed indeed for a time; but so long as it is successful it involves limitation, and therefore ignorance, and therefore pain. ' No! it is not separateness you should hope and long for,' says the Buddhist. " it is union—the sense of oneness with all that now is, that has ever been, that can ever be—the sense that shall enlarge the horizon of your being to the limits of the universe, to the boundaries of time and space, that shall lift you up into a new plane far beyond, outside all mean and miserable care for self. Why stand shrinking there? Give up the fool's paradise of " This is I," and " This is mine." It is a real fact—the greatest of realities—that you are asked to grasp. Leap forward without fear! You shall find yourself in the ambrosial waters of Nirvana, and sport with the Arahats who have conquered birth and death!'

" This theory of Karma is the doctrine which takes the place in the Buddhist teaching of the very ancient theory of 'souls,' which the Christians have inherited from the savage beliefs of the earliest periods of history.

" The history of an individual does not begin with his birth, but has been endless ages in the making; and he cannot sever himself from his surroundings, no, not for an hour. The tiniest snowdrop drops its fairy head just so much and no more, because it is balanced by the universe. It is a snowdrop, not an oak, and just that kind of snowdrop, because it is the outcome of the Karma of an endless series of past existences. It did not begin to be when the flower opened, or when the mother plant first peeped above the ground, or first met the embraces of the sun, or when the bulb began to shoot

**above the soil, or at any time which you and I can fix. . . . We may put a new and deeper meaning into the words of the poet:**

**" 'Our deeds follow us from afar;**
**And what we have been makes us what we are.' "**

The objection may be urged against the Buddhist conception that we do not choose to look upon the men who in future times will represent the incarnation of our Karma as identical with ourselves; we prefer to look upon them as altogether different beings. But here the Buddhists will have the advantage. The identity obtains whether it be recognized or not. It is real, for the laws of nature recognize it; it is an established fact. These future incarnations of our Karma inherit our character, together with all its blessings and its curses, in the same way as "I" of to-day am benefited or hampered by my actions from the days of my childhood, it matters little whether I choose to recognize the identity of myself or not.

We can have no proper conception of the action of the moral law until we understand the intercoherence of soul-life. So long as we cut it up into selves, we shall never cease to be puzzled with psychical, philosophical, and moral problems which appear insolvable and incomprehensible.

The great majority of people who consider themselves as orthodox Christians are no doubt believers in the âtman theory of the soul, postulating a self as the agent behind soul-life and looking upon it as the soul-proper; yet the great representative authorities of Christian orthodoxy, such men as the Apostle St. Paul, Thomas Aquinas, Eckhart, Tauler, Ignatius Loyola, Tholuck, and many others show strong tendencies to the doctrine of anâtman, or the surrender of the self as the soul proper. Christians are shocked at the nihilism of the Buddhist whose highest aspiration it is to root out his soul, viz., his âtman or self, in order to attain Nirvâna and become a Buddha, but they take no offence when St. Paul says: "I am crucified with Christ, yet *not I* but Christ liveth in me."

## NIRVÂNA

We have learned that it is as natural as it is erroneous for men exclusively trained in Western modes of thought, to look upon the principal doctrine of Buddhist psychology as a bare and flat denial of the soul. In the same way and for similar reasons it is as natural as it erroneous for western minds educated in Christian schools to look upon the Nirvâna of Buddhism as an annihilation, and to characterize Buddhist ethics as quietism.

Nirvâna, the ideal goal of the fully enlightened disciple of Buddha, is the most important term in the religious system of Buddhism; it is the cornerstone of the whole structure, and yet, judging from the various interpretations of the word and the controversies that have been waged about its meaning, its application must be either very ambiguous, or it contains great difficulties for Western minds.

The common definition of "Nirvâna" among all Buddhists is "deliverance," viz., deliverance from evil, or salvation. The question is, what is the nature of this deliverance?

The etymology of the word is obvious enough Nirvâna means "extinction," viz., the "extinction of self," which is generally supposed to be the definition of the term given by the Hinayâna school of the old southern Buddhism.* Those representatives of the Mahâyâna school of Japan, however, who visited the World's Parliament of Religions, are wont to describe Nirvâna as "the complete attainment of truth." In their conception, Nirvâna is attained by the extinction of the illusion of self, with all it implies, covetousness, lust, and all sinful desires.

The main issue of all the discussions concerning the term Nirvâna is the problem whether it must be conceived as a positive or a negative state of ex-

* Northern Buddhists make a distinction between Hinayâna or "small vehicle" (viz., of salvation) and Mahâyâna or "great vehicle"; the former is the Southern, the latter the Northern school of Buddhist thought; the former prefers to some extent negative and philosophically strict definitions, while the latter aims at positive and religious expressions; the former represents upon the whole more faithfully the historical traditions of Buddha, while the latter, in their aspiration to extend salvation to the broad masses of mankind, have admitted many fantastical elements. We must add, however, that these contrasts are in reality not so sweeping as they appear in a general formula, and the distinction of the Hinayâna and the Mahâyâna, although very convenient for certain purposes. is admissible only within certain limits.

istence, as an eternal rest or a life in paradise, as a complete annihilation or the bliss of absolute perfection. In order to settle this much mooted question, not by an *à priori* off-hand method, but by systematically consulting the old Buddhist authorities, the Professors F. Max Müller and Childers have collected and compared great numbers of passages in which the word Nirvâna occurs, and the result is that "there is not one passage which would require that its meaning should be annihilation," while "most, if not all," would thereby "become perfectly unintelligible."

The proposition has been made that there are several kinds of Nirvâna, but Professor Childers regards this theory as a complete failure; he says:

"An extraordinary error, originating, I think, with Burnouf, and repeated unsuspectingly by several eminent European scholars, has done much to involve the question of Nirvâna in needless doubt and obscurity. It is the belief that there are three degrees of Nirvâna, viz., Nibbâna, Parinibbâna, and Mahâparinibbâna (ordinary Nirvâna, complete Nirvâna, and the great complete Nirvâna). This idea is strangely wide of the truth, for Parinibbâna means merely Nirvâna, or the attainment of Nirvâna, and Mahâparinibbâna means nothing more than the death of Buddha."

Professor Rhys Davids sums up his disscussion of the meaning of Nirvâna in the following words:

"It is the extinction of that sinful, grasping condition of mind and heart, which would otherwise, according to the great mystery of Karma, be the cause of renewed individual existence. That extinction is to be brought about by, and runs parallel with, the growth of the opposite condition of mind and heart; and it is complete when that opposite condition is reached. Nirvâna is therefore the same thing as a sinless, calm state of mind; and if translated at all, may best, perhaps, be rendered "holiness,—holiness that is, in the Buddhist sense perfect peace, goodness, and wisdom."

Professor Childers presents us with a careful exposition of the problem in his "Pali Dictionary," *sub voce* Nibbâna, the Pali word for Nirvâna. He says:

"The difficulty is this: It is true that many expressions are used of Nirvâna which seem to imply annihilation, but on the other hand, other equally numerous and equally forcible expressions are used which clearly point to blissful existence. Thus Nirvâna is called Freedom from Human Passion, Purity, Holiness, Bliss, Happiness, the End of Suffering, the Cessation of desire, Peace, Calm, Tranquillity, and so on. How is this discrepancy to be reconciled? I reply, the word *nibbâna* is applied to two different things, first that annihilation of being which is the goal of Buddhism, and secondly, the state of blissful sanctification called *arahatta*, or Arhatship, which terminates in annihilation. This fact at once explains the apparent contradiction.

"At first sight it may appear inexplicable that the same term should be applied to two things so different as annihilation and blissful existence; but I think I am able to show that after all the phenomenon may be easily accounted for . . . . Thus, if we say 'Nirvâna is the reward of a virtuous life,' this may, strictly speaking mean that annihilation is the reward of a virtuous life; but since annihilation cannot be obtained without Arhatship, the idea that Arhatship is the reward of a virtuous life, inevitably presents itself to the mind at the same time.

"Although expressions like 'extinction is bliss' may sound strange or even ridiculous to us, who have from our earliest infancy been taught that bliss consists in eternal life, to a

Buddhist, who has always been taught that existence is an evil they appear perfectly natural and familiar; this is a mere question of education and association; the words 'extinction is bliss' convey to the mind of a Buddhist the same feeling of enthusiastic longing, the same consciousness of sublime truth, that the words 'eternal life is bliss' convey to a Christian."

Thus we have according to Professor Childers the bliss of Arhatship and the complete extinction of being, one as the cause of the other. The Arhat, on reaching the goal of Nirvâna, ceases to exist as an individual person. He says:

"The doctrine of Buddha on this subject is perfectly explicit; he even predicted his own death. Now, to be the ultimate goal of Buddhism, Arhatship must be an eternal state, for if it be not eternal, it must sooner or later terminate, either in annihilation, or in a state which is not blissful, in either case it is not the goal of Buddhism. But since Arhats die, Arhatship is not an eternal state and therefore it is not the goal of Buddhism. It is almost superfluous to add that not only is there no trace in the Buddhist scriptures of the Arhats continuing to exist after death, but it is deliberately stated in innumerable passages, with all the clearness and emphasis of which language is capable, that the Arhat does not live again after death, but ceases to exist. There is probably no doctrine more distinctive of Çakyamuni's original teaching than that of the annihilation of being."

This solution appears to be nihilistic; but it seems to me that the complete annihilation of Gautama Siddhartha does not imply the complete annihilation of Buddha. Buddha is said to have entered Nirvâna when he died. Yet at the same time we are told that Buddha had attained Nirvâna already during his life. Indeed, enlightenment and Nirvâna are, among all Buddhists of the Hinayâna as well as the Mahâyâna exact synonyms. Nirvâna, the extinction of the illusion of self, is the condition of enlightenment, or perfect understanding of truth. A Buddha is an ideal construction of a man in whom all error and the consequences of error, desires, and sin, have been abrogated; his will is purified, his thoughts are undimmed by illusions, and his mind consists of a perfect knowledge of truth.

There is among orthodox Buddhists no doubt at all that when a Buddha dies his physical existence is dissolved into its elements; and this dissolution is regarded as a final deliverance of that part of man's nature which is the cause of pain and suffering; but the truth, being that element which constitutes his Buddhahood, remains. The life in the flesh is ended, but the life in Nirvâna continues. Now, as Buddhahood is considered the aim of all evolution of life, while the by-paths of sin and error, which consist in circles of useless migrations, lead us away from our goal, Buddha is praised for having escaped the painful repetition of the course of migrations. A Buddha has reached the goal and has attained eternity. He is reborn into the world of error, only to appear as a teacher to point out to others the escape from illusion, sin, and death.

According to the orthodox Buddhist conception there is no doubt about it that the incarnation of Buddha in the person of Gautama Siddhartha has passed away. Gautama has died and his body will not be resurrected. But Buddha continues to live in the body of the Dharma, i. e., the law or religion of Buddha; and, in so far as he is the truth, he is immortal and eternal. The whole world may break to pieces, but Buddha will not die. The words of Buddha are imperishable. We read in the "Buddhist Birth Stories" the following remarkable passage which strongly reminds us of Matthew xxiv. 35.* One of the Bodhisattvas, taking the resolution of becoming a Buddha, says:

"The Buddhas speak not doubtful words, the Conquerors speak not vain words,
There is no falsehood in the Buddhas,—verily I shall become a Buddha.
As a clod cast into the air doth surely fall to the ground,
So the word of the glorious Buddhas is sure and everlasting.
As the death of all mortals is sure and constant,
So the word of the glorious Buddhas is sure and everlasting,
As the rising of the sun is certain when night has faded,
So the word of the glorious Buddhas is sure and everlasting.
As the roaring of a lion who has left his den is certain,
So the word of the glorious Buddhas is sure and everlasting.
As the delivery of women with child is certain,
So the word of the glorious Buddhas is sure and everlasting."

Christ, when taking leave of his disciples, comforts them, saying, "Lo I am with you alway even unto the end of the world," and Buddha expresses the same idea when in the hour of his death the Mallas are anxious to behold the Blessed One. Buddha says:

"Seeking the way, you must exert yourselves and strive

* *Cf.* also Mark xiii. 31; Luke xvi. 17; Luke xxi. 33.

with diligence—it is not enough to have seen me! Walk, as I have commanded you; get rid of all the tangled net of sorrow;

"Walk in the way with steadfast aim. . . . A sick man depending on the healing power of medicine,

"Gets rid of all his ailments easily without beholding the physician. He who does not do what I command sees me in vain, this brings no profit;

"Whilst he who lives far off from where I am, and yet walks righteously, is ever near me! A man may dwell beside me, and yet, being disobedient, be far away from me." (*Sacred Books of the East*, XIX. pp. 289–290.)

He who knows the truth and leads a life of truth, walking in the eightfold path of righteousness, has attained to Nirvâna and is with Buddha. And this view can only be called nihilism if Truth is an unmeaning word, and if moral aspirations are destructive of life.

There are many synonyms and explanatory epithets of Nirvâna. For an enumeration of Pâli synonyms of Nirvâna see Childers's Dictionary of the Pâli Language, pp. 272, 274, among which are such expressions as the Imperishable, the Infinite, the Eternal, the Everlasting, the Supreme, the Transcendent, the Serene, the Formless, the Void, Cessation, the Unconditioned, the Goal, the Other Shore, Rest, the True or the Truth. Nirvâna is compared to "an island which no flood can overwhelm," to a "city of peace," the "jewelled realm of happiness," "an escape from the dominion of Mâra," the tempter, or the evil one; and the disciple of Buddha, we are told, will overcome "the world of men, the world of Yama,*

* The god of Death.

and the world of gods." The Siamese always refer to it as in the phrases "Nirvâna is a place of comfort where there is no care; lovely is the glorious realm of Nirvâna." In Chapter XXVI. of the Dhammapada we read:

> "When you have understood the destruction of all that was made, you will understand that which was not made."

The most negative expression of all the synonyms of Nirvâna is the term "Void," and its mere existence in Buddhist books appears to favor the nihilistic conception of Buddhism. But what, in that case, shall we make of such sayings as "the voidness alone is self-existent and perfect"? The "abstract" may be a more appropriate translation than "the void," at least it would be less objectionable to those who have devoted themselves to the study of the philosophers of abstract thought.

It is sometimes difficult to understand the reason why an idea such as hollowness or emptiness or voidness, which to us denotes the absence of existence, has become pregnant with meaning in other languages; and we must be careful not to impute the negativism of our speech to the thought of others. Thus we find, on an old palm-leaf manuscript written in Sanskrit and preserved since 609 A. D. in the Buddhist monastery of Horiuzi, Japan, "emptiness" identified with "form"; * and that

* See page 48 in *The Ancient Palmleaves*, edited by F. Max Müller and Bunyin Nanjio. Appendix by G. Bühler. (Oxford, 1884.)

most remarkable philosopher of China, Lau-toze, gives us the key to the probable solution of the problem when he says in "Tau-Teh-King," XI.:

"The thirty spokes unite in the one nave; but it is on the empty space (for the axle) that the use of the wheel depends. Clay is fashioned into vessels; but it is on their empty hollowness that their use depends. The door and windows are cut out (from the walls) to form an apartment; but it is on the empty space (within), that its use depends. Therefore, what has a (positive) existence serves for profitable adaptation, and what has not that for (actual) usefulness.

Buddha himself abstained from making any positive statements as to the nature of Nirvâna. Whether we call it by positive or negative names is a matter of indifference and does not conduce to holiness. In this sense Buddha answers the question of Mâlukya: "Does the Tathâgata live on beyond death or does he not live on beyond death?" Buddha says:

"If a man were struck by a poisoned arrow, and his friends and relatives called in a skilful physician, what if the wounded man said, 'I shall not allow my wound treated until I know who the man is by whom I have been wounded, whether he is a noble, a Brâhman, a Vaiçya, or Çudra,'—or if he said, 'I shall not allow my wound to be treated until I know what they call the man who has wounded me, and of what family he is, whether he is tall, or small, or of middle stature, and how his weapon was made with which he has struck me.'"

This much is certain, that Buddha, while speaking of the bliss of Nirvâna, denied the continued existence of man's individualized body. Arhatship was eternal to him, but the Arhat's body dies.

Surrounded by these difficulties and contradictory opinions, let us bear in mind how close the resemblance is between the Buddhist idea of Nirvâna and the Christian hope of Heaven. It has often been remarked that many passages of the sacred writings of Buddhism would remain perfectly intelligible if we replace the word Nirvâna by Heaven. This would, in one respect, be very misleading ; Christians cling to the idea that in heaven the personality of the soul is preserved as a separate and discrete entity. The Christian hope of resurrection longs for a preservation of the ego, not of the mind. And on this point Buddhism is very unequivocal. Buddha denies the existence of any soul-substratum, or ego-entity ; he rejects the old Brâhmanical doctrine of the âtman, or self, which is said to be the metaphysical subject of man's sensations, thoughts, and volitions. But while there is an obvious difference between Nirvâna and Heaven, there is also a close resemblance not only of allegorical expressions and descriptions of the mystics, but also in the attempt at defining its nature in exact terms. There are some remarkable passages in the New Testament, one of which indicates not less clearly that the final aim of Christ's mission is the obliteration of personality by saying, "that God will be all in all," (1 Cor. xv. 28) and this final aim is characterized in the words: "There remaineth therefore a rest for the people of God" (Hebr. iv. 9). Comparing this rest to a great Sabbath the Apostle says: "He that is entered into his rest, he also has ceased from his own works as God did from his. Let us labor therefore to enter into that rest." And Jesus himself says, "Take my yoke upon you . . . and ye shall find rest unto your souls." In the face of these passages we can scarcely say that Christianity regards Heaven as a locality, and when we try to define positively what the orthodox Christian position is, or ought to be, we shall find ourselves implicated in no less intricate historico-philological problems than our Pâli scholars are in their investigations of Nirvâna. When Christian missionaries discovered some Christian color-prints of Jesus and biblical stories in Thibet, the Lama (as we read in Schlagintweit's "Buddhism in Thibet," p. 99) presented to them his view of the Christian salvation, as follows:

"Christianity does not afford final emancipation. According to the principles of their religion, he said, the pious are rewarded with a re-birth amongst the servants of the supreme God, when they are obliged to pass an eternity in reciting hymns, psalms, and prayers in his glory. Such beings, he argued, are consequently not yet freed from metempsychosis, for who can assert that in the event of their relaxing in the duty assigned them, they shall not be expelled from the world where God resides and in punishment be re-born in the habitation of the wretched."

Schlagintweit adds:

"He must have heard of the expulsion of the bad angels from Heaven."

The Lamaistic misconception of the Christian Heaven seems to be analogous to the Christian misconception of the Buddhist Nirvâna. One is quite as excusable as the other.

Schlagintweit says, that "genuine Buddhism rejects the idea of a particular locality being appropriated to Nirvâna," and Nâgasena says to King Milinda, "Nirvâna is wherever the precepts can be observed . . . it may be anywhere." When these passages are compared with the doctrine of Jesus, who says: "The kingdom of God is within you," we should not be astonished to find some mystic Lamas of Thibet declare that since the Christian doctrine of Heaven, according to Christ's own teaching, is purely internal and does not imply the positive existence of a domain somewhere in space, it implies an utter and desolate nihilism.

Schlagintweit * says: "The sacred Buddhist books declare at every occasion that it is impossible positively to define the attributes and properties of Nirvâna." A Thibetan Buddhist scholar might say the same thing to his countrymen in explanation of the Christian conception of Heaven.

If we were to hunt for Christian expressions of Heaven which are similar to the Buddhist similes of Nirvâna, we could find plenty of them, especially in the sermons of the mystics. Those who are inclined to philosophical speculation present the closest approach to a so-called negative formulation: Heaven, not otherwise than Nirvâna, is praised as an utter extermination of self; self disappears in the omnipresence of God, and reappears only as the transfigured standard-bearer of the cause of righteousness.

Whether or not this view is to be regarded as

* *L. c.*, p. 99.

nihilism should be judged from the course of ethics which is derived from it. If Buddhistic ethics are correctly characterized as quietism, we can justly classify its doctrines as nihilism. Now we find that the same objections made by Western people must have been made in Buddha's time by men trained in the schools of Brahmanism; there is a passage in the Mahâvagga in which Buddha very plainly expounds his view of action and non-action. He admits that he teaches a certain kind of quietism, but he vigorously rejects the quietism of indolence and inactivity. We read in VI., 31, 4:

"Sîha, the general, said to the Blessed One: 'I have heard, Lord, that the Samana Gotama denies the result of actions; he teaches the doctrine of non-action, and in this doctrine he trains his disciples. Now, Lord, those who speak thus, . . . do they say the truth or do they bear false witness against the Blessed One, and pass off a spurious Dhamma as your Dhamma?'"

The answer given by Buddha is as follows:

"There is a way, Sîha, in which one speaking truly could say of me: 'The Sama*n*a Gotama denies action; he teaches the doctrine of non-action; and in this doctrine he trains his disciples.'

"And again, Sîha, there is a way in which one speaking truly could say of me: 'The Sama*n*a Gotama maintains action; he teaches the doctrine of action; and in this doctrine he trains his disciples.'

"And in which way is it, Sîha, that one speaking could truly say of me: 'The Sama*n*a Gotama denies action; he teaches the doctrine of non-action; and in this doctrine he trains his disciples?' I teach, Sîha, the not-doing of such actions as are unrighteous, either by deed, or by word, or by thought; I teach the not bringing about of the manifold conditions (of heart) which are evil and not good. In this way, Sîha, one speaking truly could say of me: 'The Samana Gotama, etc.'

"And in which way is it, Sîha, that one speaking truly could say of me: 'The Samana Gotama maintains action; he teaches the doctrine of action; and in this doctrine he trains his disciples?' I teach, Sîha, the doing of such actions as are righteous, by deed, by word, and by thought: I teach the bringing about of the manifold conditions (of heart) which are good and not evil. In this way, etc."

In the same strain Buddha explains his doctrine of annihilation and contemptibleness, not as an absolute annihilation, but as an annihilation of sin and man's hankering after sin. He says:

"I proclaim, Sîha, the annihilation of lust, of ill-will, of delusion. . . .

"I deem, Sîha, unrighteous actions contemptible. . . .

"He who has freed himself, Sîha, from all conditions (of heart) which are evil and not good, which ought to be burned away, who has rooted them out, and has done away with them as a palm tree is rooted out, so that they are destroyed and cannot grow up again—such a person do I call accomplished in Tapas."* (*Sacred Books of the East*, Vol. XVII, pp. 110, 114.)

Far from preaching quietism, Buddha's sermons, parables, and sentences abound in exhortations to indefatigable and energetic activity. We read in the Dhammapada:

"He who does not rouse himself when it is time to rise, who though young and strong is full of sloth, whose will and

* The literal meaning of Tapas is "burning"; it means self-mortification. Buddha rejects self-mortification and substitutes for it the eradication of all sinful desire.

thought are weak, that lazy and idle man will never find the way to knowledge [enlightenment].

"If anything is to be done, let a man do it, let him attack it vigorously."*

The difficulty to a western mind in the comprehension of the term Nirvâna lies mainly in our habit of conceiving the nature of the soul in the old Brâhmanical sense of an ego-entity as the doer of our acts, the perceiver of our sensations, and the thinker of our thoughts. In ninety-nine cases out of a hundred, he who denies the existence of that metaphysical being is understood by people educated in our present modes of thought as denying the existence of our soul itself.

Buddha taught the non-existence of the self, and understood by self the âtman of the philosophers of his time. Again and again he inculcates the emphatic injunction that the illusion of self must be overcome. The illusion of self is the secret cause of all selfishness; it begets all those evil desires (covetousness, greed of power, and lust) of which man must free himself. As soon as the illusion of self is overcome, we cease to think of injuring others for the benefit of ourselves.

The Buddhist conception of Nirvâna is most assuredly not the annihilation of thought, but its completion and perfection. We read in the Dhammapada, verse 21:

"Earnestness is the path of immortality (Nirvâna), thought-

*Ibid., pp. 68 and 75.

lessness the path of death. Those who are in earnest do not die; those who are thoughtless are as if dead already."

This does not savor of nihilism.

That Nirvâna is the domain of the ideal, the realm of pure forms, appears very clearly from the Nirmana Sutra and other Chinese sources, in which Nirvâna is defined as "the permanent state of being," which is attained by letting go the conditions of impermanence, viz., materiality and egoity or rupa and âtman. Nirvâna is the attainment of the state where there is neither birth nor death, and is illustrated by the simile of the "guest" and the "dust," as contrasted to the "rest" of pure space. Man is a guest in this world and is in a condition of constant commotion as are the dust particles hovering in a sunbeam. Nirvâna, however, is comparable to the immutability of pure space which, while everything is changing, remains at rest.*

Nirvâna is commonly described in negative terms, but it is positive which is explained in a conversation between an unbeliever and Buddha, related in the Parinirvâna Sutra (Chap. xxxix. 1) as follows:

"There was a Brahmatchari called Basita, who resumed the conversation thus: 'Gotama! Is that which you call Nirvâna a permanent state of being or not?' 'Nirvâna consists in the absence [non-existence] of sorrow. Yes, Brahmatchari, it may be so defined.' Basita said: 'Gotama, there are four kinds of condition in the world which are spoken of as non-existent: the first, that which is not as yet in being, like the pitcher to

---

**A Catena of Buddhist Scriptures, from the Chinese*. By Samuel Beal, pp. 99 and 157.

be made out of the clay; secondly, that which having existed, has been destroyed, as a broken pitcher; third, that which consists in the absence of something different from itself, as we say the ox is not a horse; and, lastly, that which is purely imaginary as the hair of the tortoise, or the horn of the hare. If, then, by having got rid of sorrow we have arrived at Nirvâna, Nirvâna is the same as 'nothingness,' and may be considered as non-existent; but, if so, how can you define it as permanence, joy, personality, and purity.

"Buddha said: 'Illustrious disciple, Nirvâna is one of this sort, it is not like the pitcher not yet made out of the clay, nor is it like the nothingness of the pitcher which has been broken; nor is it like the horn of the hare, nor the hair of the tortoise, something purely imaginary. But it may be compared to the nothingness defined as the absence of something different from itself. Illustrious disciple, as you say, although the ox has no quality of the horse in it, you cannot say that the ox does not exist; and though the horse has no quality of the ox in it, you cannot say that the horse does not exist. Nirvâna is just so. In the midst of sorrow there is no Nirvâna, and in Nirvâna there is no sorrow. So we may justly define Nirvâna as that sort of non-existence which consists in the absence of something essentially different."

Buddhism is commonly classified as pessimism. This is true in so far as the Buddhist recognizes the existence of suffering, but it is not true if by pessimism is to be understood that world-pain which gives up life and the duties of life in despair. Says Oldenberg, speaking of the Buddhist canon:

"Some writers have often represented the tone prevailing in it, as if it were peculiarly characterized by a feeling of melancholy which bewails in endless grief the unreality of being. In this they have altogether misunderstood Buddhism. The true Buddhist certainly sees in this world a state of continuous sorrow, but this sorrow only awakes in him a feeling of compassion for those who are yet in the world; for himself he feels no sorrow nor compassion, for he knows he is near his goal which stands awaiting him, noble beyond all else."

The good tidings of Buddha's religion are not so much the recognition of the existence of pain and care as the conquest of evil and the escape from suffering. The following verses from the Dhammapada have no pessimistic ring:

"Let us live happily then, not hating those who hate us! Among men who hate us, let us dwell free from hatred!

"Let us live happily then, free from ailments among the ailing! Among men who are ailing, let us dwell free from ailments!

"Let us live happily then, free from greed among the greedy! Among men who are greedy, let us dwell free from greed!"

The Buddhist Nirvâna, accordingly, can only be conceived as a negative condition by those who are still entangled in the illusion of self. Nirvâna is not death but eternal life, not annihilation but immortality, not destruction but indestructibility. Were truth and morality negative, Nirvâna would be negative also; as they are positive, Nirvâna is positive. The soul of every man continues in what Buddhists call his Karma, and he who attains Buddhahood becomes thereby identical with truth itself, which is everlasting and omnipresent, pervading not only this world system, but all other worlds that are to be in the future. For truth is the same to-day as it will be to-morrow. Truth is the water of life, it is the ambrosia of the soul. The more our mind rids itself of selfishness and partakes of the truth, the higher shall we rise into that domain where all tribulations and anxieties have disappeared, for there sin is blotted out and death conquered.

# BUDDHISM AND CHRISTIANITY.

CHRISTIANITY, including Roman and Greek Catholics, the Protestants and all the smaller sects, may lay claim to about twenty-six per cent. of the inhabitants of the earth, and ranks, in number of adherents, as the second greatest religion. It is considerably surpassed by Buddhism, which is calculated by Prof. Rhys Davids to count five hundred million adherents, or forty per cent. of all the inhabitants of the earth.* The next religions † in order are Hinduism with thirteen, and Islam with twelve and

* The objection has been made by Sir Monier M. Williams that the Chinese Buddhists are at the same time Confucionists and Taoists, therefore he claims that if the number of Buddhists were reduced to those who are true Buddhists, and nothing but Buddhists, Christianity could easily be proved to be numerically the first religion of the world. This may be true, but is this method of using statistics legitimate? Would it not in that case be fair to apply the same restriction to both sides? The number of Christians would shrink in no less degree if we counted the real Christians, or at least the confessed Christians only, which in the United States would reduce them to the churched people who are less than one-tenth of the entire population.

† For details see the statistical tables on pp. 4–5 of Rhys Davids's *Buddhism* published in the series of *Non-Christian Religious Systems*, London, 1890.

one half per cent. In addition we have one half per cent. Jews, and eight per cent. of other creeds of less importance.

Now it is a strange fact that Buddhism and Christianity, constituting together sixty-six per cent., which is considerably more than one half of mankind, possess several most important features in common, and their agreement cannot be a product of mere chance. It is well known that many Christian missionaries * were quite at a loss to account for so many striking coincidences. Bishop Bigandet, the Apostolic Vicar of Ava and Pegu, writes :

"Most of the moral truths, prescribed by the Gospel, are to be met with in the Buddhistic scriptures. . . . In reading the particulars of the life of the last Buddha, Gaudama, it is impossible not to feel reminded of many circumstances relating to our Saviour's life, such as it has been sketched out by the Evangelists."

The Rev. Hampden C. Du Bose, a Protestant missionary, says about Romanism and Buddhism : †

"The traveller who notes the similarity between those two great systems of faith and worship must on comparison conclude that Romanism is Buddhism prepared for a foreign market,—Buddhism adapted to a Western civilization. The question troubled the earlier Catholic missionaries, and 'Prémare ascribed these ceremonies to the Devil, who had thus imitated holy mother Church, in order to scandalize and oppose its rights.' 'To those who admit that most of the Romish ceremonies are borrowed from Paganism, there is less difficulty in accounting for the resemblance.'"

---

* Quoted in *The Monist*, Vol. IV, No. 3, p. 418.

† *The Dragon, Image, and Demon*, p. 290.

And the Jesuit missionaries, Huc and Gabet, express their views of the subject as follows: *

"Upon the most superficial examination of the reforms and innovations introduced by Tsong-Kaba into the Lamanesque worship, one must be struck with their affinity to Catholicism. The cross, the mitre, the dalmatida, the cope, which the Grand Lamas wear on their journeys, or when they are performing some ceremony out of the temple; the service with double choirs, the psalmody, the exorcisms, the censer suspended from five chains, and which you can open or close at pleasure; the benedictions given by the Lamas by extending the right hand over the heads of the faithful; the chaplet, ecclesiastical celibacy, spiritual retirement, the worship of the saints, the fasts, the processions, the litanies, the holy water, all these are analogies between the Buddhists and ourselves. Now, can it be said that these analogies are of Christian origin? We think so. We have indeed found, neither in the traditions nor in the monuments of the country, any positive proof of their adoption, still it is perfectly legitimate to put forward conjectures which possess all the characteristics of the most emphatic probability.

There are some other less striking, but by no means less remarkable similarities that obtain between the cults of Buddhism and Christianity, and it would take volumes to explain them all. We mention only one more instance which is the "tee" in Buddhist pagodas, which is represented by a canopy over Roman Catholic altars. The Buddhist tee is originally an umbrella, viz., "the umbrella of sovereignty" which when executed in stone assumed a square form. There are many tees in existence which are over 2,000 years old. The old-

* *Travels in Tartary, Thibet, and China*, Eng. 2d Ed., p. 50.

est tee that still preserves the exact shape of an umbrella is still found in the caves of Ajanta. The canopy in the Roman Catholic ritual is explained as the divine Presence that overshadows the altar.

The Jesuit missionaries believe that the Buddhists adopted their rituals from Roman Catholic missionaries. They say:

> "It is known that, in the fourteenth century, at the time of the domination of the Mongol emperors, there existed frequent relations between the Europeans and the peoples of Upper Asia. We have already, in the former part of our narrative, referred to these celebrated embassies which the Tartar conquerors sent to Rome, to France, and to England. There is no doubt that the barbarians who thus visited Europe must have been struck with the pomp and splendor of the ceremonies of Catholic worship, and must have carried back with them into the desert enduring memories of what they had seen. On the other hand, it is also known that, at the same period, brethren of various religious orders undertook remote pilgrimages for the purpose of introducing Christianity into Tartary; and these must have penetrated at the same time into Thibet, among the Si-Fan, and among the Mongols on the Blue Sea. Jean de Montcorvin, Archbishop of Peking, had already organized a choir of Mongol monks, who daily practised the recitation of the psalms and the ceremonies of the Catholic faith. Now, if one reflects that Tsong-Kaba lived precisely at the period when the Christian religion was being introduced into Central Asia, it will be no longer matter of astonishment that we find, in reformed Buddhism, such striking analogies with Christianity."

How improbable is this theory! Nay, it is impossible in the face of the fact that the Lamaistic ritual dates back to the time of Fa-Hien. Although it is quite probable that Nestorian rituals, which is the shape in which Christianity reached Thibet in the seventh century, may have modified the Buddhist rituals considerably, we cannot deny that many of the most salient features of Thibetan Lamaism, such as the usage of rosaries, incense burning, the chanting of psalmodies, tonsures, etc., are unquestionably older than Christianity itself. Various church institutions, such as monkhood, processions, relic worship, etc., are not founded on the New Testament, and their origin in Christianity cannot be explained from the life history of Christ. The coincidences between Buddhism and Christianity are the more puzzling as they include so many trivial externalities.

The idea of a Buddhistic origin of Christianity has been suggested more than once; but it is incumbent upon us to state that some of the men who must be regarded as the most competent to judge this matter are either extremely reticent or scorn the suggestion as quite impossible. While it is true that Arthur Lillie and Rudolf Seydel, who have done most to make the theory popular, introduce many vague speculations, we cannot regard a refutation of some of their vagaries as sufficient to settle the question. No argument has as yet been offered to dispose of the hypothesis, which possesses, to say the least, a great probability in its favor. It is our intention here to enumerate some of the most salient facts so as to show them in their full importance, in the hope that specialists will give us more light on the subject. We repeat the motto which Albrecht

Weber inscribed upon the title page of his *Indische Literaturgeschichte:*

> "Nil desperari!
> Auch hier wird es tagen."

The agreement of the ethical spirit of both religions, Buddhism and Christianity, appears the more striking from our being confronted with an obvious difference between their dogmatologies. Christians believe in God, soul, and immortality, while Buddhists aspire to reach Nirvâna. They have no such terms as God and soul. On the contrary, they reject the ideas of a personal Creator of the world and of an indissoluble soul-unit, an âtman, or ego-entity in man, and thus they are decried by Christians as atheists and deniers of the existence of the soul. Having explained in a previous article that Buddhism is not negative, that its Nirvâna is neither more nor less positive than the Christian heaven, and that Buddha only rejects the gratuitous assumption of a metaphysical soul-agent behind the soul, not the existence of the soul itself, we shall now review the most obvious similarities and dissimilarities of Buddhism and Christianity; and we come to the conclusion that, *supposing no historical connection exists between the two faiths, their agreement must be regarded as very remarkable;* for in that case we must recognize the fact that *both Buddhists and Christians, facing the same problems of life, solve them in a similar spirit although using different modes of expression.* It would go far to prove that *the basic truths of both religions are deeply rooted in the nature of things* and cannot be supposed (as is the theory of supernaturalistic dualism) to stand in contradiction to the cosmic order of the world or to the laws according to which social institutions develop.

### BUDDHA AND CHRIST.

Let us briefly recapitulate the similarities that obtain between Buddhism and Christianity.

As St. John prepared the way for Christ, so Sumedha is anxious to be of assistance in clearing the path for Buddha. The people tell him:*

> A mighty Buddha has appeared,
> A Conqueror, Lord of all the world,
> Whose name is Dîpamkara.
> For him is being cleared the way,
> The path, the track to travel on.—Verse 51.

Sumedha replied:

> "For a Buddha do ye clear the road?
> Then, pray, grant also me a place!
> I, too, will help to clear the way,
> The path, the track to travel on."

As according to Isaiah "every valley shall be exalted and every mountain and hill shall be made low" at the coming of the glory of the Lord (Isaiah, xl, 3–5), so we read in the Sumangala Vilâsinî (Buddhagosa's Commentary on the Dîgha Nikâya) that

*Introduction to the Jatakas. See H. C. Warren's *Buddhism in Translations*, p. 12.

where the Buddha walks, "elevations of ground depress themselves and depressions elevate themselves; wherever he places his foot, the ground is even and pleasant to walk upon."—(H. C. Warren, *Buddhism in Translations*, p. 92.)

According to the sacred legends, Buddha, like Christ, was of royal, not of priestly, lineage; and his life while he was still a babe was jeopardized on account of the transcendent glory of his future. The chapter entitled "The Fear of Bimbisâra," * contains a parallel to the story of Herod's massacre of the infants in Bethlehem. The state ministers of Maghada make inquiry if there be any one capable of depriving the king of his regal power. Two of their messengers find among the Shâkyas an infant newly born, the first begotten of his mother, who would either become a universal monarch or a Buddha. On their return they exhort the king "to raise an army and destroy the child, lest he should overturn the empire of the king." But Bimbisâra (unlike Herod of the New Testament) refuses to commit the crime. The Christian story of the massacre of children is probably derived from the older Brâhmanical legend of Krishna, who is persecuted as an infant by the tyrant of Madura. The latter, unable to find the boy, ordains the massacre of all the children of male sex born during the night of Krishna's birth.

Both Buddha and Christ led a life of poverty. Both wandered about without a home, without a

* Beal, *Romantic History of Buddha*, pp. 103–104.

family, without property. They lived like the lilies of the field, and preached to all people, to rich and poor alike, without distinction of class, the gospel of the deliverance from evil.

Buddha is called Dharma-raja, the king of truth, and Christ before Pilate repudiates the idea that his kingdom is of this world. He is frequently represented by Christians as the King of Truth. Buddha is called Shâkya-simha, the lion of the Shâkya, while Christ is the lion of Judah. Buddha charges his disciples to carry the message of the glorious doctrine everywhere, saying "desêtha, bhikkhave kalyano dhammo," i. e., "Expound, O Bhikkhus, the happy truth." The word "Kalyâno" is translated in Chalmers' dictionary by "fortunate, blest, happy; beautiful, charming, pleasant; good, virtuous," and if *kalyàno dhammo* had to be rendered into Greek, we would consider the term εὐαγγέλιον as a most appropriate translation. There is no essential difference between the English "gospel," i. e. good spell, and the Pâli *kalyâno dhammo*, i. e., the good doctrine.

The same story which is told of Mary in the Apocryphal gospel of the Infancy of Mary (Chap. 6) is told of Buddha in the Jataka (Warren, Buddh. in Trans., p. 47). Both are reported to have walked soon after their birth, while still helpless babies, to the astonishment of their parents and other spectators. Only there is this addition, that the Buddha baby also speaks and announces his greatness in the words: "The chief am I of all the world."

How strangely Christian are the injunctions so frequently found in Buddhist scriptures, to have faith and to make use of the time of grace. We read, for instance, in the Jataka: *

If in this present time of grace,
You do not reach the happy state
Long will you suffer deep remorse.

Both Buddha and Christ, according to the canonical books of their respective religions were hailed soon after their birth, as the saviours of the world, by celestial spirits, by a religious prophet, and by sages. Dêvas, like the angels in the Christian Gospel, sing hymns. Asita is the Christian Simeon; the Nâgarâjas are the Magi. Aged women are also mentioned, who, like Anna, bless the baby.†

We read in the Tibetan *Life of Buddha*: ‡

"It was the habit of the Çakyas to make all new-born children bow down at the feet of a statue of the yaksha Çakyavardana; so the king took the young child to the temple, but the yaksha bowed down at his feet. . . . When the king saw the yaksha bow at the child's feet he exclaimed, 'He is the god of gods!' and the child was therefore called Devatideva."

---

* *Buddhist Birth Stories.* Translated by T. W. Rhys Davids, p. 157.

† See Ashvaghosha's *Life of Buddha*, verses 39–40.—*Sacred Books of the East*, (afterwards cited as S. B. of E.) vol. xix, pp. 1–20.

‡ *The Life of Buddha and the Early History of His Order, Derived from Tibetan Works in the Bkah-Hgyur, Bstan-Hgyur*, translated by W. Woodville Rockhill, p. 17. See also S. Beal, *Romantic History of Buddha*, p. 52.

The apocryphal Gospel of Pseudo-Matthew contains a similar passage: *

"Now it came to pass that when the most blessed Mary, with her little infant, had entered the temple, all the idols were prostrate on the earth, so that they all lay upon their faces wholly shattered and broken."

Both Buddha and Christ excelled their teachers. Both were greeted by a woman who was delighted with their personal beauty. The "noble virgin Kisâ Gotamî" bursts forth into the song:

"Blessed indeed is the mother,
Blessed indeed is the father,
Blessed indeed is the wife,
Who owns this lord so glorious."

—*Birth Stories*, p. 80.

This reminds one of the incident mentioned in Luke xi, 27:

"And it came to pass, as he spake these things, a certain woman of the company lifted up her voice, and said unto him, Blessed is the womb that bare thee, and the paps which thou hast sucked."

The word *Nibbuta*, i. e. "blessed, happy, peace," reminds Buddha of *Nibbuti*, i. e., *Nibbana*.† He says:

"By what can every heart attain to lasting happiness and peace!

---

* *The Apocryphal Gospels*, tr. by B. Harris Cowper, 4th ed., p. 63. See also *The Arabic Gospel of the Infancy*, *ibid.*, p. 178.

† *Birth Stories*, p. 80, and Spence Hardy, *Manual*, p. 160.

"And to him whose mind was estranged from sin the answer came. 'When the fire of lust is gone out then peace is gained; when the fires of hatred and delusion are gone out, then peace is gained; when the troubles of mind, arising from pride, credulity, and all other sins, have ceased, then peace is gained!' Sweet is the lesson this singer makes me hear, for the Nirvâna of Peace is that which I have been trying to find out. This very day I will break away from household cares! I will renounce the world! I will follow only after the Nirvâna itself!"

In a similar spirit Christ replies (Luke xi. 28):

"Yea, rather blessed are they that hear the word of God, and keep it."

Both Buddha and Christ were tempted by the Evil One.*

Both Buddha and Christ confessed their mission to be the establishing on earth of a kingdom of righteousness; † they sent out their disciples to preach the gospel. Said Buddha:

"Go ye now, O Bhikkhus, and wander, for the gain of the many, for the welfare of the many, out of compassion for the world, for the good, for the gain, and for the welfare of gods and men. Let not two of you go the same way. Preach, O Bhikkhus, the doctrine which is glorious in the beginning, glorious in the

---

* Compare Ashvaghosha's *Life of Buddha*, chapter xiii, "Defeats of Mâra, S. B. of E., vol. xix, p. 147, with Luke iv. 2, Matth. iv. 1–7, i. 13.

† See the *Dhamma-chakka-ppavattana-Sutta*,—viz., on "The Foundation of the Kingdom of Righteousness,"—S. B. of E., vol. xi. p. 146, and Bigandet, p. 125.

middle, glorious in the end, in the spirit and in the letter; proclaim a consummate, perfect, and pure life of holiness. There are beings whose mental eyes are covered by scarcely any dust, but if the doctrine is not preached to them, they cannot attain salvation. They will understand the doctrine. And I will go also, O Bhikkhus, to Uruvelâ, to Senâninigama, in order to preach the doctrine." *

Both Buddha and Christ refused to find recognition by pandering to the superstitions of those who seek for signs; † Buddha positively forbade miracles.‡ And yet to both innumerable miracles were attributed.

Of both we read that they walked on the water. The origin of the Buddhist legend can be traced to the allegorical expression of crossing the stream of worldliness (samsâra) and reaching the other side, which is the shore of celestial rest (Nirvâna). There is no such spiritual meaning in Christianity, or, if there was one, the metaphor has been obliterated.

As St. Peter by the strength of his faith crossed the waters of Lake Galilee, so we read in the *Jataka* § that one of Buddha's disciples accomplished the same feat.

* See *Mahâvagga* i, ii, p. 112, S. B. E., vol. xiii.; compare also Ashvaghosha's *Life of Buddha*, p. 183, with Mark iii, 14, and Luke ix. 2.

† See Luke xi. 16, and *passim*.

‡ See W. W. Rockhill's *Life of Buddha*, pp. 68–69.

§ The *Jataka* translated from the Pâli by various hands under the editorship of E. B. Cowell, No. 190, vol. ii, p. 77. Similar stories are frequently met with in Buddhist literature. See, for instance, the Chinese edition of *Buddhaghosha's Parables*, translated by Samuel Beal, Boston, 1878.

The signs of the appearance of a Christ are the same as the signs of the birth of Buddha. We read in the Jataka: *

"And the Thirty-two prognostics appeared, as follows: an immeasurable light spread through ten thousand worlds; the blind recovered their sight, as if from desire to see this his glory; the deaf received their hearing; the dumb talked; the hunchbacked became straight of body; the lame recovered the power to walk; all those in bonds were freed from their bonds and chains; the fires went out in all the hells."

How similar is Christ's reply to the disciples of St. John the Baptist!

At a marriage-feast both Buddha and Christ miraculously helped the host to entertain his guests. In Buddha's presence, as we are told in the story of the marriage-feast at Jambunada,† a small supply of food proves over and over sufficient for a great number of guests. The idea of turning water into wine, at the marriage at Cana,‡ is un-Buddhistic.

Both Buddha and Christ tried asceticism for a time, and carried their fasts to the extreme. We read:

"Each day eating one hemp grain, his bodily form shrunken and attenuated, seeking how to cross (the sea of) birth and death, exercising himself still deeper and advancing further." (Ashvaghosha's *Life of Buddha*, verse 1007.)

But both gave up these methods of gaining holiness by self-mortification for a middle way.§ Both

* Warren, p. 44.

† *Fu Pen Hing Tsi King*, translated by Beal.

‡ John ii. 1, et seq.

§ *Dhammapada*, verse 227: Chinese version of the *Dhammapada*, translated by Beal, p. 122.

were in consequence of it suspected by former believers of flagging in religious zeal.*

Both Buddha and Christ were powerful preachers, fond of parables, and concentrating their teachings in pithy aphorisms, which were both impressive and easily remembered. Both were keen thinkers, and invincible in controversies, as a rule, bringing the debate to a climax by presenting a dilemma, and always pressing the moral application of their theories. Both exercised an extraordinary influence; they looked into the hearts of men and swayed their minds through purity of motive and the authoritative earnestness of their personality. Both objected to the traditional method of clinging to the letter of religious belief which is satisfied with rituals and prayers, and both substituted for it the spirit of religious devotion and moral conduct.† Both loved to express their sentiments in paradoxes, such as, "By giving away we gain; by losing our soul we preserve it; by non-resistance we conquer," and both spoke in parables.‡ Many subjects of their parables are the same; as such we mention the sower § and

* Compare Ashvaghosha's *Life of Buddha*, verses 1024, and 1222–1224, with Luke vii, 19, Matth. xi, 3.

† As an instance of Buddha's method of spiritualizing religious rites see the *Sîgâlovâda Sutta* in *Sept Suttas Pâlis*, by M. P. Grimblot (Paris), p. 311.

‡ "'Powerful in making comparisons,' is one of Buddha's characteristic names."—Beal, foot-note to Ashvaghosha's *Life of Buddha*, verse 1915, S. B. of E., xix, p. 280.

§ *Sutta Nipâta*, p. 11–15, S. B. of E., Second Part.

the lost son; * the worldly fool who builds a large residence with store-rooms, but dies suddenly; † the comparison of good deeds to seeds sown on good and bad soil, according to the nature of the people, illustrating the truth that in bad people the passions choke the growth of merit. Buddha calls the Brahmans, and Christ the Pharisees, "blind leaders of the blind." ‡

Both Buddha and Christ show an unexpected graciousness toward a woman sinner; § and a Buddhist disciple had an encounter with a woman at a well analogous to that of Christ in Samaria. ‖

Both Buddha and Christ were, like Krishna, ¶ transfigured shortly before death, ** and above all, both inculcated the utter extinction of desire, lust, and hate in their very germ, so as to forbid all assertion of self, even the resistance to evil, and both demand the practice of love of enemies. ††

* *Saddharmapundarika* iv.

† Beal, *Translation of Chinese Dhammapada*, p. 77.

‡ Compare Matthew xv. 14, with *Tevigga Sutta*, i. 15, and *Lalita Vistara*, p. 179. See also Beal's *Romantic History of Buddha*, p. 106, where the phrase occurs, "Like a blind man who undertakes to lead the blind."

§ See the story of Ambapâli in *Mahâvagga* vi. 30. The courtesan Ambapâli is called "Lady Amra" in the Chinese version of Ashvaghosha's *Life of Buddha*, p. 255–256.

‖ Compare John v. et seq., with Burnouf's *Introduction*, p. 205.

¶ The transfiguration of Krishna serves the purpose of strengthening the faith of his followers in the presence of danger. See Jacolliot, *The Bible in India*, p. 306.

** Compare Matthew xvii. 2, and Mark ix. 2, with *Mahâparinibbâna Sutta* iv. 47, 52.

†† Compare *Dhammapada*, 5, "Hatred ceases by love," and

SIMILARITIES IN TEACHING.

There are, in addition, numerous coincidences in their utterances, so that many of the sayings of Christ and Buddha appear like two different reports of the same speech. Thus we read in the *Sutra of Forty-two Sections*, 10:

"It is difficult for the rich and noble to be religious."

And Christ said (Matthew xix. 24, Mark x. 25, and Luke xviii. 25):

"And again I say unto you, It is easier for a camel to go through the eye of a needle, than for a rich man to enter into the kingdom of God."

Christ says: "Love your enemies," and we read in the Dhammapada:

Hatred does not cease by hatred, hatred ceases by love only. This is an old rule."

The Dharma is frequently compared to living waters, as in John iv, 14, vii, 38, Rev. xxi, 6, xxii, 17, and to a pearl, or a jewel, as in Matthew xiii, 45–46, while Nirvâna is described as a city of peace and an island of jewels,* similarly as the new Jerusalem.

Yashas, the noble youth of Benares,† visits Buddha in the night, like Nicodemus;‡ but if Nicodemus

many other passages, with Matthew v. 44, "Love your enemies."

* See *Dhammapada*, p. 181.

† Ashvaghosha's *Life of Buddha*, p. 180, *Mahâvagga*, i. 7.

‡ See John iii. 2.

had been a Brahman, he would not have been mystified by Christ's proposition of the necessity of a spiritual rebirth; he would have understood the expression. The term "twice born" or "reborn" is still among Buddhists a title of honor given to priests and other men of distinction.

The coming of the Tathâgata (Buddha) is likened to the wind. We read in *The Questions of King Milinda*, page 148:

> "As the great and mighty wind which blew, even so, great king, has the Blessed One blown over the ten thousand world-systems with the wind of his love, so cool, so sweet, so calm, so delicate."

How similar, although less clear, is the passage in John iii. 8:

> "The wind bloweth where it listeth, and thou hearest the sound thereof, but canst not tell whence it cometh, and whither it goeth: so is every one that is born of the Spirit."

The Dharma (viz., religion) is said to be like the salt of the ocean, "one in taste throughout, which is the taste of salvation." This reminds us of Jesus saying that his disciples are the salt of the earth; * and the exhortation is made by both Buddha and Christ to lay up treasures that are incorruptible and inaccessible to thieves.†

* *Questions of King Milinda*, iii. 7, 15, and *Chullavagga* ix. 1, 4, which compare with Matthew v. 13.

† Compare *Nidhikandasutta*, the treasure chapter, where we read of "A treasure that no wrong of others and no thief can steal," with Matthew vi. 20.

Giving is praised in preference to receiving. In Ashvaghosha's *Life of Buddha*, 1516–1517, we read:

"Giving away our food, we get more strength; giving away our clothes, we get more beauty," etc. (S. B. of E., p. 215.)

In *The Questions of King Milinda* we find among the discussions concerning apparent contradictions explained by Nagasêma, that "the Dharma of the Tathâgata shines forth when displayed" (p. 264), which is contrasted with the injunction, "Do not let the Dharma . . . . fall into the hands of those unversed with it" (page 266). Both passages find their parallels in the Christian Gospel, the former in Matthew v. 16, "Let your light shine before men," and the latter in Matthew vii. 6, "Do not cast your pearls before swine."

Buddha says (in the *Sutra of Forty-two Sections*, 28) "Guard against looking on a woman," and (in Buddhaghosha's *Parables*, p. 153) he comments upon the law "commit no adultery," that it "is broken by even looking at the wife of another with a lustful mind." Christ expresses the same idea in almost the same words, saying: "Whosoever looketh on a woman to lust after her, has committed adultery with her already in his heart." (Matthew v. 28.)

The sentence, "If thy right eye offend thee pluck it out," (Matthew v. 29), finds a parallel in the words:

"Better far with red-hot iron pins bore out both your eyes, than encourage in yourself lustful thoughts." (Ashvaghosha's *Life of Buddha*, 1762–1763.)

"The armor of God" is described by St. Paul (Eph. vi. 13–17):

"Wherefore, take unto you the whole armor of God, that ye may be able to withstand in the evil day, and having done all, to stand.

"Stand, therefore, having your loins girt about with truth, and having on the breastplate of righteousness;

"And your feet shod with the preparation of the gospel of peace;

"Above all, taking the shield of faith, wherewith ye shall be able to quench all the fiery darts of the wicked.

"And take the helmet of salvation, and the sword of the Spirit, which is the word of God."

This reminds us of Ashvaghosha's *Life of Buddha*, 1761–1762:

"Take, then, the bow of earnest perseverance, and the sharp arrow-points of wisdom.

"Cover your head with the helmet of right thought, and fight with fixed resolve against the five desires."

In the *Lalita Vistara* (page 122) we read of the "World" that "it is like a city of sand. Its foundations cannot endure," which reminds us of Matthew vii. 26.

Matthew xxiv. 35: "My words shall not pass away," finds a parallel in *Buddhist Birth Stories*, p. 18: "The word of the glorious Buddhas is sure and everlasting."

Both Buddha and Christ point out to their adherents the good example of worldly people. Buddha says, when rebuking his disciples for improper behavior:

"Even the laymen, O bhikkhus . . . . will be respectful, affectionate, hospitable to their teachers. Do you, therefore, O bhikkhus, so let your light shine forth that you having left the world . . . . may be respectful, affectionate, hospitable to your teachers," etc. (*Mahâvagga* V. 4, 2, xvii. p. 18.)

And Christ says:

"If ye love them which love you, what reward have ye? Do not even the publicans the same? And if ye salute your brethren only, what do ye more than others? Do not even the publicans so?" (Matth. v. 46–47.)

Christ complains, in Matth. xi. 16–19, of the childish nature of the people whom no one can satisfy, neither John the Baptist who did not eat and drink nor the Son of man who did eat and drink. In the same spirit Buddha says:

"They blame the man of many words, they blame the patient and quiet man, they also blame the man who seeks the happy medium." (See Beal's *Translation of the Chinese Dhammapada*, sect. xxv. p. 122. Compare *Pâli Dhammapada*, v. 227).

It is a curious coincidence that Christ, when speaking of the signs of the coming of the Son of Man, mentions "the fig tree's putting forth leaves" (Matt. xxiv. 32), while we read in the *Saddharma-pundarîka*, ii. 134–136, S. B. of E., p. 58:

"At certain times and at certain places, somehow do leaders appear in the world......just as the blossom of the glomerous fig-tree is rare, all so wonderful, and far more wonderful is the law I proclaim."

As the coming of the Son of man, so his parting

from life is expressed in words which present a certain similarity to Buddhistic passages. Christ says:

> "Ye shall not see me" (St. John. xvi. 16),

and again (Matt. xxiv. 23.)

> "If any man shall say unto you, Lo, here is Christ, or there, believe it not."

The *Brahmajâla Sutta* (translated by Gogerly in *Sept Suttas Pâlis*, p. 59) although in a different sense also speaks of Buddha that he shall not be seen again. We read:

> "That which binds the teacher to existence is cut off, but his body still remains. While his body still remains he will be seen by gods and man, but after the termination of life, upon the dissolution of the body, neither gods nor men will see him." (P. iii.)

Self-sacrifice is the lesson of Christ's death; the same lesson is taught by Buddha in one of the Samkaapâla birth stories, where he offers himself for food to a hungry Brahman. Buddha says:

> "They pierced me through with pointed sticks,
> They hacked me with their hunting knives,
> Yet 'gainst these Bhojans raged I not,
> But kept the precepts perfectly." *

A similar passage occurs in the Greater Sutasoma Birth-story, where Buddha says:

> "I kept the promise I had made
> And gave my life in sacrifice."

---

* Warren, p. 35.

At the close of his career Buddha promised that, when needed, another Buddha would arise who will be known as Meitreya, he whose name is kindness, and in a similar mood Christ prophesies the coming of the Comforter, that will guide them into all truth and complete his work.

While the resemblances between Christ and Buddha are exceedingly great, there is a passage in the Epistle of St. James which has puzzled all translators, because it contains a Buddhist term which was no longer understood among Christians. The endless circuit of becoming is compared to a wheel, in the hands of Mara, the Evil One, which is frequently painted by Buddhist artists. St. James speaks of the tongue as a fire, saying: "Behold how great matter a little fire kindleth. He continues:

*οὕτως ἡγλῶσσα καθίσταται ἐν τοίς μέλεσιν ἡμῶν, ἡ σπιλοῦσα ὃλον το σῶμα καὶ φλογίζουσα τὸν τροχὸν τῆς γενέσεως, καὶ φλογιζομένη ὑπὸ τῆς γεέννης.*

[Thus the tongue that defileth the whole body standeth among our limbs, and it sets on fire the wheel of becoming and is set on fire by hell.]

The Latin version retains the term *rota nativitatis.* "The wheel of being born," but the English version of King James replaces the term by "course of nature." The reappearance of this peculiarly Buddhist term in the New Testament is certainly most startling and perplexing.

### CHRISTIAN AND BUDDHISTIC SENTIMENTS.

There is a strange agreement between Christian and Buddhistic sentiment as expressed in hymns and religious poetry. The well-known crusader's song which, it is said, was sung by Christian warriors on their march to Palestine, to a beautiful rhythmic march-melody, concludes with the following verse:

> "Fair is the moonshine,
> Fairer the sunlight
> Than all the stars of the heavenly host.
> Jesus shines brighter,
> Jesus shines purer
> Than all the angels that heaven can boast."

How much does this resemble the following verse in the Dhammapada (verse 387):

> "The sun is bright by day,
> The moon shines bright by night,
> The warrior is bright in his armor,
> The Brahmana is bright in his meditation,
> But Buddha, the awakened,
> Is brightest with splendor day and night." *

There is not the slightest evidence that the crusader's hymn is an echo of the verse of the Dhammapada. How naturally similar sentiments develop under the same conditions of mind may be learned from the following poem which we quote from "The Ten Theophanies," by the Rev. William M. Baker. We take the liberty only of making a few changes in the order of the verses and replace Christian terms by Buddhistic expressions. The sentiment remains unaltered and shows how thoroughly the religious literature of the one religion can be utilized

* *Sacred Books of the East*, Vol. X, p. 89.

for the other. The poem which may be entitled either "Lifting the Veil of Maya" or A Glimpse of Nirvâna," reads in its revised version as follows:

"Melt, oh thou film-flake, faster,
  Rend, thou thin gauze, in two,
O *Buddha*,* overmaster,
  Break in effulgence through!
I know how very nearly
  I draw unto thy realms.
I know that it is merely
  A film which overwhelms
These eyes from rapturous seeing,
  These ears from rapturous sound,
This self from *Buddha*-being,
  This life from broken bound.
O sacred *light*, o'erflow thee!
  Rush *æons* into one,
That earth and heaven may know the
  Eternal rest begun!"

### THE MURDER OF PARENTS.

Remarkable as these parallels are, some of which are apparently incidental, some striking, some simply curious, the list is by no means exhausted.† Let me

*The italics indicate the changes made. Line 3 reads in the original "Eternal heaven, o'ermaster"; line 11, "This self from God-like being"; line 13, "day" in place of "light"; and line 14, "æons" (which stands for the Buddhist term "kalpas") in place of "Sabbaths."

†Rudolf Seydel calls attention to a curious similarity of sound between important names, such as Mâyâ and Maria, Ananda and Johannes, Sariputra and Peter, Devadatta, and Judas, each two of these characters, strange to say, being representatives of the very same type and playing the same parts, those in Buddha's, these in Christ's life. But we have

now add a passage in which the Buddhist version may be hoped to throw light upon the Christian narrative.

Christ's words in Matth. x. 21, "The children shall rise up against their parents and cause them to be put to death," have startled Christians in no less degree than an analogous passage in the Buddhist canon has the Buddhists. We read in the *Dhammapada*, verse 295:

"A true Brahman goes scathless, though he have killed father and mother and two holy kings and an eminent man besides."

Says the translator in the footnote on page 71:

"D'Alois following the commentary explains mother as lust, father as pride, the two valiant kings as heretical systems, etc."

And Beal quotes in the Introduction to his *Translation of the Chinese Dhammapada* the following Buddhistic comment:

"Is not love (*Tanhâ*) which covets pleasure more and more, and so produces 'birth'—is not this the mother (*mâtâ*) of all? And is not 'ignorance' (*avidyâ*) the father (*pitâ*) of all? To destroy these two, then, is to slay father and mother. And again, to cut off and destroy those ten '*kleshas*'

---

to add that the names Miryam, and Simeon Kephas, the Hebrew originals of Maria and Peter, resemble their Buddhistic counterparts very little and exhibit a remarkable instance of an incidental resemblance warning us not to take even striking coincidences as evidences of appropriation.

(Ch. *shi*) which like the rat or the secret poison, work invisibly, and to get rid of all the consequences of these faults (i. e., to destroy all material associations), this is to wound a Rahat. And to cause offence and overthrow a church or assembly, what is this but to separate entirely the connexion of the five *skandhas?* ('five *aggregates*,' which is the same word as that used above for the church). And again to draw the blood of a Buddha, what is this but to wound and get rid of the seven-fold body by the three methods of escape. ......And in order to explain and enforce this more fully, the World-honored One added the following stanzas:

> Lust, or carnal desire, this is the mother,
> 'Ignorance,' this is the father,
> The highest point of knowledge, this is Buddha,
> All the 'kleshas' these are the Rahats.
> The five skandhas, these are the priests,
> To commit the five unpardonable sins
> Is to destroy these five
> And yet not suffer pains of hell."

Christ's startling prediction that "the children will rise against their parents and cause them to be put to death" bears an obvious likeness to these Buddhistic passages and will, on the supposition of an historical connexion between both religions, find, if considered in the light of the above quotation, a natural explanation.

### THE DOCTRINE OF NON-RESISTANCE.

In pushing their doctrine of kindness and love of enemies to the utmost extreme, both Buddha and Christ seem to have had but little regard for the ethics of struggle. We purposely say "seem," for the doctrine of non-resistance is one of many paradoxes which admit of a perfectly satisfactory explanation; it has been interpreted by orthodox Christian theologians and also by Buddhists to mean that a man's disposition of heart must be such that he does not defend his right because it is *his*, but because it is *right;* that selfishness and personal vanity must not be our motives of action; and that a man must be willing to give up, if need be, not only what is taken from him, but other things in addition. Thus we are told by Christian exegetists, that Christ does not demand of us to give up the mantle to him who robs us of our coat, for Christ himself defended his right when unjustly beaten. Christ himself carried on a bitter warfare against those whom he called hypocrites, and generations of vipers. He showed the belligerent spirit of his zeal when he cast out those who bartered in the temple and held pigeons for sale, which act was probably an emphatic protest against bloody sacrifices, so extremely offensive to the Essene brotherhood. And Buddha, too, with all his gentleness, was himself a powerful, although always kindhearted, controversialist; and his disciples are frequently compared to warriors who with spiritual weapons had unflaggingly and zealously to struggle for the truth.

## THE SANGHA AND THE CHURCH.

There are also striking resemblances in the development of the Sangha, or Buddhist brotherhood, and the Church. Universality is a marked feature of both religions. Thus Buddhism, as well as Christianity, is possessed of a missionary spirit; anxious to let everybody partake of the blessing of their religion, they sent out apostles to all known countries of the earth. Councils were held to settle disputes as to the right doctrine. A sacred literature originated first of the Master's sayings, with incidental mentionings of the occasions on which they were uttered; and later hagiographers undertook to tell the whole story of his life. There is an increasing tendency perceptible in the development of both Buddhistic and Christian thought, of more and more exaggerating the marvellous and of adding legendary elements. The ancient Buddhist chaityas, or assemblage halls, with nave, aisles, and apse, bear a close resemblance to Christian churches; and the Buddhist wheel reappears as the rose window above the main entrance of cathedrals.

There were monks in Buddhism long before Christianity existed; and Buddhist monks wear rough garments, live under the same, or almost the same, restrictions, have tonsures, and employ rosaries. They live as hermits or in cloisters, and the clergy of Tibet possess a hierarchy with institutions which are quite analogous to that of the Roman Catholic Church. They have processions, they baptize,* they sprinkle with holy water, and use the confessional.

* It is difficult to say whether or not baptism was established among the early Buddhists; if so, it is probable that the ceremony is older than Buddhism. We find bathing in the Ganges

There are analogies even of sects and heresies. The Doketistic heresy believed that Christ, because he was God, could have suffered no pain; his whole being was uncontaminated with material existence, and his body was mere appearance, a sham—hence the name of the sect from δοκεῖν, to seem. This view is represented in the apocryphal "Gospel according to St. Peter," in which we read (verse 10): "And they brought two malefactors and crucified the Lord between them; but he kept silence, as *feeling* no pain." Doketism is also one of the Buddhist heresies, as may be learned from a passage quoted from the *Fo-pan-ni-pan-king*, an expanded rendering of the *Parinirvâna-Sutra*, translated into Chinese by Dharmaraksha (*Sacred Books of the East*, Vol. XIX, p. 365, et seq). The Tathâgata says to Chunda, the smith:

"To those who as yet have no knowledge of the nature of Buddha, to these the body of Tathâgata seems capable of suffering, liable to want (but to others it is not so); at the time when Bodhisattva received the offering of food and drink (he was supposed to have eaten the food). . . . so now having received your offering, he will preach the law. But still, as in the former case he ate not, so neither does he eat now."—Transl. by Samuel Beal, *l. c.*, p. 367.

There are two incidents which link Buddhism and

---

mentioned as a religious rite in Ashvagosha's *Life of Buddha*, verses 164–165. But no further explanation is given concerning it. Was it an ablution, or did it symbolize the crossing of the stream of samsâra? It is remarkable that St. Paul (I. Cor. iv. 1–4) says that the crossing of the Red Sea was the baptism of the children of Israel.

Christianity together, in a quite peculiar way. On the one hand, Buddha has been received among the Christian saints under the name of St. Josaphat,* so that in this respect the followers of Buddha must appear to Christians as a kind of a Christian sect, however incomplete their dogmatic Christianity may be. On the other hand Buddha prophesied that the next Buddha after him would be Maitrêya, the Buddha of kindness, and without doing any violence to Buddha's words, this prophecy *may* be said to be fulfilled in Jesus of Nazareth. Thus the Christians may be said to be Buddhists that worship Maitrêya under the name of Christ.

### THE MAIN DIFFERENCE.

The similarities of Christianity and Buddhism are the more remarkable as among the dissimilarities there is one which exhibits an almost irreconcilable contrast. All those members of the various Christian denominations who call themselves its orthodox representatives, regard the belief in a personal God (an Ishvara) as the foundation of their religious faith.

* Josaphat is a corruption of Bodhisattva. For a detailed account of the Barlaam and Josaphat literature see Rhys David's *Buddhist Birth Stories*, pp. xxxvi, et seq. Rhys Davids says on p. xli : "It was Prof. Max Müller, who has done so much to infuse the glow of life into the dry bones of Oriental scholarship, who first pointed out the strange fact—almost incredible, were it not for the completeness of the proof—that Gotama, the Buddha, under the name of St. Josaphat, is now officially recognized throughout the whole of Catholic Christendom as a Christian saint!"

No wonder that they characterize Buddha's religion as atheism, denouncing it as unsatisfactory, or even nihilistic, and vigorously repudiate any kinship which might be supposed to obtain between both creeds.

The God-idea, representing the ultimate authority of conduct, is so fundamental in Christianity that Christians cannot think of any atheistic religion; they actually identify religion with belief in God and, indeed, we confess that it is remarkable how Buddhists can dispense at all with the God-idea.

We grant that no religion can exist without a belief in the existence of an ultimate authority of conduct; but in this sense Buddhism, too, teaches a belief in God. The Abhidharma, or Buddhist philosophy, distinctly rejects the idea of a creation by an Ishvara, i. e., a personal Creator; but it recognizes that all deeds, be they good or evil, will bear fruit according to their nature, and they teach that this law, which is ultimately identical with the law of cause and effect, is an irreversible reality; that there are no exceptions or deviations from it. Thus, law takes to some extent the place of the God-idea, and Buddhists gain a personal attitude to it, similarly as Christians do when speaking of God, in quite a peculiar way. The doctrine of the Trikâya, or the three bodies, teaches us that Buddha has three personalities; the first one is the Dharma-Kâya, or the body of the law: it corresponds to the Holy Ghost in the Christian dogmatology. The second personality is the Nirmâna-Kâya, or the body of transformations; it is transient in its various forms, and its most important and latest appearance has been Gautama Siddhârtha. This corresponds to the second person of the Christian, Trinity, to God the Son, or Christ. But there is this difference: that the Nirmâna Kâya appeared before Gautama Siddhârtha in many other incarnations and will reappear in this and other worlds again; for every one who has attained enlightenment and reached the ideal of perfection is a Tathâgata, a Buddha, a preacher of moral truth. It is in agreement with this conception that Philo speaks of Moses as a former incarnation of the Logos. The third personality of Buddha is called Sambhoga-Kâya, or the body of bliss. It is the Christian idea of God the Father. Buddha in his capacity as Sambhoga-Kâya is described as eternal, omnipresent, and omnipotent. He is the life of all that lives and the reality of all that exists. Thus he is the All in All, in whom we live and move and have our being.

Buddhistic atheism, apparently, is not wholly unlike Christian theism.

Christianity possesses in the idea, and, indeed, in the very word "God," representing the authority of moral conduct, in a most forcible manner, a symbol of invaluable importance; it is an advantage which has contributed not a little to make Christianity so powerful and popular, so impressive and effective as it has proved to be. In this little word "God," much has been condensed, and it contains an unfathomable depth of religious comfort.

No serious thinker who has ever grappled with

the problem of the God-idea can have any doubt that the conception of God as an individual being is a mere allegory, which, however, symbolizes a great truth which it is difficult to explain to untrained minds in purely scientific terms. There is a disadvantage and there is also an advantage in mythological terms. Let us here as everywhere learn from various methods of presenting a truth. Let us prove all and hold fast that which is good.

## BUDDHISTIC ART.

The spirit of Buddhism also exhibits a palpable affinity with Christian conceptions in its art productions, which, we have every reason to believe, originated uninfluenced by either the technique or the taste of the Western civilization. The difference between Western and Eastern taste is as strongly marked in religious art as in the other walks of life. Nevertheless there is an unmistakable coincidence of aspiration, which will strike any one who visits the Buddhistic departments of the Musée Guimet at Paris, or glances over the *Illustrated Guide* of its collections. We reproduce here a few pictures which seem to us especially instructive, because they express sentiments which are not foreign to the student of Christian art.

1. Mi-rô-Kou, or Maitrêya, the Buddha to come, of gilded wood (Sixteenth Century), seated upon a lotus in an attitude as if ready to rise and proclaim to the world the Gospel of the Good Law. The halo

I. MI-RÔ-KOU, or MAITRÊYA.

2. BODHISATTVA

3. SAM-BÔ.

4. Kouan-yin.

5. AMIDA (BUDDHA AMITÂBHA).

6. The Devil as a Buddhistic Monk.

round his head and the divinely glorious attitude of his whole person remind us of Roman Catholic conceptions of Christ, such as can be found in abundance in all Catholic countries, especially in Southern Europe and in the Spanish colonies of America.

2. Bodhisattva, the teacher of the law, also of gilded wood (Fifteenth Century), stands upon the lotus in the attitude of a preacher. In contrast to the statue of Mi-rô-Kou it emphasizes the human in Buddha and reminds us of the Protestant conception of Christ, which found its noblest representation in Thorwaldsen's famous statue.

3. Sam-bô, or the Buddhistic trinity, again representing Roman Catholic taste, shows the three jewels, the Buddha, the Dharma, and the Sangha. The Dharma (in one sense the Christian logos, in another the Holy Ghost) being most appropriately represented by written words, nor is it impossible that its higher position may indicate a certain superiority over the Buddha and the Sangha. For the Buddha is the incarnation and the Sangha the continued proclamation of the Dharma.

4. Kouan-yin, a peculiar conception of Buddha (made of porcelain), represents Buddha in one of his female incarnations as the goddess of charity and motherly love. The resemblance to Roman Catholic representations of Mary, the mother of Christ, is obvious, and the coincidence loses none of its force when we consider that the mythological conception of Kouan-yin is radically different from that of Mary. Buddha is conceived not as the object of motherly

love, not as the infant, but as Love itself. The statues on both sides of the chair are Hoang-tchen-saï, the disciple of Kouan-yin, and Loung-nou, the servant of Kouan-yin; the former in an attitude of worship, the latter holding in his hands a luminous pearl. The necklace of Kouan-yin contains an ornament in the shape of a cross of the Renaissance.

5. Amida (Buddha Amitâbha), of carved wood and gilded (Twelfth Century), an art production of the Tendai sect. The statue exhibits a softness of outline that reminds of Kouan-yin. Buddha's attitude and the grace of his appearance is here almost womanly, and might among Roman Catholics serve as a statue of the Virgin.

6. The Devil as a Buddhistic monk, carved wood of the Seventeenth Century, finds many parallel productions on the pinnacles of Gothic cathedrals. There is little probability that the Japanese artist who, with great ingenuity and humor, sculptured this admirable statue, ever heard of Rabelais, whose verse from Book IV, chapter xxiv, has become an English proverb, which, according to Bartlett's *Familiar Quotations*, page 772, reads as follows:

> When the Devil was sick, the Devil a monk would be:
> When the Devil was well, *the devil* a monk was he."

There is not only an obvious similarity in the religious ideas and objects of devotion, but even in religious satire, which cannot be explained by imitation, but must have originated independently in Buddhism as in Christianity.

### THE CONNEXIONS BETWEEN THE EAST AND WEST.

The question whether Christianity and Buddhism have a common origin is perhaps less important than it appears, yet there attaches to it a peculiar interest because there is a numerically very strong section of Christians who would not allow that the noble ethical maxims of Jesus of Nazareth could have developed according to the laws of nature in the normal progress of evolution. There is certainly very little probability of a borrowing on the part of Buddhism, as it is in all its essential features considerably older than Christianity. Buddha lived in the fifth century before Christ. The Buddhistic canon was settled at the time of the second council which took place about 250 B. C., and Ashoka's rock inscriptions, which contain the gist of Buddha's doctrine and testify to its established existence, date from the same period. This excludes at once the supposition that Buddhism is indebted to Christianity for its lofty morality and the purity of its ideals.

We must add that it remains not impossible (although not probable) that Buddhism, as it developed in its later phases in the North, has received from Christianity some modes of worship for which there would have been no place in the older Buddhism. Thus, Prof. Samuel Beal believes that Christian ideas and forms of worship must have been imported into Northern India as early as 50 A.D. He considers it as highly probable that King Gondoforus of the Legenda Aurea is identical with Gondophares, the founder of the Scythian dynasty in Seistan Vandahâr and Sindh, coins of whose reign are mentioned by General Cunningham. (*Arch. Survey of Ind.*, II, p. 59.) Professor Beal trusts that the old legend of St. Thomas's visit to India is confirmed; he does not consider, however, the possibility, which is not improbable, that the legend of St. Thomas may, like the St. Josaphat story, be a Christianized Buddhist legend. We waive the question and confine ourselves to stating that the evidences which Professor Beal introduces to prove the possibility of a Christian influence upon later Buddhism go still farther to establish the possibility of a Buddhistic influence upon Judea before the time of Christ's appearance. Professor Beal says (p. 133–134):

"The Parthian prince, Pacorus, was, as Josephus tells us, in possession of Syria and at Jerusalem. . . . Then again, the marriage of Chandragupta with a daughter of Seleucus, and the apparent knowledge possessed by the grandson of Chandragupta, the great Asoka, with the Greek King Antiochus, and his embassy to four other Greek kings,—all this shows that there must have been some connexion between India and the Western world, from the time of the establishment of Greek influence in the valley of the Oxus."

There were plenty of channels through which Buddhist doctrines could reach Palestine.

Speaking of the similarity between the Buddhist story of the wise judge and the account of Solomon's judgment, as told in the Book of Kings, Prof. Rhys Davids mentions the commercial relations that obtained in those early days between Judea and

India. He says (*Buddhist Birth Stories*, pp. xlvi.–xlvii.):

"The land of Ophir was probably in India. The Hebrew names of the apes and peacocks said to have been brought thence by Solomon's coasting-vessels are merely corruptions of Indian names. . . . But any intercourse between Solomon's servants and the people of Ophir must, from the difference of language, have been of the most meagre extent; and we may safely conclude that it was not the means of the migration of our tale.

"Though the intercourse by sea was not continued after Solomon's time, gold of Ophir, ivory, jade, and Eastern gems still found their way to the West; and it would be an interesting task for an Assyrian or Hebrew scholar to trace the evidence of this ancient overland route in other ways."

In order to prove the possibility of an exchange of thought between India and Judea, it is not even necessary to fall back upon these old commercial relations which are difficult to trace, for we know for sure that since Alexander's time the connexions between the East and the West in general, and especially between Buddhist countries and Judea, were quite intimate. Ashoka's rock inscriptions alone are sufficient to prove that official legations had been dispatched from India to the most important neighboring countries and to Western Asia for the sole purpose of making a strong propaganda for Buddha's religion and the Buddhistic principles of universal kindness and compassion for the suffering. The second edict mentions a legation to King Antiochus for mere humanitarian purposes. It reads as follows:

"Everywhere in the kingdom of the king Priyadarshin,* beloved of the gods, and (among those) who (are) his neighbors, as the Codas, the Pandyas, the prince of the Satiyas, the prince of Karalas Tâmraparnî, the Yavanas † king Antiochus and (among the) others who (are) the vassal kings of Antiochus—everywhere the king Priyadarshin, beloved of the gods, founded two (kinds of) hospitals—hospitals for men and hospitals for animals. Wherever there were no healing herbs to be found, whether herbs fit for men or herbs fit for animals, to all such places and in all such places, he issued orders to have such herbs brought and planted. Also where there were no healing roots and fruits he issued orders to have (them) brought and planted. And along the roads he had trees planted and wells dug for the use of man and beast."

The thirteenth edict speaks directly of a missionary legation for spreading Buddha's religion. The first part of the inscription is mutilated. The German translator, Professor Bühler, says that from the few correctly read words of a version of the same edict preserved near Shâhbâzgarhî, and from the fragment of the Ginâr inscription, the thought of the missing lines can be restored. Having expressed remorse at the atrocities committed before his conversion in Kaliriga, the king states that it is his intention from now on to make no more conquests by the sword, but is determined to take from his free neighbors everything that can possibly be endured. He adds that even the wild tribes in the forest ought to be participants of this kindness, and concludes with the remark that he has no other desire than to

* This is the customary appellation of Ashoka.

† The Yavanas are the Greeks.

treat all beings with indulgence, justice, and clemency. The part still extant reads:

"(The beloved of the gods wishes) . . . for all creatures . . . forbearance, justice, and clemency! But the following is judged of the greatest consequence by the beloved of the gods, namely, conquest by the law (Dhammavijaye.) This conquest is made by the beloved of the gods as well here (in his own kingdom) as among all his neighbors. For at a distance of six hundred Yojanas lives the (king) of the Yavanas (Greeks), called Amtiyoga (Antiochus) his neighbor, and beyond him are four, 4, kings, one named Tulamaya (Ptolemæus), one called Aikyashudala (Alexander); (further), towards the South the Codas (Colas) and the Pamdiyas (Pândyas) as far as Tambapamni (Ceylon), likewise the Hida king among the Vishas (Bais), and Vajis (Vrijis), the Yavanas (the Greeks) and the Kambojas (Kâbulis), among the Nâbha tribes of Nabhaka, among the Bhojas and Pitinikas, among Andhras and Pliadas (Puliadas)—everywhere is the doctrine of the law of the beloved of the gods followed. Even those to whom the envoys of the beloved of the gods do not go, follow the law, as soon as they have heard the comments issued by the beloved of the gods according to the law, his sermon of the law, and they shall follow it in the time to come. The conquest which by this means is everywhere accomplished fills (me) with a feeling of joy. Firmly founded is (this) joy, the joy at the conquest by the law. But (this) joy is in sooth merely something slight. The beloved of the gods holds that only of worth which has reference to the Beyond. But this religious edict was written for the following purpose. To what purpose? That my sons and grandsons (to the end of time) shall deem no other kind of conquest desirable, that if a conquest by weapons should be absolutely necessary they should exercise mercy and clemency, and that they shall only regard conquest by the law as real conquest. Such a (conquest) brings salvation here to you. But all (its joy) is the joy of effort. This, too, brings salvation here and beyond."*

* Translated from the *Zeitsch. für Morgenl. Gesellschaft*, Vol. XIV. pp. 135, 136.

Thus there cannot be the slightest doubt that Buddhist missionaries were sent to Western Asia in the third century before the Christian era and must have made attempts to preach Buddhism.

Concerning the importation of Buddhist tales, Professor Rhys Davids says (p. xliii.):

> "We only know that at the end of the fourth, and still more in the third, century before Christ there was constant travelling to and fro between the Greek dominions in the East and the adjoining parts of India, which were then Buddhist, and that the birth stories, viz., the Jataka were already popular among the Buddhists in Afghanistan, where the Greeks remained for a long time."

Shall we assume with Rhys Davids that a great number of Jataka tales, such as the legend of the Kisâ-Gotamî,* the story of the ass in the lion's skin, the jackal and the crow, and other prototypes of the so-called Æsopean fables, found their way to Greece, there to reappear in Greek literature, while the main ideas of Buddha's religion remained utterly unknown in the West? No Western traveller, we are bid to believe, ever heard of them in the East, and no Eastern traveller ever mentioned them in the West. And yet we know that the Buddhists were burning with zeal for propagating their religion, and the Sangha sent out missionaries into all quarters of the world. It would be strange if Buddhist missionaries had gone to all neighboring countries except to Palestine, and that all kinds of Buddhist stories and wise saws

*See Jacob H. Thiessen, *Die Legende von Kisâ-Gotami*, Breslau, 1880.

were translated into other tongues, but not the essential doctrines of their sacred literature.

### POSSIBLE BUDDHISTIC ORIGIN.

The probability that an influx of Buddhistic doctrines took place is very strong; nevertheless we do not press the theory that Christianity was influenced by Buddha's religion, but regard it as a mere hypothesis. Here is a proposition of how matters might have been:

It is certain that Buddhist missionaries, had they come to Palestine, would not have attacked the religion of the country, but would, in accordance with their traditional policy, have adapted themselves as much as possible to the current ideas of the people. They would have preached the gospel of Buddha, and would have tried to proclaim their message in the very terms of the Jewish creed. The soil was prepared for them by Isaiah and other prophets who objected to bloody sacrifices. It would be quite in accord with their methods pursued in other countries to adopt the Messiah idea, and to embody the Jewish notions into their faith. The Buddhist missionaries did not cling to Gautama Siddhârtha; they would always be as ready to preach the Buddha of the past as the Buddha to come. Since Buddha himself had proclaimed the coming of Maitrêya, the Buddha of Kindness, must it not have appeared possible to Buddhists living in Judæa and observing the religious earnestness of the Jews, that Maitrêya was to rise among the Jews? This would explain not only the origin of the Essene movement, which otherwise appears very obscure, but also the change of the worldly idea of a Jewish Messiah into the conception of a spiritual saviour of the whole human race from sin. The first symptoms of this change are found already in the Jewish Apocrypha, especially in the book of Esdras, in which "the Son of David" begins to be called "the Son of Man," an expression that was adopted by Jesus. The great mass of the Jews of the time of Jesus still expected a Messiah who would be like Judas Maccabæus, a warrior and a worldly king, a redeemer from foreign oppression, yet the Essenes and the disciples of John regarded the various dignities which tradition attributed to the Messiah, as mere similes. In their idea the Messiah would be an ascetic hermit and a wandering preacher, more like Buddha than like Herod, for his kingdom was not of this world; he was the Dharmarâja, the king of truth.

As the Brahman god, Brahma, continued to play an important part in the Buddhist mythology, so we ought to expect that Buddhist missionaries would not have attempted to deny the existence of Jehovah. Yet, knowing the sternness of Jewish monotheism, we can understand that the Jewish God could not take a place inferior to Buddha; and as Buddha on the other hand was superior to all gods, both God and Buddha could only be identified, so that Christ could say: "I and the Father are one."

Considering the fact that later Buddhism developed out of its own elements a cosmic authority of conduct which practically serves the same purpose as the Christian God-idea, we cannot regard it as strange that Buddhists who lived in Judæa should have adapted the Jewish theism to the trikâya of their own faith. The result could only be a trinity conception such as taught by the church.* Now if a Buddhist brotherhood had settled in Judæa, they would have recruited themselves from Jews, and we can fairly assume that they naturally would have set on foot a movement like that of the Essenes, and the first Christian society at Jerusalem with its communistic ideals, its martyr spirit, and its invincible faith in the kingdom of truth.

### F. MAX MÜLLER'S OPINION.

Prof. F. Max Müller, who, when he first became acquainted with Buddhism, was a severe critic of its doctrines, has gradually changed his views and has at last, in spite of himself, come to the conclusion that Christianity has originated under Buddhist influences. We here reproduce the report of the lecture of his, published in the Journal of the Mahabhôdi Society.

" Professor Max Müller lectured at the rooms of the Royal Society of Literature, Hanover Square,

* The development of the Christian Trinity is still shrouded in darkness. We know from passages in the Apocryphal Gospels that the Holy Ghost was identified by some of the old Christians with the Logos ; and some considered the Third Person of the Deity as a feminine presence and the Mother of Christ.

London, on "Coincidences." The Lord Chancellor took the chair, and there was a large company of ladies and gentlemen, including the Rev. Canon Wilberforce.

"The Professor said that two Roman Catholic missionaries travelling in Thibet were startled at the coincidence between their own ritual and that of the Buddhist priesthood. The latter had crosiers, mitres, dalmatics, copes, services with two choirs, five-chained censers, blessings given while extending the right hand over the people, the use of beads, worship of the saints, processions, litanies, holy water. The missionaries attributed these coincidences to the Devil, determined to scandalize pious Roman Catholics. There the matter rested.

"When the ancient language of the Brahmins began to be seriously studied by such men as Wilkins, Sir William Jones, and Colebrooke, the idea that all languages were derived from Hebrew was so firmly fixed and prevalent that it would have required great courage to say otherwise. Frederic Schlegel was the first to announce that the classic languages of Greece and Italy, and Sanskrit, the sacred language of India, were offshoots of the same stem. It might be laid down as a general principle that if a coincidence could be produced by natural causes, no other explanation need be sought. This however, could not be the reason why mitres, copes, dalmatics, crosiers, and many other things, exactly, like those in the Roman Catholic Church, existed in Thibet. The conclusion was forced upon those who first studied the subject without passion, that there must at one time have been communication between Catholic priests and the Buddhists, and it was an historical fact that Christian missionaries were active in China from the middle of the seventh to the end of the eighth century. They had monasteries and schools in different towns, and were patronized by the Government. Here, then, was a coincidence explained in a fairly satisfactory manner.

"Other coincidences between Buddhism and Christianity had been pointed out again and again, but too often in the impassioned tone of theological controversy. Coincidences between all the sacred books of the world existed and Professor Müller ventured to say that they ought to be welcomed, for surely no truth lost value because it was held not only by ourselves but also by millions of human beings whom we formerly called unbelievers.

"Some of the coincidences between Buddhism and Christianity belonged to the ancient period of the former. They included confessions, fasting, celibacy of the priesthood, and even rosaries, and, as they were honored in India before the beginning of our era, it followed that if they had been borrowed the borrowers were Christians.

"How, it might be asked, had knowledge of these things been spread! Through the fact that Buddhism in its essence was a missionary religion. We heard of Buddhist missionaries being sent to every part of the known world in the third century before Christ.

"Indian and Buddhist influences had long been suspected in the ancient Greek fable and some parts of the Bible. The story of the ass in the lion's skin was to be found in Pâli. Probably it was true that the germs of some famous stories existed among our Aryan ancestors before their separation, but the form would be that of the proverb. Some difficulty had been caused by the question whether the fables common to Greece and India had travelled east or west. The Greeks themselves never claimed that kind of literature as their invention, though they made it their own by clothing it in Greek forms. Moreover, the fable had many traces of Eastern origin, and they abounded in Sanskrit literature. They were constantly appealed to in India, and were incorporated in the sacred canon of the Buddhists. Formerly doubtful, Professor Max Müller had, after conscientious study, become more and more convinced that India was the soil that originally produced the fable as we knew it.

"Again there were in the Old and New Testaments stories which had been traced to the Buddhist Jataka, and, indeed, nobody could look at Buddhism without finding something which reminded them of Christianity. The Professor did not allude to things essential to Christianity; he spoke rather of the framework.

"Under the disguise of St. Josaphat, Buddha himself had been raised to the rank of a saint in the Roman Catholic Church, and the Professor saw no reason why Buddha should not retain a place among saints, not all of whom were more saintly than he.

"The story of the judgment of Solomon occurred in the Buddhist canon, but in a somewhat different form. We read there of the man who had no children by his first wife, but one son by his second wife. To console the first he gave her the custody of the child. After his death, each of the wives claimed the boy. They went before Misaka. He directed them to try which could pull the child from the other by main force. As soon as he began to cry, one of the women would pull no longer, and Misaka declared that she was the true mother. The Professor considered this story truer psychologically than the judgment of Solomon. To look upon the latter, as actually dating from the time of Solomon, could hardly commend itself to Hebrew scholars of the present day.

"The parable of the Prodigal Son was found in the Buddhist sacred books. So was the story of the man who walked upon the water so long as he had faith in his divinity, and began to sink when his faith failed. Such a coincidence could not be set down to accident, and it must be remembered that the date of the Buddhist parable was anterior to that told by St. Luke.

"Then there was the parable of the loaves and fishes. In Buddha's case he had one loaf, and after he had fed his five hundred brethren, as well as his host and hostess and the people of a monastery, so much bread was left that it had to be thrown into a cave.

"If such coincidences between the Buddhist sacred books and the Bible could be accounted for by reference to the tendency of our common humanity, let analogous cases be produced. If they were set down as merely accidental, let similar cases be brought from the chapter of accidents.

"Max Müller's own opinion was that at least they were too numerous and complex to be attributed to the latter cause. He had tried to lay the case before his hearers like a judge summing up for a jury. He would only ask them to remember that the Buddhist canon in which these coincidences were found, was certainly reduced to writing in the first century before the Christian era. All, however, that he felt strongly was that the case should not remain undecided." *

It is often assumed that if the priority of Buddhism were proved, it would imply that Christianity would have to be regarded as a deteriorization of Buddhism ; it would deprive Christianity of all claim to originality, beauty, and truth. We might on the same argument say that Anglo-Saxon is a degenerated form of Low German, or that the polar bear is a degenerated species of the grizzly bear, or even that civilized man is a deteriorated anthropoid. Christianity embodies in its world-conception the best thoughts of the past from all quarters of the globe. The Logos idea was derived from Neo-Platonism,

* *Journ. Maha-Bodhi Soc.*, v, 4.

the God-idea is a Jewish tradition, baptism an Essenian rite, the holy communion partly reminds us of an ancient Larathustrian cult, partly appears to be a substitution of bread offerings in the place of bloody sacrifices; * the love of enemies was preached in a similar form five centuries before Christ in the far East. The idea of a world-Saviour is Buddhistic. In a word, none of the elements of Christianity is radically new; nevertheless, the whole in its peculiar

* Justinus Martyr (Apol. I., 86), referring to a similar rite of distributing bread among the worshippers and handing them a chalice of water to drink that obtained among the Parsees, accuses the Devil of aping the Lord. While it is not impossible that the Parsees of Justinus's time had adopted some features of the Christian Sacrament, it is certain that the institution of the haoma-offering was an old established ceremony in Zarathustra's religion. It is of Aryan origin. Haoma is the Vedic *Sôma*, and the holy meat of Myazda, small pieces of which were eaten on little cakes called "draona," consecrated in the name of deceased persons, are the Vedic *hotrâ*. And it is said that he who drinks of the white haoma or Gao-kerena will on the day of resurrection become immortal. (See Darmstetter's *Introduction to the Zend Avesta in S. B. of E.*, IV., p. lxix and also the note on p. 56.) Zarathustra calls "the sacred cup and the haoma the best weapons to strike and repel the evil-doer Angra Mainya." (*Ibid.* p. 206.)

It is possible that among the Essenes of Palestine Buddhistic influence replaced the intoxicating haoma by water, while the Greek to whom wine was a symbol of holy enthusiasm again changed the water into wine.

The original meaning of breaking the bread must have been that in the new dispensation a loaf is sacrificed on the altar and not an animal. The oldest account of the Lord's last supper is found in Cor. xi. 23 et seq., and it is noteworthy that St. Paul neither mentions the Paschal Lamb nor the wine.

combination is decidedly original and marks the beginning of an era which, at least in the West, stands in strong contrast to all the ages past.

### PARALLELISM WITH LAU-TSZE.

Although it is true that the coincidences between Buddhism and Christianity are remarkable and numerous, and that their differences are easily accounted for, we will nevertheless concede that both religions may have originated independently. We possess the strange case of a similar parallelism to both Buddhism and Christianity in Lau-tsze's philosophy which can hardly be suspected of being borrowed from either. We quote a few passages from his *Tau Teh King*, which was written more than five hundred years before Christ, and almost a century before Buddha. The Chinese word *tau* bears a peculiar likeness to the Greek term *logos*. It means "word," "reason," and "path or way" at the same time. The first sentence of the *Tau Teh King* reminds us of the first verse of the fourth Gospel in the New Testament, and many other passages breathe the spirit of Christian ethics. We read in the *Tau Teh King:*

"The *Tau* (word, reason, path, or briefly logos) that can be *taued* (reasoned, argued with, walked on, or spoken) is not the Eternal Tau. The name which can be named is not the Eternal Name. (Sec. 1.)

"Tau produced unity; unity produced duality; duality produced trinity; and trinity produced all things. (Sec. 42.)

"Lay hold on the great form (of Tau), and the whole world will go to you.

"Tau, in its passing out of the mouth, is weak and tasteless. If you look at it there is nothing to fill the eye. If you listen to it, there is nothing to fill the ear. But if you use it, it is inexhaustible. (Sec. 35.)

"The great *Tau* is all-pervading. It can be on the right hand and also at the same time on the left. All things wait upon it for life, and it refuses none. When its meritorious work is done, it takes not the name of merit. In love it nourishes all things, and does not lord over them. It is ever free from ambitious desires. It may be named with the smallest. All things return home to it, and it does not lord over them. It may be named with the greatest.

"This is how the wise man, to the last, does not make himself great, and therefore he is able to achieve greatness. (Sec. 34.)

"Recompense injury with goodness. (Sec. 63.)

"The *Tau* of Heaven may be compared to the extending of a bow. It lowers that which is high, and it raises that which is low. (Sec. 77.)

"He who knows others is wise. He who knows himself is enlightened.

"He who conquers others is strong. He who conquers himself is mighty.

"He who knows when he has enough is rich. (Sec. 33.)

"The good I would meet with goodness. The not-good I would also meet with goodness. Virtue is good. The faithful I would meet with faith. The not-faithful I would also meet with faith. Virtue is faithful. (Sec. 49.)

"He that humbles (himself) shall be preserved entire. He that bends (himself) shall be straightened. He that is low shall be filled. He that is worn out shall be renewed. He that is diminished shall succeed. He that is increased shall be misled. Therefore the sage embraces Unity, and is a pattern for all the world. He is not self-displaying, and, therefore, he shines. He is not self-approving, and, therefore, he is distinguished. He is not self-praising, and, therefore, he has merit. He is not self-exalting, and, therefore, he stands high." (Sec. 22.)

The Buddhistic-Christian spirit of Lau-tsze's philosophy is so striking that the suggestion has been made to trace its origin to the same sources in India from which Buddhism has sprung. But considering the fact that Buddha is almost a hundred years younger than Lau-tsze this assumption is barely possible, not probable. And must we not grant that the Christian ethics if true may naturally develop in any country and in any age?

## NOTHING AND THE ALL.

There are many remarkable agreements of all kinds which are due, not to a borrowing, but to a similarity of the circumstances which give rise to an idea or an event. So an Indian chief, who cannot be suspected of ever having read Cæsar, replied to the invitation of the President of the United States in almost literally the same terms as Ariovistus.

Among many peculiar coincidences of Buddhistic conceptions with ideas of thinkers who never came in contact with Buddhistic traditions, let me mention only one. Passerat, a late Latin poet of the sixteenth century, a native of France, (as quoted by Charles F. Neumann in his *Catechism of the Shamans*, London, Oriental Transl. Fund, 1831) says in one of his verses:

> "Nihil interitus et originis expers
> Immortale Nihil, Nihil omni parte beatum.
> Felix cui Nihil est."

This expression, praising the happiness of him who

has attained "the Nothing which knows the beginning and end of all things, the immortal nothing, which is blessed throughout," would be natural in the mouth of a Buddhist, to whom the word conveys different associations than to us, but it is startling when pronounced by a poet who in his surroundings had no chance of hearing the praises of Nirvâna.

### A REACTION AGAINST DUALISM.

The similarity between Christianity and Buddhism must, at least to some extent, be due to a similarity of conditions. And such a similarity of conditions existed; yet here again we have good reason to believe that these very conditions were imported from India. If Buddhism was not directly transplanted to Palestine, it still remains quite probable that the seeds at least from which it sprang were sown by Buddhists in the soil of Galilee.

The main basis of all the agreements between Buddhism and Christianity lies in their similar attitude towards a dualistic and pessimistic world-conception. It is sufficiently known how Buddhism developed from the Sâmkhya system, and there can be no question that Christianity presupposes the prevalence of similar ideas in the minds of the people among whom Jesus Christ lived and taught—not among the learned only but among the multitudes.

The Essenes formed a faction among the Jews standing in opposition to both the conservative and old orthodox Pharisees and the liberal and Hellenized Sadducees. All that is known about the Essenes reminds us of Buddhistic monk fraternities and Hindu ascetics. There was a similar movement in those days among the learned Jews of Alexandria, which developed into Neo-Platonism, represented mainly by Philo (who died 54 A. D.), Plotinus (205–270), and Porphyry (232–304).

Lassen traces Neo-Platonism and Gnosticism back to India, and Professor Weber suggests the derivation of the Græco-Christian Logos-idea from the Indian "Vâch" (i. e., voice, speech, word), calling attention to the fact that the divine "Vâch," which in Sanskrit is a feminine noun, appears in numerous passages as the consort of Prajâpati, the Creator, in union with whom and by whom he accomplished his creation. Professor Garbe, in his remarkable article in *The Monist* (Vol. IV., No. 2), not only confirms these suppositions, but, following Leopold von Schroeder's suggestion, offers abundant evidence for the derivation of Pythagoric views from the same source, India, which thus seems to have been the cradle of all our philosophies.

Two things seem certain, to which heretofore the attention of investigators has not as yet been called: that gnosticism, with all the kindred aspirations of the therapeutæ in Egypt and the Essenes in Palestine, is a pre-Christian movement which prepared the way for Jesus as well as for the missionary work of the Apostle St. Paul and that this movement was developed from seeds that had drifted into the West from the religious life of India.

We consider the hypothesis of a historical connexion between Buddhism and Christianity as quite probable; yet at the same time must say that whether it is true or not is of little consequence. There are enough parallels concerning which we can be sure that they are not due to a borrowing, and such parallelism alone as obtains between Lautsze on the one hand and Buddhism and Christianity on the other hand, is sufficient to prove that the evolution of both religious may have taken place independently, according to a natural law.

Whether or not the Sâmkhya philosophy and its offshoot, Buddhism, were transplanted from India to the Western world, we find that the Hindus not less than the Græco-Judæan thinkers arrived at a crisis in their religio-philosophical evolution in which they perceived the difference between soul and body, mind and matter, spirituality and sense-appearing reality. This difference once understood, leads easily to wrong conclusions. Before a monistic solution of the problem is sought, the dualistic view naturally presents itself first to a superficial consideration as the simpler conception. It was quite correct to regard mind as the all-important element of man's life, but it was a mistake, although it seemed quite plausible by way of contrast, to look upon matter as the source of all evil. Thus the Sâmkhya philosophers, and, in agreement with them, the Neo-Platonists, believe in the existence of two realities, matter and soul (or rather souls, for they assume a boundless plurality of individual souls), while material existence is looked upon as the cause of all misery and pain. The body is said to be that which hampers the mind and imprisons the soul as in a dungeon, while spiritual existence, or that which produces the illumination of consciousness in man, is praised as infinite perfection and divine bliss. Thus the world is cut in twain, and the logical consequence of this dualism is pessimism. This world of ours, the world of bodily existence in which, as they say, the soul is imprisoned, is a domain of suffering (note here also the parallelism with Plato), and the highest aim of human exertion must be salvation from the bondage of matter. Hence asceticism and self-mortification. The death of the body was longed for because promising the liberation of the soul. Now Buddha, as well as Christ, rejected pessimistic ethics; yet it is noteworthy that they did not denounce it as altogether wrong; they only forbade the enforcement of it among their disciples, and regarded it as a lower and insufficient method of attaining salvation, or rather as a phase through which he who seeks deliverance must pass. They themselves had passed through it and rejected it. Therefore they suffered it still, but boldly disavowed its principles in their own conduct.

Thus, in the dualism of both the Sâmkhya philosophy and the Essenic ethics, as also in Neo-Platonism, a great truth, the idea of the all-importance of mind, was linked to fatal errors, viz., the duality of mind and matter, the fiction of a purely spiritual empire, and the escape from the material world to the spirit realm through the suppression and gradual mortification—mortification in the literal sense of the word, which means the reducing to a state of being dead—of all bodily existence.

Buddha and Christ were confronted by the same dualism and facing the same problem of salvation, solved the problem in the same way. Both abandoned the traditional dualism and its pessimistic applications. After having tried world-flight, fasts, and self-mortification, they gave up all further attempts at uplifting the mind by a vain struggle against the body. Yet neither Buddha nor Christ surrendered the truth contained in the dualism of their predecessors. They recognized that the purpose of life lay not in the sphere of material reality, but in the realm of mind; that the life is more than meat, and that all worldly goods serve only as means for our spiritual needs. As to the problem of evil, they surrendered the dualistic method of deliverance through asceticism for a monistic ethics of righteousness. Both Buddha and Christ found that the source of sin lay deeper than in the complications of mind with matter; that material existence is innocent of wrong-doing, and that mind alone makes or mars the world. Lust, vanity, and hatred do not reside in the objects of our senses, but in our hearts. A wrong-directed mind is the source of sin, and a purification of the mind from its sinful desires is the sole condition of salvation. Accordingly, both Buddha and Christ abandoned world-flight and self-mortification; they both returned to the world and gave offence to those who were still under the sway of a dualistic morality; they lived among the people, preaching the new way of salvation and the attainment of the kingdom of heaven that is within us.

In saying that Buddha and Christ abandoned the ethics of dualism and proposed a new system of morality that might properly be designated as monistic, we do not maintain that either Buddha or Christ taught a monistic philosophy. Neither Buddha nor Christ were philosophers, although the former can be called a philosopher with more propriety than the latter. Both were religious leaders; Christ more so than Buddha. Buddhism and Christianity are religions and not philosophies; yet from their first appearance when their founders began to preach the new doctrine, they ushered in an era of monistic thought. By discarding pessimistic principles and proposing a melioristic morality they led the way towards a monistic world-conception. The philosophy underlying their religious faith already shows a monistic trend.

As religions are slowly expanding and developing in the course of their evolution, so they cannot have originated without due preparation. Their growth is due to natural causes and takes place according to natural laws. St. Paul is generally considered as the founder of the Gentile Church; however, the existence of a Christian congregation in Rome to which he addresses the most important one of his epistles, is alone an undeniable evidence that he was one only among many missionaries of the new faith. Apollos, it is said in Acts xviii. 24, "taught diligently the things of the Lord, knowing only the baptism of John," and Paul coming to Ephesus, found "certain disciples who had not so much as heard whether there was a Holy Ghost" and were baptized unto John's baptism.* This is noteworthy. It proves that there were at that time, when Christian missionaries began to preach, Christian-like congregations who differed but slightly from those baptized in the name of Jesus Christ. It is not impossible that such communities of so-called "disciples" (which was also the name of the first Christians) were scattered, even in the life-time of Christ, over the whole Roman empire; in other words, the germs of Christianity existed before Paul organized them into Christian churches.

As the Gentile Church originated before Paul, so a pre-Christian Christianity must have begun to grow before Jesus. Apollonius of Tyana, is an exponent of this spirit. He was in many respects similar to Jesus of Nazareth, and the legends which his pious admirers told of his life bear so much resemblance to the Christian Gospels and Apocrypha that Christian fanatics have jealously destroyed the greatest part of them.† In a similar way Buddhism

* Acts xix. 1–2.

† "After his death Apollonius was worshipped with divine honors for a period of four centuries. A temple was raised to him at Tyana, which obtained from the Romans the immunities of a sacred city. His statue was placed among those of

developed in India on parallel lines with Jainism. If Gautama Siddhârtha had not appeared, Jnyâtaputra, the founder of Jainism, might have taken his place. *Vice versa*, if Buddhism which had grown so much more powerful than Jainism, had not been rooted out in India, might not Jainism have been absorbed by it so as to disappear entirely? And if Jesus of Nazareth had not become the Christ of the Western world, might not Apollonius have played a similar part in history? We do not mean to say that Apollonius was nearly as grand or sympathetic a figure as Jesus, we only say that his character was of that type from which mankind would be inclined to select their Christs, their Buddhas, their Saviours. He was in many respects suitable to serve as a centre of religious crystallization, and the sacred legends would have so moulded his personality as to make of him an incarnation of the highest moral ideal of the age. In other words, if Jesus had not appeared, we might have substantially the same religion.

## EVOLUTION IN RELIGION.

It is the habit of all religious devotees to look

the gods, and his name was invoked as a being possessed of superhuman powers. The defenders of paganism, at the period of its decline, placed the life and miracles of Apollonius in rivalry with those of Christ; and some moderns have not hesitated to make the same comparison. There is no reason to suppose, however, that Philostratus entertained any idea of this sort in composing his life of Apollonius."—*Encl. Brit.*, Vol. II., p. 189.

upon their religion as a fixed dogma. So many Buddhists imagine that true Buddhism consists in the teachings of Gautama Buddha, and Christians in the same way trust that the whole breadth and depth of Christianity was developed by Jesus Christ in his sermons, parables, and the example he set in his life. This is not so. Buddha and Christ were the founders, the one of Buddhism, the other of Christianity. It may be true that the most important features of both religions can be traced to their personal authority, but there are many phases in the development of mankind (so, for instance, the abolition of slavery) which were not thought of at the time either of Buddha or Christ. Neither Buddha nor Christ gave us in their sermons a rule for dealing with the slave problem; yet we can truly say that their spirit of brotherly love was a most important factor in its final solution. The development of Christianity was not completed with Christ's crucifixion, nor was Buddhism completed at Buddha's death; both continued to grow and to work out the problems of life in the spirit in which their founders had set the example. They are still growing, and we must be careful not to judge them according to the past alone, but consider the life that is in them now and also their future potentialities.

Buddhism and Christianity have not only developed the germs which were sown by their founders, but have also assimilated the religious experiences of other nations.

The original Christianity of the church at Jerusalem changed when it spread over the Roman empire; and it changed again when introduced among the Teutonic races of the North. Our present Christianity, for instance, contains more of the Teutonic race ethics than many of us, especially our clergy, are aware of and is very different, indeed, from the original Christianity of the communistic church at Jerusalem. Buddhism, too, has undergone changes. The Hinayâna of southern Buddhism is marked by a certain negativism, while the Mahâyâna of northern Buddhism makes the positive aspect of the Dharma and of Nirvâna more prominent. Among the Tibetans this tendency of the Mahâyâna doctrines has developed a fantastic mythology and the ecclesiastical institutions of Lamaism, while the more sober Japanese appear to be quite scholarly and freer from superstition.

### THE SUPERNATURAL IN THE NATURAL.

Taking it for granted that Buddhism and Christianity have not influenced each other and are of independent growth, their similarities will have to be regarded as the more remarkable, since they will then all the more render a special revelation theory redundant. They are a most powerful argument for a sweeping latitudinarianism, and will, if properly understood, crush the last remnant of sectarianism in Christianity. Shall we say that the injunctions: "Recompense injury with goodness," and "hatred does not cease by hatred; hatred ceases by love," have naturally developed the one in China and the other in India, while the same lofty moral thought could be attained in Judæa only through a supernatural revelation? No, the supernatural will develop everywhere according to the eternal laws of nature.

The sky, in old folk-lore tales, is conceived as a glassy bowl that covers the earth, and the Indians imagine themselves favored by Manitoo, the Great Spirit, who located them under the very top of the heavens. Let us not imitate their narrow-mindedness by believing that we alone are blessed with the zenith of a religious revelation. God spoke not through Moses alone nor through Jesus alone. God has left no one without a witness, and he speaks to every one of his children in the same way, if they but open their minds to perceive his revelation. The Zenith is over the heads of every one who raises his eyes to look up to it, and there is no part of nature but it contains the supernatural. The natural is supernatural all through. Thus we need not wonder that the foundation-stones of Buddhism and Christianity are the same; they are of a universal nature.

We deny the existence of the supernatural in a dualistic sense; but suppose we call such higher features of nature as appear in man's ethical aspirations hyperphysical or supernatural because they rise above the lower and purely physical elements of the universe, we must confess that the supernatural lies hidden in the natural and is destined to grow from it according to the cosmic laws of existence. All living creatures face the same universe and are confronted with the same problems of life; must we not, in the end, all come to the same conclusions, and, however different may be the modes of presenting them, adopt the same rules of conduct? In the light of a unitary world-conception the agreement between various religions ceases to be startling and finds, even on the assumption that they have developed quite independently, its natural explanation. Yea, we are justified in assuming that if there are beings on other planets, they, too, will develop in the course of their religious evolution a religion of deliverance from evil by the eradication of all selfhood with its vanity, lust and hatred, and by walking in the noble path of righteousness. Among them, too, a saviour will rise to bid them renounce their self and all selfishness, and to take refuge from the evils of existence in an all-embracing love.

### HINÂYÂNA, MAHÂYÂNA, MAHÂSÊTU.

Recognizing a continued evolution in the religions of mankind, we do not look upon later Buddhism with the same contempt as is customary among many Buddhist scholars. It is true that the old Buddhism of the Hinâyâna school has preserved the old traditions more faithfully and is more philosophical than religious, while the Mahâyâna school which now obtains in the North, especially in Thibet, in China, and in Japan, is more religious than philosophical, almost hiding Buddha's doctrines under an exuberant outgrowth of fantastical superstitions.

We must, nevertheless, recognize in this progress from the Hinayâna, or the small vehicle of salvation, to the Mahâyâna, or large vehicle of salvation, an advance in the right direction. Buddha had taught his disciples the path of salvation and had inculcated an unbounded love for all mankind, including one's enemies. It was quite natural that his followers were anxious to extend the blessings of salvation to all mankind. The Hinâyâna is a religion for the thinker, for the wise, for the strong; it is not a gospel to those who are poor in spirit, who are ignorant, who are weak; and yet it was the principle of the Master's all-comprehensive compassion to save *all* the world! What was more natural to a true-hearted Buddhist than to make the blessing of Buddha's religion accessible to the multitudes? The small canoe of the Hinâyâna sufficed for every one only to save himself and no one else. But what did a Buddhist care for his own salvation? A true Buddhist had ceased to be troubled about himself. He wanted to save others. Thus the general idea of a Mahâyâna, a large conveyance of salvation, of a great ship to cross the stream of worldliness, of sin, and suffering, was a logical consequence of Buddha's doctrine, even though the methods with which this idea was realized may in many respects be regarded as a failure. Yet in judging the Mahâyâna system and its fantastical offshoots, we must consider the mental state of those nations for whom it was adapted, and it may be that a purer religion would have failed utterly where cruder allegories of what appears to us as childish superstitions exercised a beneficent influence. The Mahâyâna has changed the savage hordes of central Asia, from whom proceeded the most barbarous invaders, dreaded by all their neighbors, into a most kind-hearted people, with a sacred passion for universal benevolence and charity.

Considering the development from a Hinâyâna conception to a Mahâyâna practice as an advance, we can still less regard Christianity, even if its derivation from Buddhism were certain, as a deterioration. Buddhism, viz., the original Buddhism of Buddha, is more philosophical and more abstract than Christianity, but Christianity is more religious. Buddhism, viz., again, the original Buddhism of Buddha, is free from all mythological elements while Christianity employs a number of allegorical expressions which are both appropriate and forcible. There is the dogma of the personality of God, of the Sonship of Christ of the quickening influence of the Holy Ghost, of the personality of Satan, of angels and devils, of heaven and hell ; and even to-day the belief in the literal meaning of all these religious symbols is counted among many Christians as the test of orthodoxy. A belief in the letter replaces the belief in the spirit. But what does it matter that during the development of the Church the letter of symbolically expressed truth, has crystallized into temporarily fixed dogmas, which sometimes threatened to ossify the properly religious spirit of Christianity ? The symbolism of Christianity is after all its dross only; its essence is that ethical spirit which it has in common with Buddhism. The Christian dogmatology, if properly recognized in its symbolical nature, is most beautiful, expressive, and true, but if taken in its literal meaning commits us to irrational absurdities. He who believes in the letter of a myth, or a dogma, or a religious allegory, is a pagan, and Christian paganism is not less absurd than Lamaistic or any other paganism. Nevertheless, he who believes in a myth that contains in the garb of a parable a religious truth, and accordingly regulates his moral conduct, is better off than he who is void of any faith. The truth hidden in the myth teaches him and serves him as a guide; it comforts him in affliction, strengthens him in temptation, and shows him in an allegorical reflexion the bliss that rests upon righteousness. The Hinâyâna, in its abstractness, it appears to us, is indeed insufficient for the masses of mankind, and had to change into a Mahâyâna system before it could conquer almost half the world. Christianity, however, is more perfect even than the Mahâyâna of Buddhism, as a vehicle of salvation for the masses of mankind. While the schools of Buddhism may be compared to ships that cross the stream, Christianity is like a large and solid bridge. Christianity is a Mahâsêtu. A child may walk over in perfect safety. Christianity is, as St. Augustine says, like a water in which a lamb can wade while an elephant must swim. It is difficult to explain spiritual truths to an untrained mind, for even philosophers find it difficult to understand why we must free our souls from the thought of self and overcome all vanity, lust, hatred, and illwill. But a young Christian heart finds it very natural. Without going through all the painful experiences which lead to the abandonment of selfishness, a Christian child having received Jesus and his all-comprehensive love into his heart is, on the start of his life, placed in the right moral attitude towards the world. Christianity (and this is both its strength and its weakness) has been especially successful in teaching surrender of self without at the same time disturbing the egotism so strongly developed in the Western nations. Thus Christianity extends religious bliss not only to the ignorant who do not understand the problem of life of which Christian ethics present a practical solution, but also to those whose eyes remain still covered with the veil of selfhood; yea, even to the little children who have never as yet heard of sin or the cause of sin. There is no more characteristic saying of Christ's than his words: "Suffer little children to come unto me."

No fault can be found either with Christianity or the symbols of Christianity, but blame rests with those who claim that the Christian symbols do not merely contain the truth in the language of parables, but that they are the truth itself, the absolute truth which must be accepted in blind faith whatever be the verdict of a rational inquiry or scientific criticism. The Christian whose faith consists in obedience to the spirit of Christ's ethics can shake hands with the Buddhist and say, we are brethren; our religions solve the problems of life in a similar spirit, although we differ in our modes of expression. The Christian, however, whose faith is a belief in the letter of his dogmas will regard the Buddhist, be he ever so highly educated, as a pagan and Buddha as a false prophet or even "an impostor." * The latter kind of Christianity is still regarded as orthodox, but the time will come and is near at hand when its flagrant paganism will be recognized by the very authorities of the Church. The former kind of Christianity will be established as the only true Christianity, and the old narrow orthodoxy of bigotry and blind faith will be supplanted by the new broad orthodoxy of scientific truth.

Christianity, at present the second largest religion in the world, can very well become the universal religion of mankind, but there is one condition which must be fulfilled before it can gain the victory. It must discard all paganism; it must become conscious of the symbolical element of its symbols; it must with impartial justice recognize the truth wherever it be; it must be courageous enough to acknowledge its own errors of former misinterpretations, and appreciate the good that is contained in other religions; in a word, it must become a cosmic religion—truly catholic and orthodox.

What is more orthodox than that which with methodical exactness has been proved to be true, and what is more catholic than science? We must

* See Spence Hardy in his *Legends and Theories of the Buddhists*, p. 207.

learn to understand that science is a religious revelation.

This, in essence, is the lesson which a comparison of Buddhism with Christianity can teach us : Above any Hinâyâna, Mahâyâna and Mahâsêtu is the Religion of Truth, and the truth reveals itself everywhere, to every one who has the religious spirit to seek it, and dares to find it.

# CHRISTIAN CRITICS OF BUDDHISM.

## THE MISSIONARY PROBLEM.

Missions are highly recommendable. They are in themselves a good thing and ought to be continued with vigor and enthusiasm. That religion is dead which does not missionarize. No worse objection can be made to the free-thinkers of to-day, who frequently boast of representing the world-conception of the cultured and the intelligent, than their utter want of the missionarizing spirit. Free thought can become worthy of consideration only when it begins to missionarize. So long as free-thinkers do not bring sacrifices for a wide propagation of their views their faith is plainly of a negative kind. A positive faith always engenders an enthusiasm to spread it. Missionarizing, far from being "ill-judged and unreasonable" is a sure symptom of the life that is in a religion. But while missions ought to be encouraged, we ought to spread at the same time the right spirit of missionarizing.

The missionary who wants to spread his faith must not revile the people whom he wants to convert. He must not distort nor misrepresent their religious views, and not unnecessarily desecrate what is sacred to them. There are Christians among whom the opinion prevails that the good qualities of pagan religions are an obstacle to Christianity. Whenever such views obtain it is a sure sign that the right missionary spirit is missing. Let a missionary always look for the good sides of other religions, and let him carefully search for all the points of contact. Only by utilizing the good in paganism, only by gaining the sympathy of the pagans, can Christianity hope to conquer.

When St. Paul came to Athens he did not revile the Greek gods. On the contrary, he looked for some point of contact, and found it at last in an inscription written upon the altar dedicated to the Unknown God. Praising the scrupulous and conscientious religiosity of the Athenians, he proceeded to preach to them the Unknown God whom they had unwittingly worshipped.

There is a papal brief still extant written by Gregory the Great, in the year 601, and addressed to the missionary monk Augustine, in which the policy of a very ingenious method of missionarizing is outlined. The Pope was apparently a practical psychologist who knew how to treat men and make innovations acceptable. Whatever criticism may be made on the Pope's advice as being a kind of compromise with paganism, it certainly shows great keenness and good judgment. The success of his missionaries in England was a good evidence of the cleverness of his methods. Churches were built right on the shrines and sanctuaries of the old gods, and the pagan festivals were continued under Christian names. Pope Gregory says:

"Because they (the Anglo-Saxons) are wont to slaughter at the feasts of the devils (i. e., of the pagan gods) many oxen and horses, it is decidedly necessary to let these feasts be continued and have another *raison d'être* given them. On kirmess and on the commemoration days of the holy martyrs, whose relics are preserved in those churches which are built on the spots of pagan fanes, a similar feast shall be celebrated; the festive place shall be decorated with green boughs and a church sociable shall be held. Only the slaughter of animals shall no longer be held in honor of Satan, but in praise of God, and the animals shall be slaughtered for the sake of eating them, and thanks shall be given for the gift to the Giver of all goods." *

Gregory advises not to destroy the pagan temples, but to transform them into churches. He urges the adoption, as much as possible, of pagan rites, and the substitution of the names of saints for the names of heroes and gods. In the same spirit Bishop Daniel writes to Winfrid, commonly called Boniface (Epist. xiv., 99), to be tolerant, patient, and to avoid all objurgation lest the pagans be embittered. "A missionary should not at once repudiate the genealogies of the gods, but should rather use them to prove their human character. He should propose questions which would set the pagans to thinking about the origin of the world and the origin of the gods, whence the gods came and what be the origin of the first god, whether they continue to generate

* See Beda Venerabilis, *Hist. Eccles. Britorum*, I., Chap. 30.

new gods, and, if not, when they had discontinued increasing, and, if they continued increasing, whether their number would by-and-by be infinite."

Leo the Great utilized the pagan art of Rome for Christian art. He changed the statue of Jupiter into St. Peter, and the goddess Anna Perenna became St. Anna Petronela, who is still worshipped in the Campagna. And the Christian missionaries imitated the Pope's method. The Teutonic eschatology of Muspilli, which is the destruction of the world by fire, was Christianized by German converts in a poem where Elijah and other saints and archangels take the place of the Teutonic gods, whose original features are unmistakably preserved.

This method of missionarizing had its serious drawbacks, and led for a time to a great confusion of Christian and pagan beliefs. Thus the Danish king, Suen Tuesking, when starting on an expedition to England, made a treble vow to the god Bragafull, to Christ, and to St. Michael. And we read of Ketil, an Irish warrior, who in all ordinary cases called upon Christ, but whenever there was a matter of grave importance he addressed himself to Thor.* It is true that many pagan institutions and customs survived, but after all in the long run the evil influences were overcome, and the good only remained. A pagan festival, the Yuletide, has now become the most celebrated Christian feast, bearing the name Christmas, and Christianity was not the loser by it.

I do not mean to say that Christian missionaries

* Roskoff, *Geschichte des Teufels*, Vol. II., pp. 10–13.

should temporize with heathen error or compromise with heathen institutions; not at all; I only mean to say that Christian missionaries should not imitate St. Augustine's maxim, who regarded all virtues of the pagans as shining vices, but that they should joyously recognize and hail everything good in pagan religions. I simply stand up for rigid justice, and would demand of every missionary a sympathetic comprehension of that religion which the people to whom he is sent have embraced.

Are there not many institutions, moral convictions, habits and modes of thought in pagan countries which are unnecessarily antagonized by our missionaries? Should not Christian missionaries, in order to be successful, first of all have regard for the religious views which they intend to overthrow? Should they not recognize the noble aspirations of pagan saints and prophets, such as Buddha and Confucius? It would be better for Christianity if the pagan nations themselves began to send missionaries to Christian countries. For there is nothing more spiritually healthful than a severe competition among those who cherish the confidence of having found the truth.

We regret to say that the spirit in which the missionary addresses unbelievers is, upon the whole, offensive. He comes to non-Christians like an enemy who wants to destroy that which they regard as the highest and best, and the result is that they only gain converts of the lowest type, who become converted solely for the sake of worldly advantages and are a disgrace to the religion to which they become affiliated.

The proper spirit for a missionary would be to go to unbelievers, to reside among them in their own style of living and give them a practical example of his views of life. He should go to other countries and inquire into the significance of the people's religious convictions. He should say to them, "The people of our country are interested in your welfare and in your conceptions of truth. Please let me know what you believe, and when you have told me what you believe I will, if you are willing to listen to me, tell you what we believe. We believe that we are right and you believe that you are right. Let us compare our views, and whatever I can learn from you I wish to learn, and, *vice versa*, I expect that whatever you can learn from me you will consider, and, whatever the truth may be, we shall both be glad to accept it." If missionaries come in this spirit to other countries Christianity will no longer be identified with beef eating in China and with liquor drinking in India. There would be no prosecution. Missionaries could without fear of danger enter into the remotest corners of China. They would not be hated, but would be welcomed, and we hope that a time will come when all religions will exchange missionaries in the same way that the government of our nation sends ambassadors to other nations and in turn receives their representatives.

The reason why the Christian missions of the present day are, upon the whole, a lamentable failure, is due mainly to the haughtiness with which Christ's religion is offered to the pagans. Christians are so deeply impressed with Christ's humility that they are not aware of the pride which they themselves exhibit. There is, for instance, a missionary hymn whose melodious rhymes are frequently heard in Christian churches. The verses are beautiful, but they are marred by an undisguised contempt for the heathen ; yet no missionary seems aware of it. The first stanza is grand and full of inspiration ; it reads :

> " From Greenland's icy mountains,
> From India's coral strand,
> Where Afric's sunny fountains
> Roll down their golden sand ;
> From many an ancient river,
> From many a palmy plain,
> They call us to deliver
> Their land from error's chain."

That is genuine poetry, and how praiseworthy in spirit ! But the poet continues :

> " What though the spicy breezes
> Blow soft o'er Ceylon's isle,
> Though every prospect pleases,
> And only man is vile ;
> In vain with lavish kindness
> The gifts of God are strown,
> The heathen in his blindness
> Bows down to wood and stone."

The Singhalese people are neither vile nor idolatrous ; they are famed as the gentlest race on earth, and their religion is Buddhism. Their worship consists in flower offerings at Buddha-shrines, but even the most ignorant of them are aware of the fact that a Buddha statue is not the Buddha himself. Protestants make similar accusations against the Roman Catholics, when they ought to distinguish between practices resembling idolatry and idolatry itself.

If Buddhists sent missionaries to our country who sang such stanzas to us, how should we like it? It is certain that missionary hymns which denounce the people of Ceylon as "vile" do not help Christians to make converts among them.

The hymn continues:

> "Can we, whose souls are lighted
> With wisdom from on high,
> Can we to men benighted
> The lamp of life deny?"

The poet intends to glorify "the light from on high," but he exalts himself as belonging to those "whose souls are enlightened with wisdom from on high"—which makes a great difference! His noble zeal for spreading the truth appears as pharisaical self-conceit, and can only give offence to those whom he wishes to convert. Thus it is natural that when Christian missionaries speak of love, Buddhists accuse them of haughtiness and pride.

Missionaries do not only unnecessarily offend the pagans by showing a contempt for their persons, their religion, their morals and their nationality, but also require of their converts a surrender of habits and customs which they cannot give up without cutting themselves loose from their traditions, which necessarily and naturally have become most sacred to them. It should be as little necessary for a Chinaman to sever himself from the noble traditions of his nation if he becomes a Christian, as it would be for a Jew to look upon his race as the outcasts of God. Jew-Christians might continue to abstain from pork, and Buddhist vegetarians who become Christians might remain vegetarians after their conversion.

In the Russian Church it is customary for converts to curse the faith to which they formerly belonged, and we are informed that the present Empress was the first instance in which an exception of this un-Christian ordinance had been made. She was permitted to become a Greek Catholic without cursing the Lutheran denomination, in which she was reared.

There are customs in China expressive of the sacredness of family traditions which a convert is expected to renounce on account of the religious character of family reunions.

In a book on China entitled *The Dragon, Image and Demon*, by the Rev. Hampten C. Du Bose, which contains much valuable information, but is written in a spirit that does not become a Christian missionary, we find the following statement on Ancestral Halls in China. The Rev. Mr. Du Bose says:

" These buildings are not so conspicuous as the idol temples, but they are very numerous, as any family or clan may have its temple, generally marked by the funereal cedar. Here the 'spirit tablets' of departed forefathers are kept, 'containing the simple legend of the two ancestral names carved on a board,' and 'to the child the family tablet is a reality, the abode of a personal being who exerts an influence over him that cannot be evaded, and is far more to him as an individual than any of the popular gods. The gods are to be feared and their wrath deprecated, but ancestors represent love, care, and kindly interest.' If the clan do not own an ancestral hall, there is 'in every household a shrine, a tablet, an oratory or a domestic temple, according to the position of the family. It is a grand and solemn occasion when all the males of a tribe in their dress robes gather at the temple, perhaps a great 'country seat,' of the dead, and the patriarch of the line, as a chief priest of the family, offers sacrifice.

"Much property is entailed upon these ancestral halls to keep up the worship, but as this expense is not great, all the family have shares in the joint capital, and the head of the clan sometimes comes in for a good living. At baptism converts to the Christian faith renounce their claim to a share in this family estate because of its idolatrous connections.

"In these halls the genealogical tables are kept, and many of the Chinese can trace their ancestry to ten, twenty, thirty, and sometimes even to sixty generations. These registers are kept with great care, and may be considered reliable.

"'Should a man become a Christian and repudiate ancestral worship, all his ancestors would by that act be consigned to a state of perpetual beggary. Imagine, too, the moral courage required for an only or the eldest son to become a Christian, and call down upon himself the anathemas not only of his own family and friends, but of the spirits of all his ancestors.

"When we preach against this form of paganism it seems as heathenish to the Chinese, as if at home we taught a child to disobey his father and despise his mother. 'It forms one of the subtlest phases of idolatry—essentially evil with the guise of goodness—ever established among men.'"

Du Bose is well-meaning, but a partisan; he is a Christian pagan, who believes that the institutions of his sect and nation alone afford salvation. His book is an instance of the wrong spirit that prevails among many Christian missionaries. It is not free from misrepresentations, but lacks all consideration of, and reverence for the accomplishments of great men that are of another creed and another race. Of the founder of Tauism, Du Bose says, p. 345:

"His name * [*sic*] is Laotsze, which means literally 'old boy,' or, judging from some things that are said about him, the wild Western appellation 'old coon' is not inappropriate."

Du Bose calls Buddha "the Night of Asia," as if Asia would have been better off without Buddhism. As for Buddhistic superstitions, which every Buddhist will grant prevail among the uneducated classes, we would say that Buddha can be made as little responsible for them as Christ is responsible for Christian crusades, witch prosecutions, and heresy trials, which were once quite common over all Christendom.

Christian missionaries ought to be bent on preserving all that is good in the Chinese character. They must not ruthlessly break down those features which are characteristic of the Chinese. If missionaries cannot find a *modus vivendi* for converts by which they can preserve their hallowed family relations and continue to hold their ancestors dear, we cannot blame the Chinese Government for regarding

* Lautsze, which means "the old philosopher," is not a name, but an appellation. His proper name is *Er*, his family name *Li*. *Tsze* means child and philosopher at the same time.

Christian missionaries as a public nuisance. We respect the Saxon chief who, on hearing that all his ancestors were in Hell, withdrew from the baptismal font and preferred eternal damnation with his fathers to the bliss of the Christian Heaven in the company of Christian monks.

Missionarizing should not cease, but should be raised to a higher level. It should be done in brotherly love, not with contempt or in a spirit of pharisaic self-conceit. The rules which ought to be observed by all of us are well set forth by the Rev. George T. Candlin, of Tien-tsin, a Christian missionary to China, who personally and in friendliness met the Buddhist and Confucian delegates from Eastern Asia on the platform of the Religious Parliament. He writes:

"We must begin by giving one another credit for good intentions. I do not see why we may not commence at once by the leading representatives of the various faiths who were present at Chicago, including all the distinguished representatives of Christianity, with Mr. Mozoomdar, Mr. Dharmapâla, Mr. Vivekananda. Mr. Ghandi, the Buddhists of Japan, the high priest of Shintoism, and our friend Mr. Pung entering into direct covenant with each other:

"1. Personally never to speak slightingly of the religious faith of one another. This I understand does not debar the kindly and reverential discussion of differences which exist, or the frank utterance of individual belief.

"2. Officially to promote among their partisans, by all means in their power, by oral teaching, through the press, and by whatever opportunity God may give them, a like spirit of brotherly regard and honest respect for the beliefs of others.

"3. To discourage amongst the various peoples they serve as religious guides, all such practices and ceremonies as not constituting an essential part of their faith, are inimical to its purity and are the strongest barriers to union.

"4. To promote all such measures as will advance reform, progress and enlightenment, political liberty and social improvement among the people of their own faith and nationality.

"5. To regard it as part of their holiest work on earth to enlist all men of ability and influence with whom they are brought into contact in the same noble cause.

"To these articles I can heartily subscribe myself. I do not see why others may not."

### A BUDDHIST TRACT.

During the World's Fair the interest taken in other religions, especially in Buddhism, grew to such an extraordinary degree that some Christians began to fear for Christianity and tried to counteract the favorable impression which the foreign delegates had made on the Chicago public. The idea prevailed that missionary work was redundant because the followers of Buddha, Zoroaster, Mohammed, and Confucius were on a par with the followers of Jesus Christ, and no longer needed the Gospel. To counteract the evil influence of this opinion, a leaflet was published for distribution at the entrance of the Art Palace, in which the Religious Parliament was being held. The leaflet fell into my hands, and, being of extraordinary interest, I cannot help calling attention to it, and shall be glad to contribute my share to its wide circulation.*

*The leaflets can be had at five cents each, ten for 25 cents, or $1.50 per hundred, from W. E. B., 332 Lake street, Oak Park, Illinois.

The leaflet contains the reprint of a Chinese placard, being a religious tract that exhorts men to conversion. The occasion on which the placard was produced is described in *The Far East*, as follows:

"Gan-kin was full of death. There was a great drought. No rain had fallen for six months. The city was parched and dry. Foul odors and pestilential gases, resulting from indescribably unsanitary conditions, bred fevers and cholera and death. There was no water to wash in, and hardly any to drink. The children died. The beasts died. The people died. The crops failed. Famine threatened the city. Who was to blame? Above all, who was to help?

"Kaolaishan, disciple of Buddha, had an inspiration. The Buddhist priest Che had spoken. Gan-kin had forgotten his words; this miserable state of things was quite to be expected; but the town should remember once more. If he were to remind Gan-kin, it would be an act of merit. He would gain. The town would gain. He might avert the famine.

"And so it came to pass that the words of the Buddhist priest Che were once more in vogue at Gan-kin. Kaolaishan did his work thoroughly. He printed a large tract. It was three feet long and one and one-half feet wide. It was posted up on the walls and distributed by thousands. Everybody who could read, read it. Everybody who could pray, prayed it. It enjoined a constant repetition of Buddha's name. His name was repeated innumerable times, for could not his name avail to avert the famine?

"The central figure on the sheet was that of the Buddhist priest. The lines of his garments were ingeniously contrived in readable characters. Three rows of dots on his shaven head showed the marks of his ordination. For every bead on the rosary in his hand he was supposed to repeat Buddha's name or a prayer. A coffin and a skeleton at the foot of the sheet represented death—a subject on which the Buddhist priest had thought."

The leaflet reproduces in fac-simile on a reduced

scale the Chinese placard, and offers a literal translation of its contents, neglecting, however, the poetic measure and the rhyme, and showing sometimes a lack of tact in the choice of words. But the translation is clear enough to render the sense and give a fair impression of the religious spirit of the original.

The motive of the publication is "to let Buddhism speak for itself." The author of the tract says:

> "Buddhism is the faith of millions to-day. Are we to believe that this faith, evolved by the ages in the process of religious development, exactly suits the requirements of these millions, and that all efforts for their evangelization are ill-judged and unreasonable attempts to foist a foreign faith upon people who do not need it any more than they need foreign clothes? Or are we to number them among 'the ignorant and those that are out of the way,' upon whom the Christ of God had compassion, whom He has died to redeem, and to whom we are responsible to carry the glad tidings of His great love and great salvation?"

*
* *

Before entering into the contents of the Buddhist tract I wish to repeat that, far from being opposed to missions, I am a strong supporter of the missionary spirit and, lest the following criticisms be misunderstood, the reader should bear in mind what has been said in the beginning of this chapter on the missionary problem.

The little Buddhist tract, translated for the purpose of ridiculing Buddhism, is apparently a gem of religious poetry, and many passages of it might grace any Christian hymn-book if the translation were only cast into an elegant literary form.

The title of the whole reads: "Tract Exhorting All Men to Invoke Buddha's Name." It consists of several parts. The first of it is a religious hymn on the vanity of all things, composed by the Buddhist priest Che, and reads, according to the translation before me, as follows:

"It is good to reform; it is good to reform,
The things of the world will be all swept away.
Let others be busy while buried in care,
My mind, all unvexed, shall be pure.

"They covet all day long, and when are they satisfied?
They only regret that the wealth of the family is small,
They are clearly but puppets held up by a string,
When the string breaks they come down with a run.

"In the domain of death there is neither great nor small,
They use not gold nor silver and need not precious things,
There is no distinction made between mean and ignoble, ruler and prince.

"Every year many are buried beneath the fragrant grass;
Look at the red sun setting behind the western hills.
Before you are aware the cock crows and it is daylight again.

"Speedily reform. Do not say: 'It is early,'
The smallest child easily becomes old.
Your talent reaches to the dipper (in the heavens).
Your wealth fills a thousands chests.
[But consider that] the consequences of your actions will follow you in future time.*

* This line deviates from the copy before me. The translator has somehow misunderstood the original Chinese, and translates "your patrimony follows you, when will you be satisfied? The rendering as given above is on the authority of Mr. K. Tanaka, a Japanese student of philosophy at the University of Chicago, whom I requested to revise the questionable passages of the translation.

"It is good to exhort people to reform.
To become vegetarian,* and invoke Buddha's name is a precious thing you can carry with you.
It may be seen that wealth and reputation are vain.
You cannot do better than to invoke Buddha's name.

"There is, there is; there is not, there is not; yet we are troubled.
We labor, we toil; when do we rest?
Man born is like a winding stream;
The affairs of the world are heaped up mountain high.
From of old, from of old, and now, and now, many return to their original.
The poor, the poor, the rich, the rich, change places.
We pass the time as a matter of course;
The bitter, the bitter, the sweet, the sweet, their destiny is the same."

* * *

"To covet profit and seek reputation the world over
Is not so good as (to wear) a ragged priest's garment, and be found among the Buddhists.
A caged fowl has food, but the gravy pot is near.
The wild crane has no grain, but heaven and earth are his.†

"It is difficult to retain wealth and fame for a hundred years,
Transmigration of souls continually causes change.
I exhort you, gentlemen, to speedily seek some way of reforming your conduct.
A man (being) once lost, a million ages (of suffering) will be hard to bear."

* * *

"A solitary lamp illumines the darkness of the night,
You get into bed, take off your socks and shoes;

* The Chinese, speaking generally, are, as a nation, vegetarians. Frequently this is a matter of necessity with them, but when strict Buddhists they abstain from animal food from religious motives.—Foot-note of the Missionary Tract.

† The crane denotes the Buddhist work.

Your three souls and seven spirits turn and follow your dreams,*
Whether they will come back in the morning light is uncertain."

* * *

"To be forgotten, grow old, and die of disease is a bitter thing,
But who has not this?
If you do not invoke Amitâbha Buddha, how can you escape punishment."

* * *

"Villainous devices, treacherous evil, hidden poison, false rejoicing,
Forgetting favors, crossing the river and then breaking the bridge (i. e., to serve oneself at the expense of others),
Losing all conscience, deceiving one's own heart; one that has done these things will live with the king of Hell.
He that has said good-bye to conscience, finds it even now difficult
To escape the punishment of the knife-hill and oil pot.
Houses, gold and silver, land, wife, family,
Grace and love, rank and lust, all are VAIN." †

[Now the Buddhist priest addresses the skeleton:—]
"How can you, sir, carry all things away with you?
A few layers of yellow earth cover all your glory."

* The three souls are three abstracts of man's psychic life, such as we make when distinguishing between mind, soul and spirit. The seven elementary spirits represent various aspects of man's vitality and the physiological processes of his system.

† The characters representing these several possessions are ranged above one large, elongated sign. This character, which is pronounced *Kong*, and corresponds pretty accurately to the Latin *vanus*, is thus shown to be the sum of man's earthly possessions and attainments; reminding one strongly of the words of the preacher—"All is vanity."—Remark of the Missionary translator.

[The inscription on the coffin reads as follows :—]

"A silver coffin worth 108,000 ounces of pure silver (about £27,000).

This man took pains to devise ingenious things, but all in VAIN.

To travel east, west, north, south, to see all life is vain ;
Heaven is vain, earth is vain, including also mysterious man.
The sun is vain, the moon is vain.
They come and go, for what purpose ?
Fields are vain, lands are vain, how quickly they change owners !
Gold is vain, silver is vain, after death how much remains in your hand ?
Wives are vain, children are vain.
They do not join you on the way to hades.
According to the '*Tatsang* classic' vanity is lust,
According to '*Panrohsin* classic' lust is vanity.
He that travels from east to west is like a bonny bee ;
After he has made honey from flowers with all his labor, all is vain.

"After midnight you hear the drum beat the third watch,
You turn over, and before you know where you are you hear the bell striking the fifth watch [indicating daylight].
To carefully think it over from the start, it is like a dream.
If you do not believe, look at the peach and apricot trees,
How long after the flowers open are they withered !
If you regard prince and minister, after death they revert to the soil,
Their bodies go to the earth, their breath to the winds,
Within the covering of yellow earth there is nothing but a mass of corruption ; they pass away no better than pigs or dogs.
Why did they not at the beginning inquire of the Buddhist priest Che ?
There is one life and not two deaths ;
Don't brag, then, before others of your cleverness.

A man during life owns vast tracts of land,
After death he can only have three paces of earth [eight feet of land by twelve in length].*

Here we must interrupt our quotation because the next following lines are apparently misunderstood by the translator. As they stand they give no sense. The translation reads as follows:

"To think it over carefully after death, nothing would be taken away;
The Buddhist priest Che has, with his own hand, written to you.
The word heart: loudly laugh!

"Not much time need be employed in writing it.
It has one curve like the moon and three dots all awry.
The feathered tribe, and the beasts also, will become Buddhas.
If you only invoke Buddha's name you will go to the kingdom where there is the highest bliss."

The translator adds the following comment in explanation:

[At this point it will be seen that the winding convolutions of the priest's robe have reached the centre of his body. Here the heart is by the Chinese supposed to be located, and a good deal of the "ingenuity" referred to in the title is contained in the fact that at this point the characters refer to the heart. Hence the exhortation to "laugh loudly." To Western minds the sudden introduction of three wholly disconnected lines breaking in upon the theme of the discourse is not sufficiently ingenious to dispense with explanation.]

The original Chinese, which in this passage, in spite of its reduction in size, is plainly legible, means (according to Mr. Tanaka's version):

* Mr. Tanaka calls my attention to the fact that the translator omitted this line but quoted it in a foot-note as the literal translation of "three paces of earth."

The Buddhist priest Che wrote with his hand the word "heart," and he laughed to himself [thinking] how little time is needed in writing it, etc.

That is to say: The Buddhist priest Che writes the character *hsin*,* which in Chinese is one of the easiest words to write, and he thinks to himself, "If only the people knew how easy it is to attain salvation! It is as easy as the writing of the word heart. Thus the whole world can be transfigured into the state of Nirvâna if only the name of Buddha be rightly invoked."

The passage reminds one of an old German hymn, which begins:

> "*Es ist gar leicht ein Christ zu sein!*"
> "'Tis easy indeed to be a Christian."

We need not discuss the significance of this statement, so similar in Buddhism and in Christianity; the truth is that the easiest thing is sometimes the most difficult to accomplish. A change of heart seems a trifling circumstance, but it implies a change of the entire man and of his whole life. The invocations of the Saviour—be his title Buddha or Christ—implies the adoption of his views of life and moral maxims.

* * *

The tract now introduces a worldly-minded man, whose egotism is characterized in these words:

**Hsin* 心 means "heart."

[An unbeliever says:—]
"I see other men die,
My heart is burning like fire.
I am not anxious about other men,
But [I tremble] because the wheel comes to me too."

The priest replies:—]
"If you wish to escape the ills of life and death,
At once invoke Buddha's name.
If in life you invoke his name
Hereafter you shall reap the highest bliss."
*Pikiu, Pikiuni, Yiuposeh, Yiupoi.*

"Virtuous men, virtuous women, and the other devotees of Buddha
Shall all together go to the Western Paradise.
On seeing this tract reflect, reflect.
*Kaolaishan*, disciple of Buddha, native of Chihli has engraved it and given away as an act of merit. The block he retains in his own keeping.
"Respect printed paper."

Such is the Chinese tract according to the Christian missionary's translation, with a few emendations of my own. Aside from the suggested change of the sense in the main passage, I have only taken the liberties which are of a purely literary character, replacing such phrases as "repeat Buddha's name" by "invoke Buddha's name," "article of death" by "domain of death," and the abbreviation "Mito" by the full name "Amitâbha Buddha," which latter form is better known.

The translator may, in spite of the mistakes which he made in several passages, be a good Chinese scholar, but he betrays his utter ignorance of Buddhism by his explanation of the words *Pikiu, Pikiuni, Yiuposeh,*

*Yiupoi.* These words are the Chinese forms of the Sanskrit words *Bhikshu*, *Bhikshuni*;* *Upâsaka*, *Upâsikâ* which means "monks, nuns; male lay disciples and female lay disciples." The translation of the Sanskrit words is given in the next following line, but the Christian missionary, in translating the placard, explains the words in a foot-note as:

> "A Buddhist charm, probably derived from Indian names. The words have no significance whatever, being merely repeated as a kind of magic."

The words *Bhikshu*, *Bhikshuni*, *Upâsaka*, *Upâsikâ*, may be unknown to those Chinese people who received no religious education, but among Buddhists they are common terms; and what shall we think of a missionary who lives in China for the purpose of converting Buddhists, but is so unacquainted with Buddhism that he regards the words with which the congregation is commonly addressed as a kind of magic? Imagine that a Buddhist came to America and would not know what the words *pastor*, *deacon*, and *church member* or *communicant* meant, and would explain them to be unmeaning words used as a charm!

* * *

The whole placard is encompassed with two rows of little circles, which surround the hymns that ap-

* In Pâli *Bhikkhu*, *Bhikkhuni*. The Sanskrit *Bhikshuni* is not an original and legitimate Sanskrit word, but one of those later terms which has been formed after the analogy of the correspondent Pâli form.

pear in the shape of a priest's picture like a frame; and at the right-hand side we read the injunction to fill out the little circles with a red pencil on each three hundred times that the Refuge formula has been repeated.

The Christian translator of the tract condemns severely the pagan habit of repeating Buddha's name innumerable times, and we do not hesitate to join him in his disapproval. But he ought to consider first that the repetition of prayers or formulas is a practical method of impressing religious truths on the hearts of the people; it is in a certain stage of culture as commendable as the method of teaching the multiplication tables by making children commit them to memory; and, secondly, that the Christians, too, have to a great extent availed themselves of this method by enjoining people to repeat the Lord's Prayer over and over again. The practice of repeating the Refuge Formula and of repeating the Lord's Prayer are on the same level, and, if it is to be condemned in one case, why should we not denounce the other as well? The Buddhist Refuge Formula (in Chinese *O-mi-to-fu*, which means "I take my refuge in Buddha") is the vow which Buddhists make to pacify their emotions, and vows are the only prayers which Buddhism allows. This prayer a Buddhist is expected to have in his heart whatever he does,—when he lies down to sleep, when he rises in the morning, when he stands, when he walks, when he is in good health, when he is sick, and when he faces death. The Christian translator says: "And there is none to answer, nor any even to hear." He continues:

> "Listen to that cry going up from thousands of trembling lips, ay, from millions of suffering hearts, daily, hourly, momentarily; a monotonous, unceasing repetition.
>
> "And remember that Jesus hears it always: that he died in response to its unspoken pain and sorrow. Remember that, having committed to us its deep, all-satisfying reply, He says to us to-day, "Go ye into all the world and preach THE GOSPEL to every creature."

This is a strong appeal to Christians for missionarizing, but it is no argument against Buddhism, or Buddhist vows. I am fully aware of the difference which it makes whether the people take their refuge in Jesus or in Buddha, for it is not the name only, but the whole world-conception connected with the name. Behind the names there are realities. But with all the difference that is implied in names, we must not imagine that there is a peculiar magic power in the name itself.

Such an educated Christian as Lavater believed that the exorcisms of Gassner were efficacious on account of the holiness of the name of Jesus. He thought that the word "Jesus" could be used like a spell, or like the charm of the Indian medicine man. And this seems to be the view of the Christian translator of the Buddhist tract before us. Shall we say that the Buddhist contemplations of the vanity of earthly life and the seriousness of death are pagan notions so long as the request is made to invoke Buddha's name, and would these same thoughts rise to the dignity of Christian sentiment if only the name Buddha Amitâbha were replaced by Jesus Christ?

Justice demands us to consider the worth of our argument also from the standpoint of our opponents. Might not Buddhists reply in the same strain? They might say: "Did not Buddha, too, send out his disciples with the words which we quote literally as follows:

"'Go ye now, O bhikshus, for the benefit of the many, for the welfare of mankind, out of compassion for the world. Preach the doctrine which is glorious in the beginning, glorious in the middle, and glorious in the end, in the spirit as well as in the letter. There are beings whose eyes are scarcely covered with dust, but if the doctrine is not preached to them they cannot attain salvation. Proclaim to them a life of holiness. They will understand the doctrine and accept it."

Apparently there is a Christianity which is not yet free from paganism and lacks charitableness in judging others. Buddhists might on the same ground regard Christian prayers as objectionable. Yet they will scarcely do so, for whatever advantages the Christian nations have over the followers of Buddha (and there can be no question about it that these advantages are great), in one respect Buddhism has the preference over Christianity. It is its breadth and comprehensiveness. Buddhists would not say of Mohammed, or Zoroaster, or Confucius that they are false prophets. Buddhists recognize the prophetic nature of all religious leaders. Sir Monier M. Williams quotes the following Buddhistic commandment:

> "Never think or say that your own religion is the best. Never denounce the religion of others."

It was Ashoka, a Buddhist emperor, who convened about two thousand years ago the first parliament of religions in which he requested the sages of his large empire to discuss the differences of their respective faiths in brotherly kindness.

Ashoka's twelfth edict declares:

> "There ought to be reverence for one's own faith and no reviling of that of others."

I have not as yet met a Buddhist who would not look upon Christ with reverence as the Buddha of Western nations.

### R. SPENCE HARDY.

As an instance of the wrong spirit that animates many (I do not say "all") of our missionaries, I refer to the book of a man for whose intellectual and moral qualities I cherish the highest opinion.

The Rev. R. Spence Hardy, the famous Buddhist scholar to whose industry we owe several valuable contributions to our knowledge of Buddhism, has written a book, *The Legends and Theories of the Buddhists Compared with History and Science*, in which he treats Buddhism with extraordinary injustice. This is not in the interest of Christianity, for it is nothing but the spirit of injustice that alienates the sympathies of non-Christian people toward Christianity.

It is strange that Mr. Hardy's unfair statements are made with no apparent malice, but from a sheer habit which has been acquired through the notion of the exclusiveness of Christianity.

In making these critical remarks I do not wish to offend, but to call attention to a fault which can and should be avoided in the future.

Spence Hardy says in his book, *The Legends and Theories of Buddhists Compared with History and Science* (pp. 138, 140):

> "The tales that are told about the acts performed by Buddha, and the wonders attendant on these acts, need only be stated, in order to be rejected at once from the realm of reality and truth. . . . These things *are* too absurd to require serious refutation."

Mr. Hardy forgets that many "tales told about the acts performed by Jesus, and the wonders attendant on the acts," too, need only be stated, in order to be rejected at once from the realm of reality and truth. Mr. Hardy recognizes the paganism of others, but he does not see that he himself is still entangled in pagan notions. What would Mr. Hardy say if a Buddhist were to write exactly the same book only changing the word Christ into Buddha and making other little changes of the same nature. Buddhists, requested by a Christian missionary to believe literally in Christ's walking upon the water or being bodily lifted up to heaven, are, as much as Spence Hardy, entitled to say: "These things are too absurd to require serious refutation." Mr. Hardy protests (p. 137):

> "I deny all that is said about the passing through the air of Buddha and his disciples, or of their being able to visit the Dêwa and Brahma worlds."

If history and science refute the miracles attributed in the later Buddhistic literature to Buddha, why not those attributed to Christ? And we must assume that Mr. Hardy does not deny that Christ descended to hell and that he passed through the air when carried up to heaven in his ascension.

Mr. Hardy speaks of "the errors of Buddhism that are contrary to fact as taught by established and uncontroverted science" (p. 135), but he appears to reject science whenever it comes into collision with a literal interpretation of Christian doctrines. Buddhism is to him a fraud, Christianity divine revelation. He says of Buddhism (pp. 210–211, 313, 207):

> "I must confess that the more closely I look into the system, the less respect I feel for the character of its originators. That which at first sight appears to be the real glory of Buddhism, its moral code, loses all its distinction when minutely examined. Its seeming brightness is not that of the morning star, leading onward to intenser radiance but that of the meteor; and not even that; for the meteor warns the traveller that the dangerous morass is near. [*sic!*] Buddhism makes a fool of man by promising to guide him to safety, while it leads him to the very verge of the fatal precipice. . . . The people who profess this system know nothing of the solemn thought implied by the question, 'How can I do this great wickedness and sin against God?' . . . The operation of the

mind is no different in mode to that of the eye, or ear, vision is eye-touch, hearing is ear-touch, and thinking is heart-touch. The man, as we have repeatedly seen, is a mere mass, a cluster, a name and nothing more. . . . There is no law, because there is no law-giver, no authority from which law can proceed."

Man is "a cluster," means that the unity of man's soul is a unification—a truth on which all prominent psychologists and naturalists of Christian countries agree with Buddha. In the same sense Hume characterized the human soul as a bundle of sensations and ideas. Man is an organism consisting of a great number of living structures, which in their co-operation constitute a well-regulated commonwealth of sentient functions. And why should there be no law if there is no law-giver? Is the law of gravity unreal because of its mathematical nature, which indicates that it is of an intrinsic necessity and requires a law-giver as little as the arithmetical law $2\times2=4$. Is $2\times2=4$ a reliable rule only if a personal God has decreed it? The moral law is of the same kind!

Buddha regards the order of the world not as the invention of either Brahma or any other God, but as an eternal and unconditional law as rigid as the number-relations, which we formulate in arithmetical propositions. Does such a view of man's soul and the nature of the moral dispensation of life indeed annul all moral responsibility? Buddhism does not employ the same symbolical terms as Christianity, but it is not devoid of an authority of moral conduct. Mr. Spence Hardy is so accustomed to the Christian terminology, that he, from the start, misconstrues all other modes of expression.

In other passages Mr. Hardy refers to Buddha's tales in which Buddha speaks of his experiences in previous existences. He says (p. 153):

> "These facts are sufficient to convince every observant mind that what Buddha says about his past births, and those of others, is an imposition upon the credulity of mankind, without anything whatever to support it from fact."

Here Mr. Hardy's naïveté can only evoke our smiles: Buddhists are no more obliged to accept the Jataka tales as genuine history, than our children are requested to believe the legends of saints or Grimm's fairy tales. There are Buddhists who believe the Jataka tales, and there are many Christians, especially in Roman Catholic countries, who believe the legends of saints.

Speaking in this connexion of the fossil remains of extinct animals, Mr. Hardy says (p. 150):

> "Of many of the curious creatures that formerly existed only a few fragments have been found. Among them are birds of all sizes, from an ostrich to a crow, and lizards with a bird's beak and feet. . . . The Himalayas contain the remains of a gigantic land tortoise. The megatherium lies in the vast plains of South America, etc., etc. . . . Now if Buddha lived in these distant ages, and had a perfect insight into their circumstances, as he tells us he had, how is it that we have no intimation whatever in any of his numerous references to the past, that the world was so different in these respects to what it is now? . . . The only conclusion we can come to is, that he knew nothing about the beasts that roamed in other lands, or the birds that flew in other skies; and that

as he was ignorant of their existence he could not introduce them into his tales."

It is right that Mr. Hardy appeals to the tribunal of science against the narrowness of a belief in the letter of the Buddhistic Jatakas; but why does he not sweep first before his own door? Unfortunately, the same objections can be made to Christ, who said: "Before Abraham was I am," apparently meaning that he had existed æons before his birth. There is a great similarity between the pre-existence of Christ and of Buddha, especially when we consider the later doctrine of Amitâbha, the infinite light of Buddhahood, which is omnipresent and eternal. While Christ claims to have existed before Abraham, he gives us no information about the fossil animals that have of late been found by geologists. Ingersoll speaks of Christ in the same way as Spence Hardy does of Buddha. He says: "If he truly was the Son of God, he ought to have known the future; he ought to have told us something about the New World; he ought to have broken the bonds of slavery. Why did he not do it? And Ingersoll concludes: "Because he was not the Son of God. He was a man who knew nothing and understood nothing." When Ingersoll speaks in these terms, he is accused of flippancy, but Mr. Hardy's seriousness is not to be doubted.

What would Christians say of a Buddhist, who, with the same logic, commenting on analogous Christian traditions, would say of Christ what Mr. Hardy says of Buddha! Mr. Hardy says:

"I have proved that Buddhism is not a revelation of truth; that its founder was an erring and imperfect teacher, and ignorant of many things that are now universally known; and that the claim to the exercise of omniscience made for him by his followers is an imposition and pretence. . . . We can only regard Buddha as an impostor."

This is strong language, and I am sorry for Mr. Hardy that he has forgottten himself and all rules of justice and fairness in his missionary zeal.

Even Buddha's broadness in recognizing the good wherever he found it, is stigmatized by Mr. Hardy. He says (p. 215):

"Buddha acknowledges that there are things excellent in other religions, and hence he did not persecute. He declares that even his opponents had a degree of wisdom and exercised a miraculous power. But this very indifference about error, as about everything else, this apparent candor and catholicity, is attended by an influence too often fatal to the best interests of those by whom it is professed."

Mr. Hardy condemns "this apparent candor and catholicity" as "indifference about error," and he adds (p. 216):

"To be a Christian a man must regard Buddha as a false teacher."

Mr. Hardy, apparently intending to palliate his harsh remarks, says:

"I am here a controversialist, and not an expositor." (P. 206.)

But even as a controversialist, he should not lower himself by making unjust accusations. It is neither right nor wise; for the liberties which he takes must be granted to his opponents; and if they refuse to use them, it is to their credit.

Mr. Hardy says: "These conclusions I have founded upon statements taken from the sacred writings," and he rejects Buddhism on account of these errors wholesale. Nor would he permit Buddhists to discriminate between Buddha's doctrine and later additions. For, says Mr. Hardy (p. 219):

"By rejecting other parts of the Pitakas as being unworthy of credence, and yet founding upon them, and upon them alone, your trust in the words they ascribe to Buddha, you do that which no wise worshipper would do, and what you have no liberty to do as a man guided by the requirements of reason."

This is a dangerous principle for Mr. Hardy to propound, for it should be applicable to all religions, and what would become of Christianity if it had to be kept under the bondage of the letter, so that we should no longer be allowed to discriminate between truth and error, but adopt or reject at once the whole fabric. If one discrepancy of the dogmatic texture of a religion with science or with reason disposes of it as a fraud, what shall we do with Christianity?

Spence Hardy's attitude toward Buddhism is typical for a certain class of Christians whose Christianity is little more than a highly advanced paganism.

Happily there are Christians who see deeper, and they feel no animosity against Buddhism on account of its many agreements with Christian doctrines. As their spokesman we quote Prof. Max Müller, who says:

"If I do find in certain Buddhist works doctrines identically the same as in Christianity, so far from being frightened, I feel delighted, for surely truth is not the less true because it is believed by the majority of the human race."

### CHARLES GUTZLAFF.

Speaking of the critics of Buddhism among the missionaries, we must not forget to mention the Rev. Charles Gutzlaff, a German, who enjoys an undeserved reputation for scholarship among people unacquainted with his writings. His two-volumed work, *China Opened*,* is full of the grossest errors, which are scarcely pardonable in an illiterate man who lived only a short time in the Middle Kingdom. Note only this tremendous mistake: Speaking of Confucius, who, as is well known, was not an original thinker or author, but a conservative preserver of the wisdom of the sages of yore, Gutzlaff says:

"Antecedent to him, China does not appear to have possessed any men of genius; or if it did possess them, both themselves and their works have long passed into oblivion."

As though Fu Hi, Yü the Great, Wu Wang, Wen Wang, and innumerable other sages, among them Lau-tsze, who were born before Confucius, had

*London: Smith, Elder, & Co., 1838. The author's name is spelled "Gutzlaff" in the English edition. The German spelling is "Gützlaff."

either not existed or passed into oblivion! The Shu King is a collection of songs, all of which are older than Confucius.

Other blunders, such as attributing to Confucius himself the well-known classic on filial piety, which is written either by Tsang-tsze or by a scholar belonging to the school of Tsang-tsze, are scattered throughout Gutzlaff's book.

Gutzlaff pretends to have read books of which he knows very little. In explanation of Lau-tsze's term *tau* (reason, logos, path), he says:

> "Commentators differ as to the meaning of this word. We cite the opinions only of the two most celebrated of them. According to the best author, Taou is the art of governing a country; but another observes, that the Taou is shapeless, or invisible, and maintains and nourishes heaven and earth. It is devoid of affection, but moves the sun and moon; it is nameless, but contributes towards the growth and sustenance of all creatures. It is something undefined, to which it is difficult to assign a name, which however may be called Taou, for want of a better."

Gutzlaff does not name these "two most celebrated commentators," for it is one of his habits never to quote authorities or to give references. But any one who ever glanced through Lau-tsze's short booklet could not have overlooked that these "opinions" are simply loose and inaccurate quotations from Lau-tsze's Tau-teh-king.

Mr. Meadows, Chinese interpreter in H. M. Civil Service, in his book, *The Chinese and Their Rebellions*, is not too severe on Gutzlaff, when he says (p. 376):

"Probably few men have excelled Dr. Gutzlaff in the capacity for rapidly inditing sentences containing a number of propositions not one of which should be correct. In fact all his labors are characterized by a superficiality, a lack of thorough research, and a profusion of unfounded assertion."

Gutzlaff's opinions on China and Buddhism would certainly not be worth mentioning if he were not sometimes regarded and quoted as an authority whose statements are willingly accepted on account of his supposed scholarship and long residence in China.

Gutzlaff devotes a long chapter to religion; speaking of Buddhism, he says:

"The life of the founder of this idolatry is enveloped in so much mystery, that his very existence has been doubted by some, whilst others have presumed, that there lived and taught, at different periods, various persons of this name."

"His name greatly varies according to the countries where his tenets have been received. Thus we have it pronounced Budha, Budhu, Budse, Gautema, Samonokodam, Fuh, or Fo, etc., all designating one and the same individual."

As if the title Buddha, the Enlightened One, were a name, and of the same kind as "Gautama"! Gutzlaff continues:

"He inculcated mercy towards animals, prohibited the killing of any living creature, and enjoined good-will towards all mankind. His disciples wrote down these instructions, which, inclusive of the commentaries, amounted to two hundred and thirty-two volumes. The writer has perused several of them in the Siamese Pale, and if ever any work contained nonsense, it is the religious code of Budhu."

Siamese can only be the language spoken in Siam, and Pale (or as it is now commonly spelled Pâli) is the vernacular spoken in the kingdom of Maghada in Buddha's time, which has become the classical language of Buddhism. What Siamese Pâli may be, no one except the Rev. Mr. Gutzlaff knows.

Gutzlaff continues in the next paragraph, "his [Buddha's] own uncle rose against him," probably meaning Devadatta, his cousin. He further says:

"The most superficial observer will discover in this system some resemblance to a spurious kind of Christianity. If we do not admit that the human mind will always have recourse to the same follies, we may presume that these ceremonies were borrowed from the Nestorians of the seventh century, a period which exactly coincides with a great reform in the Tibetian system of Budhuism.

"The providence of God, in permitting so many millions blindly to follow this superstition, is indeed mysterious. We can only adore where we are unable to comprehend. Yet, amongst all pagans, the Budhuists are the least bigoted. They allow that other religions contain some truth, but think that their own is the best, and the most direct road to heaven. Amongst the myriads of idols they worship, there are no obscene representations, nor do they celebrate any orgies."

We do not doubt that Chinese Buddhism is full of distortions and superstitions, but even here we find still preserved the purity, the breadth, and the moral earnestness of the great founder of the Religion of Enlightenment.

The Buddhistic description of Hell, as given by Gutzlaff on page 224, differs from the old-fashioned Christian Hell only in unimportant details, and the injunction to repeat the refuge formula, *O me to Fuh!* on all occasions for the sake of "having Fuh both in the mind and in the mouth," is quite analogous to the constant repetition of the Lord's Prayer, which is practised in all Christian countries. The worship of Fuh, as prescribed by various sects, is neither more nor less pagan than the worship of Christ among Christians. Gutzlaff quotes from a Buddhist work, the title of which he does not name, the following passage:

> "Let each seek a retired room, and sweep it clean; place there an image of Fuh, every day burn a pot of pure incense, place a cup of clean water, and when evening comes, light a lamp before the image. Whether painted on paper, or carved in wood, the figure is just the same as the true Fuh; let us love it as our father and mother, venerate it as our prince and ruler. Morning and evening, let us worship it with sincerity and reverence, fall prostrate before it like the tumbling of a mountain, and rise up with dignity like the ascent of clouds. On leaving the room report it [bid it farewell]; returning, let us give notice [greet it]; and even when we travel, at the distance of five or ten le, let us act as in the presence of our Fuh."

Among other extracts from "native works," Gutzlaff quotes the following passage:

> "The laws of Budhuism are boundless as the ocean, and the search after them is as little tiresome as that after precious stones. He who has transgressed them ought to repent; he who never acted against them may silently ponder upon them, and thus know the purity of exalted virtue."

Happening to know this verse as a formula in common use among the Chinese and Japanese Buddhists, I can from memory point out a few gross mistakes in Gutzlaff's translation, without even having at present the original at hand. It must read about as follows:

"The religion of Buddha is as boundless as the ocean.
The search after it is more remunerative than that after precious stones.
He who has transgressed Buddha's injunctions ought to repent.
He who has never sinned, may in silence ponder upon them.
Thus he will comprehend the purity of exalted virtue."

### G. VOIGT AND ADOLPH THOMAS.

From among the German critics of Buddhism I select for discussion two Protestant clergymen, G. Voigt and Adolph Thomas, whose remarks seem to me worthy of notice.

G. Voigt * declares that Buddhism did not originate in the whim of a maniac or in the hallucination of an enthusiast, but is born out of the very depths of the human heart. Its aspirations remind us of St. Paul's cry: "O wretched man that I am! Who shall deliver me from the body of this death!" (Rom. vii. 24.) "But," adds Mr. Voigt, "Buddha cannot deliver mankind, he cannot conquer the world because he denies it; and he cannot deny the world, because he does not conquer it. Christianity alone is the world-religion because it alone conquers

* "Buddhismus und Christenthum," in *Zeitfragen des chr. Volkslebens.* Heilbronn: Henninger. 1887.

the world" (p. 19). "Buddha's salvation is self-deliverance, and this is the first and decisive condition of the Buddhistic Gospel. It refers man, in order to gain his eternal salvation, to the proud but utterly barren path of his own deeds" (p. 22).

Here the Buddhistic scheme of salvation is the same (Voigt claims) as that of Goethe's *Faust* (p. 31), for Faust, too, does not rely on the blood of Christ, but has to work out his salvation himself. Accordingly, one main difference between Christ and Buddha consists in this, that Christ is the Saviour of mankind while Buddha only claims to be the discoverer of a path that leads to salvation (p. 35).

Mr. Voigt's statement concerning Buddha's doctrine of salvation is to the point; but we have to add that while Buddhism is indeed self-salvation, Christianity may, at least in a certain sense, also be called self-salvation. In another sense, Buddhism, too, teaches the salvation of mankind, not through self-exertion, but through the light of Buddha.

Mr. Voigt is a Protestant and a Lutheran; therefore he presses the point that we are justified not through our own deeds, but through God's grace who takes compassion on us. To Lutherans it will be interesting to know that there is a kind of Protestant sect among the Buddhists (and they are the most numerous and influential sect in Japan), the Shin-Shiu, who insist on salvation *sola fide*, through faith alone, with the same vigor as did Luther. They eat meat and fish, and their priests marry as freely as Evangelical clergymen. The statement made by

A. Akamatsu for presentation at the World's religious parliament and published in leaflets by the Buddhist Propagation Society declares:

"Rejecting all religious austerities and other action, giving up all the idea of self-power, we rely upon Amita Buddha with the whole heart, for our salvation in the future life, which is the most important thing: believing that at the moment of putting our faith in Amita Buddha, our salvation is settled. From that moment, invocation of his name is observed to express gratitude and thankfulness for Buddha's mercy; moreover, being thankful for the reception of this doctrine from the founder and succeeding chief priests whose teachings were so benevolent, and as welcome as light in a dark night; we must also keep the laws which are fixed for our duty during our whole life."

Replace the words "Amita Buddha" by "Jesus Christ" and no Lutheran of the old dogmatic type would make any serious objection to this formulation of a religious creed.

Let us now turn to points on which Mr. Voigt fails to do justice to Buddhism, not because he means to be unfair, but because he is absolutely unable to understand the Buddhistic doctrines.

Buddhism in Mr. Voigt's opinion is full of contradictions, for "the idea of retribution can no longer be upheld if there is no ego-unit" (p. 23), and "the standard of Christian morality is God, but Buddhism, ignoring God, has no such standard of morality" (p. 43). Voigt maintains:

"He who denies the living God, must consistently deny also the living soul—of course, not the soul as mental life, the existence of which through our experience is sufficiently guaranteed, but the soul as the unit and the personal centre of all mental life. In this sense Buddhism denies the existence of a soul" (p. 22).

Why can the idea of retribution no longer be upheld if the soul is a unification and not a metaphysical soul-unit? Why can Buddhism have no standard of morality, if Buddha's conception of moral authority is not that of a personal being, but that of an immanent law in analogy with natural laws and in fact only an application of the law of cause and effect? It is the same misconception which we found in Mr. Spence Hardy's arguments, when he said "There is no law, because there is no law-giver."

Adolph Thomas, another German clergyman, criticises Buddhism in a lecture which he delivered in various cities of North America. It bears the title "A Sublime Fool of the Good Lord." The lecture is a curious piece of composition, for it is a glowing tribute to Buddha's greatness and at the same time a vile jeer at his religion. Here is a translation of its best passages:

"I will show unto you, dear friends, a sublime fool of the Almighty. Miniature copies you will find, not a few, in the large picture gallery of the world's history. I show you a colossal statue. It represents Shâkyamuni, the founder of the first universal religion, to whom the admiring generations of after-ages gave the honoring title of *Buddha*, i. e., the Enlightened One. Out of the dawn of remote antiquity, through the mist of legendary lore, his grand figure looms up to us belated mortals, lofty as the summit of the Himalayas towering into the clouds above. He stands upon the heights of Oriental humanity, his divine head enveloped by the clouds of incense, sending his praise upwards from millions of temples. The equal rival of Jesus Christ cannot be otherwise than sublime.

"Buddha possesses that soul-stirring sublimity which wins the hearts with a double charm, by the contrast of natural dignity and voluntary humiliation, of nobility of mind and kindness of soul. This son of a king, who stretches forth his hand to the timid and rag-covered Tshandala girl, saying: 'My daughter, my law is a law of grace for all men,' appears at once as winning souls and as commanding respect. The cry of woe with which he departs from the luxurious royal chambers, full of sweet music and pleasures of the table, full of the beauty of women and the joys of love; 'Woe is me! I am indeed upon a charnel field!' thrills the very soul. The alms-begging hermit, to whose sublime mind royal highness was too low, the splendors of court too mean, the power of a ruler too small, must have inspired with reverence even the gluttonous and amorous epicurean. A prince who was capable of mortifying soul and body by retirement, fasting, and meditation during six long years to find a deliverance from the ocean of sorrows for all sentient beings, bears indeed the stamp of those staunch and mighty men of character, who are able to sacrifice everything for an idea. 'Son constant heroisme,' says the latest French biographer of the ancient founder of Buddhism, concerning his character, 'égale sa conviction. Il est le modèle achevé de tous les vertus qu'il prêche.'

"Buddha towers above the ordinary teacher not less by his intellectual geniality, than by his moral excellence. Five hundred years before the birth of Christ did this far-seeing thinker anticipate the most far-reaching views in the field of natural sciences and the freest social advances of the nineteenth century. This very ancient saint of the interior of Asia was a champion of free thought and liberty after the most modern conception. He looked at the world with the unsophisticated eye of a scientist of our days, seeing in it a chain of causes and effects in continuous change, birth and death, forever repeating themselves, or perhaps with the shortsightedness of a fashionable materialist, seeing in it nothing but the product of matter which to him exists exclusively. A priest of humanity centuries before a Christ and Paul broke through the barriers of the Jewish ceremonial service, thousands of years before a Lessing and Herder preached the newly-discovered gospel of pure humanity, Buddha revealed to the people of India and China, to Mongolians, Malayans, the never-heard-of truth that upon the earth and in heaven humanity alone had merit.

"The moral code of Buddhism has given a purer expression to natural morality and has kept it more free from natural prejudices and religious admixtures than any of the later religions.

"Buddha already held high the banner of philanthropic sympathy, which is perhaps the acknowledged symbol of modern ethics, and before which in our times even the arms of war give way. The humane demand that capital punishment be abolished, which Christianity only now, after nineteen centuries begins to emphasize, had already been realized in Buddhistic countries shortly after the death of the founder of their religion. And in regard to his efforts upon the field of social policy, I venture to call the reformer of India the boldest champion who has ever fought for the holy cause of liberty; for the tyranny, which he fought—that of the Brahman castes—was the most outrageous violation of the rights of man, and he that fought it was—according to the legend—the descendant of an Oriental dynasty which was of course, as every one of them, a sneer upon the liberty of the people.

"Sublime in his *earthly career* by his personal worth, Buddha has still been more elevated in his *immortality* by the extent and power of his historical effects. He is one of the spiritual kings, whose kingdom is without end and whose train-bearers are nations. The dark chasm of oblivion into which two thousand years have sunk, has not even dimmed his memory. Following the track of the victorious sun, his illustrious name has appeared like a brilliant meteor to us also, the inhabitants of the Far West, the sons of Europe and America. He who is adored like a god by three hundred and seventy millions of people in Asia, took captive also not a few strong minds of the German civilized countries. Philosophers and poets like Schopenhauer and Kinkel worshipped at his shrine.

"His words sound in our ears, also, like words of authority. The dignified pathos that pervades them conquers the souls.

'Not even feasting with the gods
Brings rest unto the truly wise;
Who's wise indeed doth but rejoice
That no desires within him rise.'

"The sublimity that lies in his description of his blessed Nirvâna is affecting: 'I have attained unto the highest wisdom, I am without desires, I wish for nothing; I am without selfishness, personal sentiment, stubbornness, enmity. Until now I was full of hatred, passion, error, a slave of conditions, of birth, of age, of sickness, of grief, of pain, of sorrow, of cares, of misfortune. May many thousands leave their homes, live as saints, and after they have lived a life of meditation, and discarded lust, be born again.'

"From the sublime to the ridiculous there is but one step. I must laugh when I think of a group of three Japanese idols. This stone monument from the history of Buddhism appears as a comically disgusting caricature of the Christian trinity.

"Here a striking connexion comes to the surface. A despiser of the gods became the forerunner of worshippers of idols; Buddha's doctrine of liberty brought in its train the tyranny of priests, his enlightened views, superstition; his humanity, the empty ceremonies of sacerdotal deceivers. His attempt at education and emancipation of the people without a god was followed by a period of a senseless and stupefying subjugation of the people; a striking contrast and lamentable failure indeed!

"What an irony of fate. Fate had different intentions from Buddha and forced Buddha to do that which was contrary to what he intended. Like a hunted deer which falls into the net of those from whom it fled, like a deceived fool who accomplishes foreign aims against his will and knowledge, thus India's sublime prince of spirits lies before us, adjudged by the power of fate from which no one can escape. One is reminded of the Jewish poetry of old: 'He that sitteth in the heavens shall laugh, the Lord shall have him in derision.' In derision did he, who governs the fates of men, place the fool's cap upon that noble head. The comedies of Aristophanes are praised, because a bitter seriousness is heard in their droll laughter. The great author of the world's drama has after all composed a far better satire than the best comic poet of this earth. The monster tragi-comedy, *Buddha and Buddhism*, which he wrote into the chronicles of the world, moves not only the diaphragm, but the heart also."

The rest of Mr. Thomas's lecture consits of caustic complaints on the increase of atheism in Christian countries. Natural science, he says, is materialistic. Schopenhauer's pessimism is gaining ascendency in philosophy, and theology tends either to the infidel liberalism of D. Fr. Strauss or favors a reaction that will strengthen the authority of the Pope. Everywhere extremes! He concludes one, of his harangues:

"It darkens! We are Buddhists and not Christians. . . . Bless us, O Shâkyamuni Gautama, 'master of cows'—which is the literal translation of 'Gautama.' Why did your worshippers not call you 'master of oxen'?"

Strange that one who ridicules Buddha cannot help extolling him in the highest terms of admiration. Mr. Thomas sets out with the purpose of calling Buddha a fool, but the subject of his speech and the greatness of the founder of Buddhism carry him along so as to change his abuse into an anthem of praise. He is like Balaam, who went out to curse Israel but cannot help blessing it. And what can he say against Buddha to substantiate his harsh judgment? The same things can be said of Christ, for the irony of fate is not less apparent in the history of the un-Christ-like Christian church than in the development of the un-Buddha-like Buddhism.

The same objections again and again! Buddha was an atheist and denied the existence of the soul. The truth is that while the Buddhist terminology radically differs from the Christian mode of naming things, the latter being more mythological, both religions agree upon the whole in ethics, and the spirit of their doctrines is more akin than their orthodox representatives, who cling to the letter of the dogma, are aware of.

## SIR MONIER MONIER-WILLIAMS.

Among the scholarly authors, of university professors who have written on Buddhism, Sir Monier Monier-Williams, Boden Professor of Sanskrit at Oxford, is one of the most distinguished and prominent authorities. Not only are his Sanskrit Dictionary, Grammar, and Manual standard works of philological scholarship, but also his translations exhibit the genius of a poet who can re-think and re-feel the ideas of bards who lived in ages long past and uttered thoughts which it is difficult for us to comprehend in their original significance. There can be no doubt but Sir Monier Monier-Williams's books on Brahmanism and Hinduism and on Buddhism give us most reliable and instructive information concerning the two great religions of India, and

I confess that their study has proved to me extremely profitable. But one point challenges my opposition; it is, not that he writes from the standpoint of a Christian, for he has not only a right, but is even under the obligation, to do so; nor is it that his works possess the character of contributions to Christian apologetics, a mission which is implied in the duties of the Boden professorship held by him: it is that he narrows Christianity to the dogmatic conception of the Anglican church creeds, and establishes on this ground distinctions which, if tenable, will not, as Sir Monier believes, lift Christianity above Buddhism, but, on the contrary, would give the first place to Buddhism and annul all the claims that Christianity may make to catholicity.

Professor Williams openly states that he has "depicted Buddhism from the standpoint of a believer in Christianity" (p. ix), and when delivering in 1888 his Duff-Lectures which form the nucleus of his book on Buddhism, he expressed his "deep sense of the responsibility which the writing of these Lectures had laid upon him and his earnest desire that they may by their usefulness prove in some degree worthy of the great missionary whose name they bear."* Even the title of the book announces that Buddhism is treated "in its contrast with Christianity."

After these statements we are prepared for an *ex parte* exposition of Buddha's doctrines which, however, considering the antagonistic attitude of Sir

* Quoted literally, only changing "me" into "him."

Monier Monier-Williams is as just and fair as can be expected. The book is valuable on account of its author's unquestionable ability in selecting and marshalling his materials in a masterly way, but it is marred by repeated attempts to belittle Buddha, "who," Sir Monier says, "if not worthy to be called the 'Light of Asia,' and certainly unworthy of comparison with the 'Light of the World,' was at least one of the world's most successful teachers." In spite of Buddha's alleged unworthiness to be compared with Christ, Sir Monier compares the two constantly; he does so in spite of himself, and all Christians do so and cannot help doing so, because the comparison forces itself upon every one who familiarizes himself with the lives of these two greatest religious leaders of mankind.

Professor Williams is undoubtedly anxious to be just toward Buddha, but we cannot help taking him to task for a certain animosity which is shown in occasional distortions of the accounts of Buddha's life and doctrines. Thus he says, when Buddha preached to his disciples, his sermon "was addressed to monks," while "that of Christ was addressed not to monks but to suffering sinners" (p. 44), as if the disciples of Christ were not in the same predicament as the monks that followed Buddha; for Christ's disciples, too, had forsaken their homes in order to devote themselves exclusively to the salvation of their souls. The term "monk" smacks of a Roman Catholic institution that has become odious in Protestant countries. On the other hand, the word "sinner" expresses a self-humiliation popular in certain Christian circles only, but offensive to those who believe in the dignity of man. Albeit, whether monks or sinners, both the disciples of Buddha and Christ were salvation-seeking men.

An actual misrepresentation, prompted by an unconscious disdain for Buddha, lies in the following passage:

> "The story is that Gautama died from eating too much pork (or dried boar's flesh). As this is somewhat derogatory to his dignity it is not likely to have been fabricated. A fabrication, too, would scarcely make him guilty of the inconsistency of saying 'Kill no living thing,' and yet setting an example of eating flesh-meat."

The fact is that according to the Mahâparinibbâna Sutta Buddha's last meal consisted of "dried boar's food," which in later works was interpreted to mean "dried boar's meat"; but it is not impossible that "boar's food" denotes some mushroom or root that was eagerly eaten by pigs. Thus it is not quite certain that Buddha's last meal consisted of meat; yet we grant that Buddha ate meat. Nevertheless, there is no report which states that Buddha ate "too much," we are only told that the meat was not fit to eat. Whatever "boar's food" may have meant Buddha taught that salvation could not be obtained by abstinence from meat alone but by purity of heart. Professor Williams probably remembers the Amagandha-sutta which sets forth that evil habits, wicked deeds, and impure thoughts defile a man, but *not the eating of flesh*— a declaration seven times emphasized in the refrain of the verses 4–10.

Accordingly, there is no inconsistency in Buddha's eating meat, yet as to the statement that Buddha ate "too much,." we can only say that it is an unjustifiable accusation which we confidently hope Professor Williams will expunge from eventual future editions of his book. Buddha probably often enough ate disgusting food on his wanderings through the country of Magadha, for he was not always the guest of kings, but more often a recipient of the hospitality of poor villagers—a fact which is not only in itself probable, but is actually mentioned in various Chinese accounts of Buddha's life, as, for instance, in the Fo-Sho-Hing-Tsan-King. Considering the hot climate of India, too, it is not improbable, that the meat Buddha ate for his last meal was tainted. Such in fact is the report of the Mahâparinibbâna Sutta, IV., 19, where we read:

> "Now the Blessed One addressed Chunda, the worker in metals, and said: 'Whatever dried boar's flesh, Chunda, is left over to thee, that bury in a hole. I see no one, Chunda, on earth nor in Mâra's domain, nor in the Brahma's heaven, no one among Samanas and Brâmanas, among gods and men, by whom, when he has eaten it, that food can be assimilated, save by the Tathâgata.
>
> "'Even so, Lord!' said Chunda, the worker in metals, in assent, to the Blessed One. And whatever dried boar's flesh remained over, that he buried in a hole."

In the face of death, and suffering from the pains of the consequence of his last meal, Buddha reveals a nobility of character, which shows that he was not only great, but also amiable. When Buddha felt that his end drew near, he said:

"Now it may happen, Ânanda, that some one should stir up remorse in Chunda, the smith, by saying, 'This is evil to thee, Chunda, and loss to thee in that when the Tathâgata had eaten his last meal from thy provision, then he died. Any such remorse, Ânanda, in Chunda, the smith, should be checked by saying, 'This is good to thee, Chunda, and gain to thee, in that when the Tathâgata had eaten his last meal from thy provision, then he died. . . . There has been laid up by Chunda, the smith, a karma redounding to length of life, redounding to good birth, redounding to good fortune, redounding to good fame, redounding to the inheritance of heaven, and of sovereign power.' In this way, Ânanda, should be checked any remorse in Chunda, the smith."

While Buddha rejected the idea of obtaining salvation through abstinence from flesh food, he certainly did not encourage the slaughter of animals for the sake of making food of them. Thus a great number of Buddhists abstain from eating fish and meat; but there are some Buddhists (I refer, for instance, to the Shin-Shiu, the largest sect of Japan) who do eat fish and flesh, and they are recognized as good Buddhists as much as Lutherans may be called good Christians.

There is no need of picking out all the passages in Sir Monier Monier-Williams's book on Buddhism which appear to be dictated by a partisan spirit favoring a dogmatic conception of Christianity and apt to prove offensive to the followers of Buddha. I shall, therefore, limit my critical remarks to the last chapter of the book, entitled "Buddhism, contrasted with Christianity" (pp. 337–563).

Professor Williams says: "Christianity is a religion, whereas Buddhism, at least in its earliest and truest form, is no religion at all." And why not? Because

> "A religion, in the proper sense of the word, must postulate the existence of one living and true God of infinite power, wisdom, and love, the Creator, Designer, and Preserver of all things visible and invisible. It must also take for granted the immortality of man's soul or spirit. . . . Starting from these assumptions, it must satisfy four requisites: (1) it must reveal the Creator, (2) it must reveal man to himself, (3) it must reveal some method by which the finite creature may communicate with the infinite Creator, (4) it must prove its title to be called a religion by its regenerating effect on man's nature."

We must add that Professor Williams apparently understands by God and soul the traditional conceptions of dogmatic Christianity; and his faith in God and soul is a mere "postulate," for in the realm of experience no trace can be found of either. Thus our knowledge of both must be attributed to a special and supernatural revelation. The word "reveal" in the passage quoted is intended to be understood in the narrow sense, as opposed to the revelations of the senses and of science.

What a poor comfort is the belief in a postulated and specially revealed God! A postulated God is distant and hidden—even to the sages of the most enlightened pagans. We are informed that what they, the "unaided," know of noble and elevating truths is a mere natural product of their investigation; it is at best what any scientist can discover by the usual methods of scientific inquiry. Their God, it appears, can only be the God of the Religion of Science, who is the divinity of existence, the eternal condition of man's rationality, the standard of all truth, and the authority of right and justice; but not a metaphysical ego-deity whose existence can only be known by an act of special revelation.

We must add that, in our opinion, the God of dogmatism is not the God of the Israelitic prophets, nor of Paul, nor of Christ. The founders of Christianity were as broad as Socrates, as Lau-tsze, and even as Buddha—though Buddha was the broadest of all. They prolaimed no *Quicunque;* the condition of salvation which they held out to the poor in spirit resembled closely the Dharma of Buddha, but not the Thirty-nine Articles of the Anglican Church, nor the confession of faith of any other Christian church. It would take too much space to reprint any one of them, be it the Augustana of the Lutherans, or the Thirty-nine Articles of the Episcopalians, or the Westminster Confession, or the decrees of the Tridentinum, or a papal bull, perhaps the famous bull of Innocence VIII., issued in 1484, which brought the terrors of the witch persecutions down on Europe.*

There is none of these but contains the most irrational and even barbarous and immoral propositions

* The bull is known by its initial words: "*Summis desiderantes affectibus.*"

proclaimed in the name of God and professing to be the true and orthodox interpretation of God's revelation. Compare any one with Buddha's Dharma, which is briefly condensed in the famous stanza:

"To abandon all wrong-doing,
To lead a virtuous life
And cleanse one's heart.
That is the religion of all Buddhas."

Buddha's religion is very much like that of Christ, but it differs greatly from the Christianity of Christian dogmatism. Christ requests men to have *faith* (i. e., Hebrew *amunah*, firmness of character, or Greek πίστις, faithfulness or fidelity), which is a moral quality implying steadfast confidence; the churches demand *belief*, i. e. taking something for granted. We cannot live without faith, but we can very well exist without belief, for we can be faithful in the performance of our duties, the correctness of which we may be able to know and understand. In fact, whenever belief is necessary, it plays a mere temporary part, for we must strive with might and main to replace it by knowledge.

Measured by the standard of Professor Williams's religious ideal, (which, being the Christianity of belief, not of faith, starts, as he expressly states it, from "assumptions," and is based upon a "taking for granted,") Buddhism is no religion at all. For, says he of Buddhism:

"It failed to satisfy these conditions. It refused to admit the existence of a personal Creator, or of man's dependence on a higher Power. It denied any eternal soul or Ego in man.

It acknowledged no external, supernatural revelation. It had no priesthood—no real clergy ; no real prayer ; no real worship. It had no true idea of sin, or of the need of pardon, and it condemned man to suffer the consequences of his own sinful acts without hope of help from any Saviour or Redeemer, and indeed from any being but himself."

Now, as I understand Buddhism, all these drawbacks are its greatest glory ; and if there is any truth in Christianity, Christianity also must possess these very same features.

Professor Williams says on page 14 :

"Buddhism—with no God higher than the perfect man—has no pretensions to be called a religion in the true sense of the word."

Remember that Christ was crucified on the charge of blasphemy. If the dogmas of Christianity have any meaning at all, they proclaim this central truth of all genuine religion, that the Deity is revealed in humanity ; God is nothing more nor less than those eternal conditions of being which beget man—i. e., the rational and morally aspiring being. Christ is God's equal. God is the Father, Christ is the Son ; and the Son and the Father are one. In a word, the significance of Christianity is that God reveals himself in the perfect man. The ideal of human perfection is identical with true divinity.

Buddhism developed the idea of Amitâbha Buddha, personifying in him the omnipresent conditions of enlightenment. There is no God higher than Buddha, and there is nothing greater in God than that which produces the ideal of a perfect man.

But Buddhism denies the existence of "a soul or ego." Very well! Did Christ ever teach that the soul of man is his ego? If the belief in an ego-soul were one of the essential ingredients of "a religion in the proper sense of the word," Christ should have enlightened us about it. He did nothing of the kind, and this being so, we must begin seriously to doubt whether Christ ever taught a religion in the proper sense of the word. Indeed if Buddha's doctrine of the soul is nihilistic and pessimistic, we must say the same of St. Paul, for he declares that he himself has been crucified with Christ, and that not he himself, i. e., Paul, liveth, but Christ liveth in him.

As to prayer we can only say that Christ did his best to abolish "real prayer," (that is, prayer in the sense of begging) by instituting for it the Lord's prayer, which is no prayer in the proper sense of the word. Christ said: "When thou prayest thou shalt not be as the hypocrites are; . . . when ye pray use not vain repetitions as the heathen do, . . . your father knoweth what things ye have need of, before ye ask him." The Lord's prayer, accordingly, is a prayer which contains no prayers whatever; the fourth supplication, "give us this day our daily bread," appears as a request, but considered in the context of the whole Sermon on the Mount, we find that Christ emphasizes the word "this day," which must be interpreted as nothing else than the injunction "Take no thought for the morrow!"

The same is true of the fifth supplication, "Forgive us our trespasses, as we forgive those who trespass against us." The burden of these words lies in the clause introduced by "as," which again is no prayer, but contains a vow.

The Lord's prayer is not so much addressed to God who "knoweth what things we have need of," but to the person who wants to pray. It is no begging, but a self-discipline. It satisfies a craving which is natural in weak-hearted persons, in adult children, but unworthy of a man. In the form of a prayer, the Lord's prayer weans Christians of praying. It teaches man no longer to pray, or to attempt to change the will of God, but to change the will of the praying person by saying "not my will but God's will must be done." "Real prayer" is a heathenish notion implicating the heart in hypocrisy.

If there is any philosopher of weight who can be called Christian it is Kant. Educated by pious parents, and himself deeply religious, he preserved of the faith of his childhood as much as possible; and hear what he says about prayer:

> "To expect of prayer other than natural effects is foolish and needs no explicit refutation. We can only ask, Is not prayer to be retained for the sake of its natural effects? Among the natural effects we count that the dark and confused ideas present in the soul are either clarified through prayer, or that they receive a higher degree of intensity; that the motives of a virtue receive greater efficacy, etc., etc.
>
> "We have to say that prayer can, for the reasons adduced, be recommended only subjectively, for he who can in another way attain to the effects for which prayer is recommended will not be in need of it.
>
> "A man may think, 'If I pray to God, it can hurt me in no wise; for should he not exist, very well! in that case I have

done too much of a good thing; but if he does exist, it will help me.' This *Prosopopœia* (face-making) is hypocrisy, for we have to presuppose in prayer that he who prays is firmly convinced that God exists.

"The consequence of this is that he who has made great moral progress ceases to pray, for honesty is one of his principal maxims. And further, that those whom one surprises in prayer are ashamed of themselves.

"In public sermons before the public, prayer must be retained, because it can be rhetorically of great effect, and can make a great impression. Moreover, in sermons before the people one has to appeal to their sensuality, and must, as much as possible, stoop down to them."

The Buddhist prayer is of the same nature as the Lord's prayer, in the sense in which we conceive it and as Kant would have interpreted its purport. It is no longer a prayer in the proper sense of the word; it is a vow. Like the Lord's prayer, the Buddhist vows teach men to take refuge in religion, and that is more than any "real prayer" can ask or do for us.

Professor Williams says (p. 544), "the main idea implied by Buddhism is intellectual enlightenment." With all deference to Professor Williams's knowledge of the significance of Buddhist doctrines, we must beg him to omit the word "intellectual." Buddha's idea of enlightenment" (in contradistinction to Christian dogmatism) certainly includes "intellectual enlightenment," but it is first and last and mainly an enlightenment of the heart.

Professor Williams says:

"What says our Bible? We Christians, it says, are members of Christ's Body—of His flesh and of His bones—of that

Divine Body which was once a suffering Body, a cross-bearing Body, and is now a glorified Body, an ever-living, life-giving Body. Hence it teaches us to honor and revere the human body; nay, almost to deify the human body.

"A Buddhist, on the other hand, treats every kind of body with contempt, and repudiates as a simple impossibility, all idea of being a member of the Buddha's body. How could a Buddhist be a member of a body which was burnt to ashes—which was calcined,—which became extinct at the moment when the Buddha's whole personality became extinguished also?"

Here we have a new Christology and a new Christian dogma which demands Christians "almost to deify the human body." The passage to which Professor Williams refers (I. Cor. vi., 15–20) cannot be interpreted in the sense that Christians "are members of Christ's body—of His flesh and of His bones." For in that very passage we read:

"He that is joined unto the Lord is one spirit."

Further says Paul:

"O wretched man that I am, who shall deliver me from the body of this death." (Rom. vii. 24.)

The New Testament treats the body as forfeited to death; and there is certainly truth in this view, although it has been wrongly interpreted in Christian asceticism and monkish morality. As to Buddha, it is well known that while he did not seek the pleasures of the body, he spurned asceticism as a wrong method of seeking salvation. Whenever Buddhists retained mortifications they did so in violation of the most unequivocal injunctions and of the historically best assured traditions of Buddha's

Dharma. As to "the Body of Buddha," Professor Williams overlooks here the well-known Buddhist doctrine that Buddha's body is the Dharma. When Buddha died, his bodily life was dissolved into non-existence, but not his doctrine. His individuality was gone, but not the enlightenment of his Buddhahood. We read in "The Book of the Great Decease" (Chap. VI., 1):

> "Now the Blessed One addressed the venerable Ânanda, and said: 'It may be, Ânanda, that in some of you the thought may arise, "The word of the Master is ended, we have no teacher more!" But it is not thus, Ânanda, that you should regard it. The truths and the rules of the order which I have set forth and laid down for you all, let them, after I am gone, be the Teacher to you.'"

Further Professor Williams says:

> "The Buddha had no idea of sin as an offence against God (p. 546). Nor did the Buddha ever claim to be a deliverer from guilt, a purger from the taints of past pollution. . . . On the contrary, by his doctrine of Karma he bound a man hand and foot to the inevitable consequence of his own evil actions with chains of adamant. He said, in effect, to every one of his disciples, 'You are in slavery to a tyrant of your own setting up; your own deeds, words, and thoughts in your present and former states of being, are your own avengers through a countless series of existences.
>
> "'If you have been a murderer, a thief, a liar, impure, a drunkard, you must pay the penalty in your next birth . . . your doom is sealed. Not in the heavens, O man, not in the midst of the sea, not if thou hidest thyself in the clefts of the mountains, wilt thou find a place where thou canst escape the force of thine own evil actions. Thy only hope of salvation is in thyself. Neither god nor man can save thee, and I am wholly powerless to set thee free.'"

Buddha teaches that the evil consequences of error, sin, and wrongdoing cannot be escaped; but evil deeds can be covered by good deeds. The passage to which Professor Williams refers is incomplete without its counter-truth, that good deeds, too, will not fail to bear good fruits. Buddha teaches:

> "As the welcome of kinsfolk and friends awaits him who has been abroad and is now returning in safety: so the fruits of his good works greet the man who has walked in the path of righteousness when he passes over from the present life into the hereafter."

To quote the one without the other would be the same as if some one cited from the New Testament the words, "He who does not believe shall be damned," and forgets to add the counter proposition, "He who believes shall be saved."

In Professor Williams's opinion, Christianity is superior to Buddhism, because it is said actually to relieve the believer from the consequences of sin. He continues:

> "And now, contrast the few brief words of Christ in his first recorded sermon. 'The Spirit of the Lord is upon Me, because He hath anointed Me to preach good tidings to the poor; He hath sent Me to proclaim liberty to the captives, and recovering of sight to the blind, and the opening of the prison to them that are bound.'"

Buddha would never have said, "the Spirit of the Lord is upon me," (which is a peculiarly Hebrew expression), and it is very improbable that Christ would ever have thought of saying anything like it.

As to the substance of this proclamation, Professor Williams will be aware that both Buddha and Christ promised to give liberty to the captives, the recovery of sight to the blind, and the faculty of comprehension to the deaf.

Professor Williams sums up:

"Yes, in Christ alone there is deliverance from the bondage of former transgressions, from the prison-house of former sins; a total cancelling of the past; a complete blotting-out of the handwriting that is against us; an entire washing away of every guilty stain; the opening of a clear course for every man to start afresh; the free gift of pardon and of life to every criminal, to every sinner—even the most heinous and inveterate."

Captain C. Pfoundes, a resident of Japan, who has made a study of Japanese Buddhism, says on the subject of the doctrine of atonement, viewing it from a purely practical standpoint:

"It is all too true, and more the pity it is that it is so, that the converts (nominal) to Christianity are largely natives whose conduct is such that by the general opinion of foreign residents such converts are not the most desirable class to employ. The true Buddhist has ever in mind the fear of punishment hereafter for misdeeds, not to be lightly atoned for. 'The naughty little boy who is always ready to say he "is sorry," if he is assured that this will obtain forgiveness,' has no counter part in true Buddhism; and the too easily purchased pardon of Christian mission teaching is viewed as a danger, from the ethical standpoint, by the educated and intelligent Asiatic."

If the essence of Christianity consists in the hope of an entire washing away of every guilty stain and getting rid of the consequences of our evil deeds, we can only hope that the civilized nations of mankind will abandon Christianity. Buddha's doctine is certainly grander and, what is more, truer than this hollow doctrine of a salvation of the guilty by the death of the innocent. Buddha, when speaking of sacrifices, rejected the idea that blood can wash away sins, and when he regarded himself as the saviour of man, he meant that he was their teacher. He claimed to have pointed out the way of salvation and to have removed the cataract from the eyes of the blind, but he expects every one of his followers to exert himself when walking on the path.

A man converted from sin is saved in the sense that henceforth he will walk in the right direction; his character is changed; he turns over a new leaf, but he cannot annihilate the past and the consequences of his former karma.

The dogma of the vicarious atonement through Christ's death is a survival of the age of barbarism; for it is based upon the savage's idea of religion which represents God as an Apache chieftain who, when offended, thirsts for the death of somebody and must be pacified with blood.

He who believes it necessary to "postulate" the existence of a metaphysical âtman-God in addition to the real God whose presence appears in the facts of experience, and of a purusha-soul in addition to the psychic realities of our life, will naturally regard the extinction of the illusion of "the thought '*I am*,'" (i. e., the error of the existence of an individual ego-self) and of an individual God-being, as dreary nihilism and "morbid pessimism." Professor Williams says:

> "What is Buddhism? If it were possible to reply to the inquiry in one word, one might perhaps say that true Buddhism, theoretically stated, is Humanitarianism, meaning by that term something very like the gospel of humanity preached by the Positivist, whose doctrine is the elevation of man through man—that is, through human intellects, human intuitions, human teaching, human experiences, and accumulated human efforts—to the highest ideal of perfection; and yet something very different. For the Buddhist ideal differs *toto cœlo* from the Positivist's, and consists in the renunciation of all personal existence, even to the extinction of humanity itself. The Buddhist's perfection is destruction."

The Buddhist perfection consists in the complete surrender of the illusion of an ego-self; and Professor Williams meant to say that the Buddhist's perfection should, from his standpoint of a believer in an ego-self, be regarded as tantamount to destruction; for he knows very well, and happily says it too, that it is not so. But so little does Professor Williams understand the positivism of Buddha's doctrine, that he regards Buddha as inconsistent, because, instead of proclaiming the ideal of destruction, or surrendering himself to quietism, Buddha rouses himself and his followers to energetic work and sympathetic usefulness.

Professor Williams says:

> "In fact it was characteristic of a supreme Buddha that he should belie, by his own activity and compassionate feelings, the utter apathy and indifference to which his own doctrines logically led."

According to my comprehension of Buddhism, Buddha need not in his ethics *belie* his own doctrines; for his ethics are an immediate consequence of his doctrines. Should not Professor Williams first suspect his conception of Buddhism, before he imputes to so profound and clear a thinker, as Buddha unquestionably was, a gross inconsistency on the main issues of his religion?

A few days ago I received a booklet entitled *Happiness*, which is a comparison of Christianity with Buddhism from a Buddhist standpoint. It is ostensibly written by a Buddhist who presents a friend and co-religionist with the impressions he receives during a sojourn in England. In spite of its crude make-up the booklet is cleverly designed and makes some good points which are decided hits on a literal belief in dogmatic Christianity. Salvation is defined by this Buddhist author as "The destruction of ego or of the misery of existence." He adds: "I find that they [the Christians] always think we mean the destruction of existence itself and not of the misery." Concerning the Christian idea of salvation he says: "They imagine they go to their heaven, ego and all: throwing their blackest sins on the shoulders of their God."

The Buddhist and Christian conceptions of religion are contrasted as follows:

"*Ours.* Destruction of *Ego* by knowledge, gratitude, and love; the practice of which is intense happiness.

"*Theirs* is more the worship of *God*, chiefly for the forgiveness of sin, as if such forgiveness were possible, without suffering; whilst ours is the destruction of the evil itself."

When speaking about the doctrine of atonement, our Buddhist author says:

"This strange idea arises I think from their notion of a despotic and capricious *God*, who forgives or condemns in a moment without reason, yet, at the same time, with this unmerciful *God* there is no forgiveness—*the debt of sin must be paid with innocent* blood, though it involve the sacrifice of his own innocent son."

Several paragraphs are devoted to prayer which with Buddhists is "contemplation and self-examination." Speaking of the Lord's prayer our Buddhist critic says:

"You would think Him [the God of the Christians] an incompetent being, when they set Him a good example—'Forgive us . . . as we forgive.' But if He followed their example He would rarely forgive them.

"Again, you would say they were praying to some evil spirit, when they beg him not to lead them into temptation."

The Buddhist and Christian conceptions of Hell are tersely condensed in these statements:

"*Ours.* The effect of obedience to *Ego*, here and hereafter, while it lasts.

"Their *Hell* is like their *Heaven*, a place—not a state—where the identical earthly bodies of nearly all humanity will be tormented in actual fire for ever; to no purpose, except to satisfy the vindictiveness of their Creator, whom they call the 'God of Love.'

"They do not see that it is the *Ego* that tortures, and not *God*; that he cannot torture, and has no *Hell*."

These quotations show how easily a religion is misrepresented, but we are sorry to say that the great mass of Christians justify the above criticism by actually believing in the letter of their dogmas. We trust that there is a nobler Christianity than Christian dogmatism, but Sir Monier Monier-Williams regards the belief in the atonement of sin by the innocent blood of Christ, the efficacy of real prayer, the reality of an ego-soul, and the existence of a personal and miracle-working God-Creator, as the essence of Christianity.

In a summary of his comparison of Christianity with Buddhism, Professor Williams says:

"Buddhism, I repeat, says: Act righteously through your own efforts, and for the final getting rid of all suffering, of all individuality, of all life in yourselves. Christianity says: Be righteous through a power implanted in you from above, through the power of a life-giving principle, freely given to you, and always abiding in you. The Buddha said to his followers: 'Take nothing from me, trust to yourselves alone.' Christ said: 'Take all from Me; trust not to yourselves. I give unto you eternal life, I give unto you the bread of heaven, I give unto you living water.' Not that these priceless gifts involve any passive condition of inaction. On the contrary, they stir the soul of the recipient with a living energy. They stimulate him to noble deeds and self-sacrificing efforts. They compel him to act as the worthy, grateful, and appreciative possessor of so inestimable a treasure.

"Still, I seem to hear some one say: We acknowledge this; we admit the truth of what you have stated; nevertheless, for all that, you must allow that Buddhism conferred a great benefit on India by encouraging freedom of thought and by setting at liberty its teeming population, before entangled in the meshes of ceremonial observances and Brahmanical priestcraft.

"Yes, I grant this: nay, I grant even more than this. I admit that Buddhism conferred many other benefits on the

**millions inhabiting the most populous part of Asia. It introduced education and culture; it encouraged literature and art; it promoted physical, moral, and intellectual progress up to a certain point; it proclaimed peace, good will, and brotherhood among men; it deprecated war between nation and nation; it avowed sympathy with social liberty and freedom; it gave back much independence to women; it preached purity in thought, word, and deed (though only for the accumulation of merit); it taught self-denial without self-torture; it inculcated generosity, charity, tolerance, love, self-sacrifice, and benevolence, even towards the inferior animals; it advocated respect for life and compassion towards all creatures; it forbade avarice and the hoarding of money; and from its declaration that a man's future depended on his present acts and condition, it did good service for a time in preventing stagnation, stimulating exertion, promoting good works of all kinds, and elevating the character of humanity."**

If Professor Williams's conception of Christianity must be accepted as true Christianity, Christianity will pass away to make room for Buddhism. Happily, Christianity is a living religion, that, having passed through the stage of metaphysical dogmatism, is still possessed of the power of regeneration, so as to approach more and more—though progress is sometimes slow—the ideal of a genuine catholicity. Those features which Professor Williams regards as the essential grandeur of Christianity, are a most serious defect; and their absence in Buddhism indicates that it is the more advanced religion. That religion only which has overcome the pagan notions of a special revelation, of atonement through blood, of wiping out the past, of the miraculous power of prayer, of the ego-consciousness as a kind of thing-in-itself, and of a creation out of nothing by a God-magician, can eventually become the religion of mankind.

For myself, I must confess that I never felt more like a true Buddhist than after a perusal of Professor Williams's description of Buddhism; for I am now more firmly convinced than ever, that our Church-Christianity can only become a scientifically true and logically sound religion of cosmic and universal significance, by being transformed into that Buddhism which Professor Williams refuses to regard "as a religion in the proper sense of the word."

Did you never read in the Scriptures, "The stone which the builders rejected, the same has become the head of the corner"?

# CONCLUSION.

BUDDHA's religion appears valuable for three reasons.

1. It is the religion of enlightenment. Buddha's principle of acquiring truth is to rely upon the best and most accurate methods man can find for investigating the truth. In his dying hour he urged his disciples to rely upon their own efforts in finding the truth, not upon the Vedas, not upon the authority of others, not even upon Buddha himself, and he added: "Hold fast to the truth as a lamp."

2. Buddha anticipated even in important details the results of a scientific soul-conception. He rejected the Brahman theory of soul-migration and explained man's continuance beyond death as a rebirth or reincarnation, a reappearance of the same soul-form. This is based on the doctrine that man's psychic nature is not a substance or entity, not an âtman or self, but consists of karma; it is the product of deeds, a form of activity conditioned by the preservation or transference of the memory of former actions. Nor did Buddha shun the unpopularity to which his message to the world was exposed, be-

cause liable to be misrepresented as a "psychology without a soul."

3. While he was bold and outspoken in his negation, he proclaimed at the same time, the positive consequences of his philosophy. The negation of the âtman-soul shows the vanity of man's hankering after enjoyment, be it in this world or in a heaven beyond, and Buddha taught that by cutting off the yearning for a heaven in any form, be it on earth or beyond the clouds, man will annihilate those conditions which produce the hell of life. When the idea of an independent self is done away with, when we understand that man's character is the form of his being as shaped by, and finding expression in, deeds, and finally, when we learn that according to our deeds this form continues in the further development of life, bearing fruit according to the nature of our deeds, the irrationality of all hatred, envy, and malevolence becomes apparent, and room is left only for the aspirations of an unbounded and helpful sympathy with all evolution of life.

Buddha is, so far as we know, the first prophet who proclaimed the paramount importance of morality in religion. At the same time he is the first positivist, the first humanitarian, the first radical freethinker, the first iconoclast, and the first prophet of the Religion of Science. The more we become acquainted with the original writings of Buddhism, the more are we impressed with the greatness of Buddha's far-seeing comprehension of both the problems of religion and psychology. To be sure, he had not the same scientific material at his disposal that we have to-day, but the fundamental problems in philosophy, psychology, and religion, are much simpler than our philosophers would make us believe. Buddha saw in great outlines the solution of the religious problem, and pronounced boldly a religion which stood in contradiction to all that which by Brahmans was considered as most essential to religion. In a word, he pronounced a religion based upon facts which should replace a religion based upon the assumptions of belief.

Many Buddhist doctrines, especially some of the most salient moral maxims, have reappeared in Christianity, where they assumed a less abstract and more concrete shape, so as to appeal more directly to the energetic races of the North.

Christianity has been to Europe what Buddhism has been to Asia, and the analogies in the history of both religions, especially the evolution of sects, the development of ritual and religious art, and the various deviations finding expression in superstitious practices, priestly pretensions, and dogmatic vagaries, are most interesting and instructive.

For the sake of purifying our conception of religion, there is no better method than a study of comparative religion; and in comparative religion there is nothing more fruitful than a tracing of the analogies and contrasts that obtain between Buddhism and Christianity.

# INDEX.

## A.



## B.



## C.

Y.



Z.